THE VINEGAR CUPBOARD

ANGELA CLUTTON

THE VINEGAR CUPBOARD

Recipes and history
of an everyday ingredient

ANGELA CLUTTON

BLOOMSBURY ABSOLUTE
LONDON · OXFORD · NEW YORK · NEW DELHI · SYDNEY

For Mum and Dad – thank you.

CONTENTS

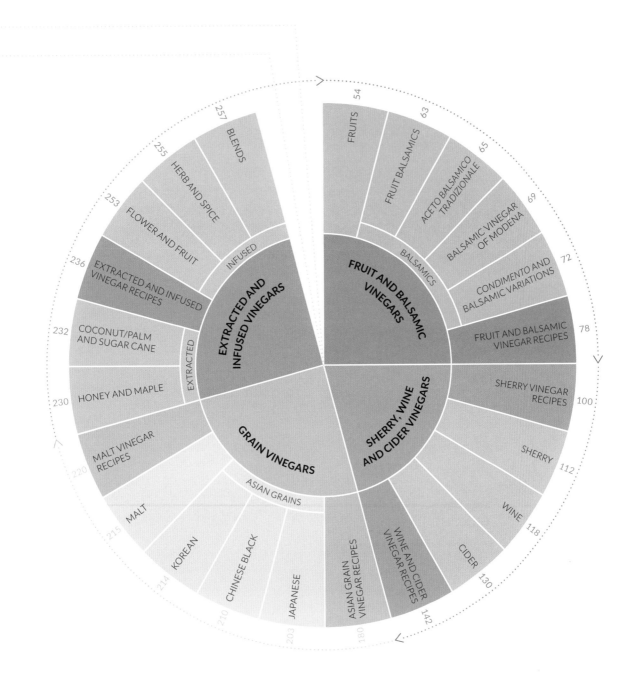

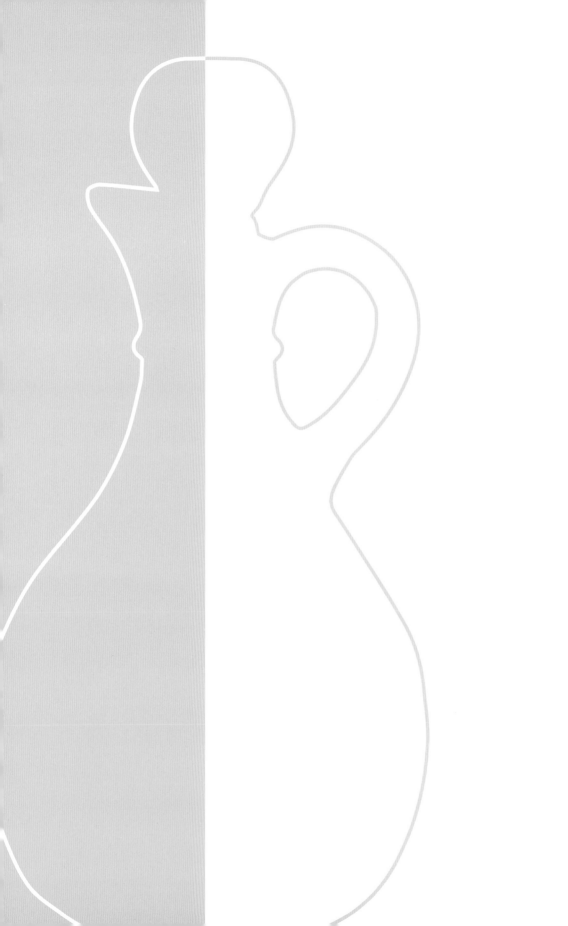

INTRODUCTION

'Think what a poem a salad would be when dressed with primrose vinegar...'

The above line, from Florence White's classic 1930's cookbook, *Good Things in England* is what first led me down the rabbit hole of vinegar discovery.

It piqued my interest because at that time – maybe ten years ago after first reading it as I sit here writing this – flower vinegars were not often found. It got me thinking that in the many eighteenth- and nineteenth-century cookbooks I am happy to have in my collection, there are plenty of vinegar recipes. But in later books, all that stops, and vinegar (in British cookbooks, anyway) is referred to much more generically. That in turn got me wondering about just what we were missing.

The answer has turned out to be: we were missing a lot.

Over the intervening years my vinegar collection has grown in size and diversity and is now fundamental to how I cook. In my teeny-tiny London kitchen there are cupboards that can barely contain the bakeware, saucepans, roasting tins and so on that are crammed in and have to be prevented from falling out when opening the doors. My vinegars, however, have a cupboard all to themselves. Perfectly positioned right by the hob. Barely an arm-raise away from whatever I am cooking. They luxuriate in comparative space, with only each other to jostle with.

I know it isn't just me who has got more into vinegar. It has been exciting to feel wider interest in vinegars growing at the same time as my own. The range of vinegars generally available to buy is expanding rapidly. It is not hard now to find fruit, herb, sherry, cider, malt, rice, balsamic and many types of red and white wine vinegars – from Rioja through to champagne – on store shelves.

I wonder how much the upsurge in interest in vinegar is the result of consumer tastes swinging away from sweet towards sour? How much is it to do with our widening interest in the provenance of food, with us wanting to know more about an ingredient and how it is made? Maybe it is on the back of the trend for fermenting, which is at the very heart of vinegar-making. With such an interest in gut health and fermented foods, is now the perfect time for a fresh look at the benefits of vinegar, too?

Most exciting of all to me as a cook is that I feel there is a growing interest in vinegars because of the role of acidity in cooking. I hope that by demonstrating the many great ways in which vinegars can be used to balance and bring flavour, *The Vinegar Cupboard* will enable even more modern cooks to make the most of this ancient ingredient. I promise, once you have used cherry vinegar to deglaze a pan used to cook duck breasts, then drizzled the resulting sauce over the meat, the doors will be blown off how your culinary mind considers vinegar. Mine were, anyway.

In this book you will find the stories behind world vinegars, interwoven with recipes for using them. Please know: there is no recipe in here that requires just one specific vinegar – or even one general type of vinegar. What I want these recipes to show is how the vinegars can be used interchangeably for varying impact and deliciousness. There is a flow between the vinegars, in their respective colour, density, acidity, flavour, aroma and culinary use. I would absolutely hate it if anyone thought a recipe could not be made because they did not have the 'right' vinegar. There are always options. And not only the options I give. As vinegar understanding grows, so does the confidence and awareness of switching vinegars round.

With very many vinegars out there all over the world, this book cannot be encyclopaedic. It isn't trying to be encyclopaedic, and nor is it a textbook (does it sound like I am getting my excuses in?). But it is embracing of the breadth of vinegars you might come across. It should help you understand them and the joy they can bring to your cooking.

I really hope that as you read about each vinegar, you will feel as if you have it in your hand – and then you will want to go out and find it so you can use it in your cooking. I honestly don't expect everyone to have a vinegar cupboard, but I'd like to think this book might get you pondering a vinegar shelf at least…

Angela Clutton
London, 2019

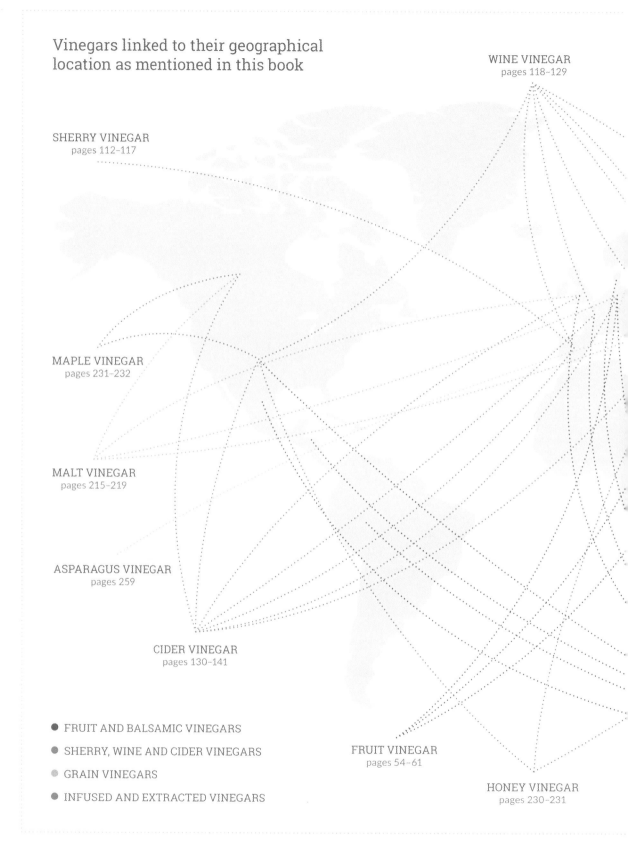

Vinegars linked to their geographical location as mentioned in this book

WINE VINEGAR
pages 118–129

SHERRY VINEGAR
pages 112–117

MAPLE VINEGAR
pages 231–232

MALT VINEGAR
pages 215–219

ASPARAGUS VINEGAR
pages 259

CIDER VINEGAR
pages 130–141

● FRUIT AND BALSAMIC VINEGARS

● SHERRY, WINE AND CIDER VINEGARS

● GRAIN VINEGARS

● INFUSED AND EXTRACTED VINEGARS

FRUIT VINEGAR
pages 54–61

HONEY VINEGAR
pages 230–231

WHEY VINEGAR
pages 259

BLACK BEAN VINEGAR
pages 259

BALSAMIC VINEGAR
pages 63-77

KOREAN VINEGAR
pages 214

CHINESE BLACK
VINEGAR
pages 210-214

JAPANESE BROWN
VINEGAR
pages 203-207

COCONUT AND PALM VINEGAR
pages 232-234

SWEET POTATO VINEGAR
pages 259

FRUIT VINEGAR
pages 54-62

SUGAR CANE VINEGAR
pages 234-235

What is Vinegar?

Every time we add a squeeze of lemon or a splash of wine to our cooking, what we are actually trying to do is give the dish the acidity to help bring out the other flavours. While lemon and wine are fine, vinegars are the very best way of doing this, and much more besides.

Choosing to use vinegar is very often literally within the reach of all of us as cooks. Most reasonably well-stocked kitchens will have at least one bottle of vinegar knocking around somewhere (even if many of those bottles go underused). The very ordinary nature of vinegar is, I think, part of the joy of discovering just how extraordinary it is, too, in terms of what it is and what it can do.

Many cultures across so many various places and times have a long-standing heritage of this wonderful alchemy of taking a raw base of sugar-rich agricultural produce and double-fermenting it into alcohol and then into vinegar. It's an ingredient shared right across the world, with each local vinegar closely tied to regional agriculture. Fruit vinegars are made according to the fruits that grow locally; wine vinegar is made in wine-producing countries; rice vinegars in the rice-producing countries... You get the idea. And it's one that runs throughout this book when considering each vinegar style.

Vinegar's long-standing connection with its local food chain has always meant that it plays an important role in the local economy and ecosystems, and in minimising food waste. Seasonal gluts of produce can be turned into vinegar rather than disposed of. Even spoiled produce – or spoiled alcoholic ferments such as 'off' wine or cider – can become vinegar rather than be wasted. Vinegar is of itself a preservative, helping to ensure the longevity of other foods. Vinegar is impressively neat, barely creating any waste in its production. And even when it does, that can be turned to an advantage, such as when making malt vinegar, where the initial stage is to extract the sugar from the grain. The spent grain is then no longer useful, but clever producers can use it to feed cattle.

All of that adds up to helping me understand why vinegar has been prevalent for so long. And it makes me wonder, too, at a time when the food community is working very hard to encourage people to look at attitudes to wasting food, whether vinegar may yet take more of a role in the protection of global food resources.

Its environmental and agricultural 'worth' are definitely part and parcel of what a vinegar is. As is the cultural significance that you will discover when you read about different vinegars. The use of local crops and local know-how in vinegar production means each different type gives an insight into a particular aspect of a global culture. Vinegar as a sociological, anthropological and historical lens? Absolutely.

But in amongst all that – and vinegar's much-lauded health benefits – what must not be forgotten is that vinegar is quite simply one of the most useful storecupboard ingredients a cook can have. Whether you have just one vinegar, a couple or a cupboard-full, there is so much you can do when cooking with it. From the alchemy of local produce, vinegar becomes the kitchen's own alchemist.

Vinegar's general uses

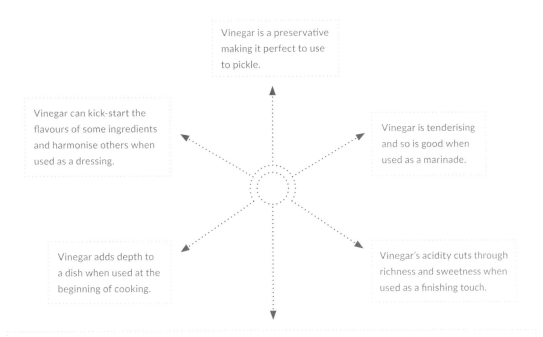

Vinegar is a preservative making it perfect to use to pickle.

Vinegar can kick-start the flavours of some ingredients and harmonise others when used as a dressing.

Vinegar is tenderising and so is good when used as a marinade.

Vinegar adds depth to a dish when used at the beginning of cooking.

Vinegar's acidity cuts through richness and sweetness when used as a finishing touch.

Typical vinegar acidity level

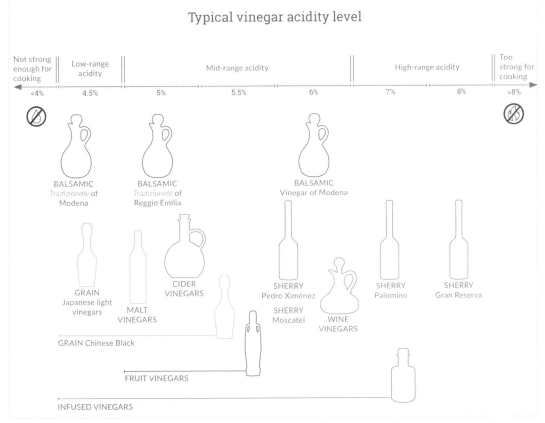

Not strong enough for cooking	Low-range acidity	Mid-range acidity	High-range acidity	Too strong for cooking
<4%	4.5%	5%	5.5%	6%	7%	8%	>8%

BALSAMIC
Tradizionale of
Modena

BALSAMIC
Tradizionale of
Reggio Emilia

BALSAMIC
Vinegar of Modena

GRAIN
Japanese light
vinegars

MALT
VINEGARS

CIDER
VINEGARS

SHERRY
Pedro Ximénez

SHERRY
Moscatel

WINE
VINEGARS

SHERRY
Palomino

SHERRY
Gran Reserva

GRAIN Chinese Black

FRUIT VINEGARS

INFUSED VINEGARS

Vinegar Through History

The story of vinegar has enticingly mysterious beginnings. What and where was that moment of discovering that an alcohol fermentation of fruits or grains had soured into vinegar? Who first took a sip, had an initial puckering, then thought, 'Hang on, there's something pretty marvellous here...'

We simply do not know, and I cannot imagine that question will ever fully be unravelled because the wonder of vinegar is that it is a global phenomenon, with the moment of discovery happening in many different ancient civilisations – totally independently of each other – several thousand years ago. It is only as time evolves into written records that we begin to get a clearer sense of vinegar's by then already well-developed cultural, medicinal and culinary significance. And we learn that as empires spread, so did vinegar love and lore, resulting in its growth and development all around the world.

Throughout this book I will be poking into the various pinch points of individual vinegar histories that I think are most pertinent to our modern understanding of why that vinegar should be valued still. Whether that is fourteenth-century France and wine vinegar; nineteenth-century malt vinegar in the context of British industrialisation; the impact of twentieth-century wartime rice shortages on Japanese vinegars, or many others. Those are particular insights into the people, places and times that affected – for better or worse – a particular vinegar.

Just as interesting, and maybe more important is the bigger picture of vinegar's place through history, which is what you will find here: insight and context into how vinegar gained momentum and spread its acidic powers across many nations.

vinegar

vinaigre
Literal French 'sour wine'

vinum 'wine'
acere 'sour'
Latin

4000 BC
Mesopotamian tablets described fermenting grain into beer and vinegar.

3000 BC
Egyptian vessels contained remnants of brewed barley acidified into vinegar.

2070–1600 BC
Legends from the Xia Dynasty told that Heita, the son of Du Kang, discovered the first rice vinegar.

1895–539 BC
The Babylonian kingdom provided evidence of palm vinegar from date trees.

1500 BC
Inscriptions on Egyptian burial tombs showed jars of vinegar being used as payment for embalming.

WORD ASSOCIATIONS

The modern English word 'vinegar' comes from the French *vinaigre*, meaning
'sour wine'. By the time the French gifted us their love of sour wine and the word
to describe it in the fourteenth century, we already had in Middle English the
alegar which was 'sour ale'. French influence was such that we subsequently lost
the language distinction between 'sour wine' and 'sour ale', and our word for 'sour
wine' became universal for all such sour ferments, not just wine.

France's *vinaigre* – just like Spain's *vinagre* – comes from the Latin *vinum acetum*.
Acetum is the word to focus on. It comes from the Latin *acere*, meaning 'sour'. Then
look at the ancient Greek word *akmé*, meaning 'sharp' or 'spike', which is the root of
the modern Greek word for vinegar, *oxos*. On top of all that, know that in the Anglo-
Saxon languages of Old English and subsequent Middle English, the 'gar' of *alegar*
and vinegar was the word for a spear.

The point of all this is to show how in ancient Greece, ancient Rome, and onward
through European civilisations, the word for vinegar has been trying to convey its
sharp, sour flavour and piercing acidity. Contrast that with the Chinese characters
for vinegar used in Japan and China, which share the same left-side character of
the brewing pot for *sake*. The language focus there is on the process. It tells us how
ancient cultures have perceived so differently their discovery of vinegar.

FROM ANCIENT CULTURES OF MESOPOTAMIA AND EGYPT
TO THE CLASSICAL WORLD AND ROME

The ancient cultures of what we now consider the Middle East provide us with
early clues to the discovery and use of vinegar. It would be a long time before
people understood how fermented sugars from fruits or grains became vinegar,
or knew how to control it, but they were certainly the happy beneficiaries of the
accidental turning of the region's produce into vinegar.

The Mesopotamian empire of much of modern-day Iraq, Kuwait and Saudi
Arabia has provided archaeologists with written tablets of around 4000 BC, which
describe a form of fermentation of grain into beer and from there to vinegar. The
Babylonian kingdom in the south of Mesopotamia has given us evidence of palm

770–476 BC
First professional vinegar-making facility developed in China during the Zhou Dynasty.

5th century BC
Large amounts of vinegar were produced in Jinyang and became very commercial.

5th century BC
Chinese scientists discovered that living organisms were necessary for acetic fermentation.

5th century BC
Japan and Korea started to adopt Chinese cultures, including the love for vinegar.

4th century BC
Xenophon wrote about the Persian process of making vinegar from palm trees.

vinegar from date trees, and also of date fruits, figs and grapes being fermented, and as they became vinegar being used for pickling and preserving.

Other archaeological discoveries have found ancient Egyptian vessels from 3000 BC containing the remnants of their brewed barley *hequa*, which acidified into vinegar. There are also inscriptions on the walls of burial tombs of 1500 BC showing that jars of vinegar were used by families as payment for embalming – indicating that it had acquired value by then, too.

From ancient Greece to ancient Rome. Where the acidity of vinegar was being used to purposely draw lead acetate – known as 'sugar of lead' – from lead pots to use as a popular sweetener. The extent to which the ancient Romans knew of its toxic elects may be questionable, but certainly they knew sour wine vinegar acted very powerfully on the raw material. (As did Cleopatra, who according to famous legend sought to flaunt her wealth to Mark Antony by dissolving an expensive pearl in a glass of vinegar and drinking it. She knew what the vinegar could do.)

Plutarch wrote in his *Parallel Lives* that the famous second-century BC Roman consul and senator, Cato the Elder, would take vinegar to quench his thirst. This would have been the *posca* of vinegar mixed with water and herbs, a favourite drink that came over from ancient Greece, where it was principally used as a medicinal tonic. The Roman people, however, took it for refreshment. Soldiers took it with them on campaigns, as it was certainly safer than drinking unknown water.

By the first century AD comes the *De Re Coquinaria* compilation cookbook of Roman recipes that features vinegar in many of its dishes. Vinegar had the full-house of appeal: refreshing, restorative, delicious. It was also safe to take on long journeys, on which it could be used as a preservative of other foods, making it little surprise that as the Roman empire spread in power and geography, vinegar spread too. That reach includes Jerusalem, where the New Testament tells us that Jesus on the cross was given a cloth soaked in vinegar – very probably *posca*. (Both the Old and the New Testaments are interesting windows into the normality of vinegar, through people using it as a drink or condiment.) It also spread to nations such as Spain and France, which may have had their own vinegar culture anyway, but then found that the Romans brought a love of it too.

FROM CHINA TO JAPAN AND BEYOND

Remember how I said at the start of this that we do not know who took that first sip of accidentally fermented vinegar and decided it was pretty good? Well, I hold on to that uncertainty even in the face of two Chinese legends that claim otherwise.

4th century BC
Hippocrates of ancient Greece advocated vinegar as a medicinal remedy.

3rd century BC
Text detailing vinegar's use as medicine recorded on silk sheets sealed in a tomb in Changsha.

2nd century BC
In ancient Rome, according to Plutarch, Cato would take vinegar to quench his thirst.

1st century BC
Cleopatra flaunted her wealth to Mark Antony by dissolving a pearl in a glass of vinegar and drinking it.

They are ascribed to two of China's famous regional vinegars. First, the Zhenjiang black vinegar which is China's most well-known vinegar. It was apparently invented during China's oldest dynasty, Xia, by Heita, the son of Du Kang, who had himself invented rice wine. What a very ingenuitive family they were. According to legend, Heita made some rice wine, set aside the remnants of the lees from making it, and when he went back three weeks later found they had become wonderfully sweet and sour. Sound convincing? Or you might prefer the legend from Shanxi province of an ancient female deity by the Fen River who invented vinegar and then, with supreme generosity, spread the vinegar know-how far and wide.

We are on surer ground with an understanding of how much China had fallen for vinegar's charms by the time of the Zhou Dynasty (1046–256 BC). That was when writings on all subjects, including vinegar, really developed in China. Not that those dates should kid anyone into thinking there wasn't vinegar in China before then. It is just that there isn't the recorded evidence for it. What we do know is that in the 800 years of the Zhou Dynasty things changed enormously in China, and those are well documented. We learn that sometime between 770 and 476 BC came the first professional vinegar-making facility; that members of the nobility would be buried with ceramic pots of vinegar when they died; and how the Royal Courts of several Chinese states engaged a vinegar-maker whose only job was to brew vinegar for the royals. I think only the origins of balsamic vinegar (see page 66) carry such associations of exclusivity. Elsewhere vinegar was mainly prized because it was cheap and easy to produce.

Vinegar did duly become more widely made and consumed, with reports by the fifth century BC of large-scale vinegar-making in Jinyang – modern-day Taiyuan – in Shanxi province. Interest in vinegar grew so much that the Chinese scientists discovered that living organisms are necessary for acetic fermentation and put a name – *shen gyi* – to those bacteria. That was some 1,300 years before the vinegar work of France's Louis Pasteur.

The Chinese love of vinegar also led to a love of vinegar in Korea and Japan. Both of those countries began through the first five centuries AD to adopt elements of Chinese culture, religion, practical know-how and language. The brewing techniques of sake and grain vinegar were part of that flow of knowledge across the seas by merchants and monks. Vinegar would take hold so fast that by the Nara period in Japan of AD 710–794, it was being taxed as a type of sake. By the Edo period of the seventeenth century, it was being produced commercially to huge popularity and culinary use across Japan.

1st century AD The New Testament states that on the cross Jesus was given a cloth soaked in vinegar.

1st century AD Roman recipes using vinegar found in *De Re Coquinaria* compilation cookbook.

1st century AD Due to vinegar's use as a preservative and the growth of the Roman empire, vinegar spread further across the globe.

5th century Vinegar was being commercially produced and began to be hugely popular across China.

8th century Vinegar was being taxed as a type of sake in Japan because of its popularity.

FROM THE MIDDLE AGES

Coming back to the history of European vinegar at the point of the Middle Ages feels rather sweeping, yet it can be justifiably dealt with in a broad brushstroke because for most of that period, from the fifth to fifteenth centuries, vinegar kept itself under the radar. Which isn't to say it wasn't widespread or fabulous or relied upon. Just that it was largely produced in rural, small-scale settings. There was no significant commercial drive behind it.

Agricultural communities produced vinegar from whatever their crops were, almost as a by-product. Often vinegars were made simply at home. To any extent that Europe had a wider production of vinegar, that rested with the monasteries. This is maybe no great surprise given all we know about the faith that has been put in the healing benefits of vinegar over the centuries, but still I find it fascinating that monks in the later Middle Ages were leading a monastic tradition of making both excellent wine and wine vinegar from the vines that grew close to the abbeys.

They were kept busy by the medieval bubonic plagues of Europe. The fight against those owed much to vinegar, with people being advised to wash with it to try to keep the germs at bay. If you happen to go to Derby you will still find evidence of how that English town tried to fight the great plague of the mid-1600s. At Friar Gate in the marketplace is the 'vinegar stone' on which would have been put a trough of vinegar, and as money was changing hands it was first put into the trough to disinfect it.

DEVELOPING A DEEPER UNDERSTANDING OF VINEGAR

From the end of the Middle Ages through the eighteenth-century Age of Enlightenment was a period of significant, well, enlightenment on how vinegar is made. Rising interest in vinegar set European scientists on a course to try to understand more about it. The question became: why and how did fermented alcohol sour into this other thing that was quite different, absolutely delicious, and massively useful as an ingredient and as a preservative? They knew that once they had cracked those questions they were only a hop, skip and a jump from being able to control and speed up the process.

There comes a point when vinegar history turns to the developing scientific understanding of how it is made. To find out more about the evolution of vinegar-making, refer to the section on 'How is Vinegar Made' (see page 22). What matters

1250–1815 European scientists' interest in vinegar rose and further research was carried out.

1300–1500 Monks made wine and wine vinegar from the vines that grew close to the abbeys.

14th century The French brought their love of sour wine to Britain.

Mid-1600s Vinegar was used to fight the plague as it was known for its sterilising characteristics.

1750–1900 The European industrialisation brought more scientific inventions for the vinegar production.

in terms of the bigger picture of vinegar history is simply that the science coincided with geographical exploration and the increased transportation of goods, and was music to the ears of commercial traders. More vinegar could be made more cheaply, meaning that the love of vinegar began to spread to other countries including those that may not have previously had their own vinegar culture.

INDUSTRIALISATION, GLOBALISATION AND LOOKING AHEAD

The industrialisation that spread through Europe in the second half of the eighteenth century and through the nineteenth century brought more scientific inventions, all intended to improve the production of vinegar.

There were definite improvements in yield, speed and control. Yet lost on the way were some regional specialities and differences – increasingly so as agricultural communities shrank. Vinegars inevitably became more homogenised. The same thing happened when industrialisation hit China in the second half of the twentieth century and changed the face of mass commercial vinegar production.

The upside to all this, though, is that vinegar-making has weathered industrialisation well. As you will discover throughout the book, a modern revival in global interest in the provenance of food has played its part. We are much more aware again now of protecting older, slower, more idiosyncratic methods of production. There is a drive towards authenticity of ingredients, and that includes a greater understanding of the value of vinegar-making of the past.

All of which I think puts modern and future vinegar-lovers in the perfect position: there is no shortage of decent-quality, mass-produced, easily available and cheap vinegar; and there are ever-growing sectors of vinegar craftspeople making more artisan products. Thanks to global connectivity we can now experience more easily the exciting vinegars of cultures other than our own. If you are reading this book, you are playing your part in that. I am optimistic for happy vinegar days ahead.

19th century
The Schützenbach method sped up and simplified the process of vinegar-making.

1864
Louis Pasteur identified the bacteria that are crucial to vinegar-making as acetic acid bacteria.

20th century
Wartime rice shortages during the twentieth century impacted Japanese vinegar production.

1940s
Frings developed the acetator which is still one of the fastest methods of vinegar-making.

Mid-1900s
China's industrialisation changed the face of its mass commercial vinegar production.

How is Vinegar Made?

I am going to try very hard to keep this simple. Some science is unavoidable, but I hope to avoid either giving a chemistry lesson (not least because I certainly don't have the science pedigree for that) or making it seem complicated (because on the whole it isn't). It all boils down to one very simple idea: natural sugars present in a base ingredient of fruit, grains, etc are fermented by yeast into alcohol. Then (in the appropriate circumstances of temperature) oxygen and bacteria ferment the alcohol into acetic acid. The acetic acid is vinegar.

Different vinegars will have different end-product acidity levels: 5–6% is the middle range of acidity and where vinegars are most useful; go below 4% and it isn't really a vinegar in any meaningful culinary way as the acidity is too low for kitchen tasks such as pickling; go above 8% and a sip might scorch the back of your throat.

THE SCIENCE OF ACETIC FERMENTATION

For thousands of years, the conversion of alcohol to acetic acid vinegar just happened, and nobody quite knew how or why. It was only as the science of chemistry evolved that understanding grew of how the process worked and the elements that were needed.

Exposure to air

The chemist Antoine-Laurent de Lavoisier (1743–94) settled upon air – or a component of air – as being the principal cause of the acetification. He gave that component the name 'oxygen', from the Greek, meaning 'acid-former'.

His was a deeper scientific insight into an idea the Dutch botanist and physician Hermann Boerhaave (1668–1738) had already developed. Boerhaave's vinegar work focused on the importance of air to make vinegar (and also of the 'vegetal substance' that appeared on it, which I'll come on to). He rightly thought that a larger surface area of alcoholic liquid allowed more air contact and therefore a quicker process, and so established a method of trickling the alcoholic liquid through wood shavings to increase the surface area that could be exposed to the air.

It is a similar idea to that developed by two German scientists: Karl Wilhelm Gottlob Kastner (1783–1857) and Johann Sebastian Schützenbach (1793–1869). Remember that name, 'Schützenbach' – it will crop up a few times in reference to modern producers who are still using the core method he worked upon.

The Schützenbach method put together two ideas: maximising exposure to air by trickling the alcoholic liquid over wood shavings on which the bacteria could grow; and using a generator to move air through the tank to speed up the process. The time taken to convert the alcohol was significantly quicker and easier to control than simply leaving the air to act on the surface of the alcohol. It was a huge stride forward in modern vinegar-making.

Vinegar production process overview

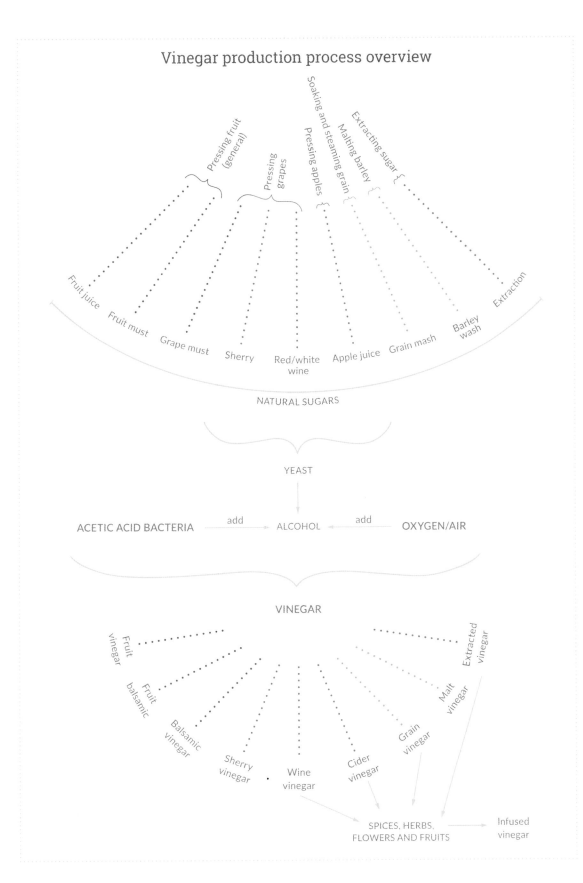

Acetic bacteria

Louis Pasteur (1822–95) was the scientist who really broke through on defining the science behind vinegar, even if he wasn't the first to articulate ideas on how a living micro-organism played a crucial role in acetic fermentation.

I've already mentioned that Boerhaave was working on it. There was also South African-born scientist Christiaan Persoon (1761–1836), who specialised in mushrooms and assumed the bacteria on the surface of vinegar to be a fungus. Their work was preceded by a Chinese text called *Qi Min Yao Shu* of around AD 500. Its ten volumes covered agriculture to veterinary medicine, brewing and cooking. They looked in detail at vinegar brewing and identified that living organisms that coated the surface of vinegar played a key role in its fermentation.

But certainly it was Pasteur who identified the organisms as a particular type of bacteria fundamental to vinegar-making, and went further than anybody else in developing our modern understanding of the process.

The bacteria are called acetic acid bacteria – sometimes known as AAB or *acetobacter* – and survive by metabolising sugar and alcohol, making acetic acid (vinegar) as a waste product. They appear after alcohol has been fermented, as long as there is heat and air to allow them to grow. There is not one AAB, but very many different types or strains that will be different from each other depending on the base ingredient of the ferment and the ensuing alcohol. The bacteria are formed by air, so the properties of local air can make a difference. All of which means that the bacteria don't just do a chemical job; they also play a really important and exciting role in developing particular vinegar profiles.

Acetic acid bacteria

also known as AAB or *acetobacter*, the bacteria which convert alcohol to vinegar.

The acetic acid bacteria do an excellent job of guzzling up the alcohol but there is always a little left behind in the vinegar-making. It is on the whole a very small amount. The permitted level of residual alcohol differs slightly between vinegars. Many vinegars will be 0.5%, though in the EU a wine vinegar can be up to 1.5%. And sherry vinegar can be allowed to be even double that. Remember, though, that the amount of vinegar being consumed at any one time is never (even for me) going to be very much. The amount of alcohol consumed via vinegar is negligible.

METHODS OF MAKING

In his published *Studies on Vinegar*, Pasteur identified the criteria that are essential for vinegar-making:

1. alcohol and its inherent sugars
2. oxygen
3. the fermenting bacteria
4. temperature between 20°C and 35°C

He had originally wanted to apply for a patent on these principles, but then decided to abandon that and put the knowledge freely into the public domain. Thank goodness, because quite where our vinegar world would be without that I don't know.

There's core process that Pasteur identified still lies at the heart of modern vinegar-making. From slow, artisanal production done with greater understanding of how it happens; through to the industrialisation and computerisation that sped up and commercialised vinegar-making; and varying methods of production in-between.

The reality for modern vinegar-makers is often a hybrid of the production methods outlined on page 27. Innovative makers of many of the vinegars I describe in detail through this book are developing their own production processes around these core principles.

A few vinegar-makers I have met are nervous of sharing too much about how their vinegar is made. 'The secret of the vinegar makers' is something I will mention later in regard to the Orléans vinegar-makers' oaths not to reveal how they do it. Sometimes it feels like that oath still applies. Why? Well, I fear that for some it may well be because they are less than proud of how they make vinegar and may want to give the impression that their process is rather more 'authentic' than it actually is. Others just want to protect their craft. For while vinegar-making is simple, it is also complicated. There is science, yes – but it also needs heart and soul, and a little magic, to do well.

RAW VINEGAR, FILTERING, AGEING AND SULPHITES

The conversion to acetic acid vinegar – whichever process is used – isn't necessarily the whole story, or even the end of the story of how vinegar is made. Other factors play a role, too.

There's the type of vessel the conversion happens in. At one end of the scale are wooden barrels, giving some characteristics of flavour to the

Sulphites

Sulphites are a natural by-product of fermentation and are present at low levels in vinegars. As they are a type of food allergen, anyone who suffers from that might need to be aware but really the levels are very low. Often so low they do not need to be on the label.

Unless – and it is quite a big unless – sulphites have actually been added to the vinegar. That used to be done a lot to act as a preservative. Then it was realised that using a preservative to preserve a preservative was probably not necessary. A properly-made vinegar does not need sulphites added in order to be safe or stored. If you see sulphites listed on the ingredients label of a vinegar you might want to wonder why.

vinegar, and allowing the vinegar to breathe. At the other are the huge steel tanks (acetator-made vinegar is always done in a steel tank).

Pasteurising is important to consider, too. Raw vinegar will contain the mother of vinegar and its flavour profile will not have been affected (i.e. damaged) by the heat of pasteurisation. Filtration can also remove flavour elements along with the mother of vinegar. It is a quirk of food fashion that premium vinegars at the moment are often raw and unfiltered. That means they are cloudy and with the mother of vinegar floating around inside – 'attributes' that used to be painstakingly avoided because they were not how consumers wanted their vinegar to be.

Then there is ageing. Where vinegars are aged after their acetic conversion, the same story applies as for making the vinegar in wood. Ageing in wood can give characteristics to the finished vinegar and allow it time to develop its flavour. Throughout this book you will discover many vinegars that are wood-aged.

The 'mother' of vinegar

the cellulose secreted by the acetic acid bacteria as they convert the alcohol into vinegar, and which binds the bacteria together. For much more on the 'mother', see page 138.

DISTILLATION AND DISTILLED VINEGAR

Everything I have said thus far is about fermented vinegar. But there is another type of vinegar you need to know about, too, if only to understand why it won't be featuring much elsewhere in this book. It is distilled vinegar, made by distillation rather than fermentation.

You will know by now that fermented vinegar is made by yeasts fermenting sugars to alcohol, then bacteria fermenting alcohol to vinegar. The key difference with distilled vinegar is that it is made from distilled alcohol, a cheap spirit with a very high alcohol content that is produced by distillation of alcohol made from all manner of things – it could be potatoes, wine, sugar beet, grains... The distilled alcohol is then converted in an acetator to very high-acidity vinegar. Where it is to be used for cooking purposes that will then be diluted to achieve 5% acidity.

Distillation means boiling and condensing the spirit to separate off diluting elements such as water to achieve the higher alcohol content. You are going to read so much elsewhere in this book about how having an interesting, delicious base alcoholic ferment plays such an important role in delivering interesting vinegar. But when it comes to distilled vinegar, the reverse of that applies.

White vinegar and spirit vinegar are other names for distilled vinegar. It is colourless, tasteless and cheap to produce. People sometimes clean with it; technically you could pickle with it. On the positive side, some producers use it as a 'clean' neutral base for allowing flavourings/infusions to really come to the fore. Those are pretty much the best things I can find to say about distilled vinegar.

Methods of Production

Minimal intervention

This is a more managed version of how vinegar has been allowed to happen for thousands of years: expose alcoholically fermented sugars to the air and to the acetic acid bacteria, keep it all within the right temperature boundaries, and you will have vinegar. This is known as surface fermentation, because the bacteria act upon the surface of the alcoholic ferment.

Where modern makers differ from their vinegar-making ancestors is in knowing how to control exposure to the air in the barrel; how to control the temperature; how to understand the bacteria; and that the bacteria 'mother of vinegar' can be added to get the batch going or give it a helping-hand.

This is what happens with modern versions of the Orléans process (see page 118), which so inspired the scientists of the eighteenth and nineteenth centuries: when a not-quite-full barrel of alcohol is converted to vinegar, some of that is removed but – crucially – some of it is left behind so that when the barrel is replenished with the next batch of alcohol there are already bacteria in the barrel to 'seed' the new batch with bacteria and begin its acetic fermentation.

Depending on the amount of alcohol to be fermented, the acetic conversion to vinegar can take months: it is time consuming. For some that is a downside, but the upside is that the base gently and slowly develops its vinegar profile of colour, flavour and smell.

If you are tempted to try vinegar-making at home, it is not hard to replicate the circumstances needed. With wine, particularly, it is simply a case of keeping it in a crock or jar with some air in there too and the mother of vinegar you can buy online. Vinegar will happen. (See page 129 for a little more on that.)

Helped along a little

Some modern makers use versions of the Boerhaave or Schützenbach wood-shaving methods mentioned earlier. It is still surface fermentation – the shavings just create more surface. It isn't always wood that is used now. It could, for example, be particular plastics that hold the bacteria well, but the idea is the same.

These methods tend to take a few weeks. Again, it depends on the volume. It is a commercially appealing process as the vinegar is given some time to evolve its flavours, but it is still quicker and more controllable than the more hands-off alternative.

Helped along a lot

The bigger commercial vinegars are made by an acetator. This is the most technological and fastest of the methods of vinegar-making. Rather than surface fermentation, this is submerged fermentation and was developed by the company Frings in the 1940s on the basis of technology developed for making antibiotics.

Very strong pumps ensure air is constantly circulated inside the tank, moving the bacteria at great speed and intensity through the alcohol. It is fast – taking barely a day to complete its acetic conversion – and very high yielding. It gives no time for the vinegar to develop flavour characteristics, but that is not to say that all acetator-made vinegar is 'bad'. It isn't. Start with a decent base ingredient of raw material/alcohol, and you can have a perfectly good baseline vinegar. It won't be particularly exciting for your senses of taste and smell. But it will do a job.

Vinegar and health

It has proven impossible to write a cookbook on vinegar without encountering its 'health-giving' associations. I never wanted to avoid them, but I do raise an eyebrow to the sheer extent of the health claims some people and some producers make. I worry too often only part of the picture is presented, and some people – and producers – are happy to keep the public underinformed and overimpressed.

Yet, many different cultures across thousands of years have expounded the benefits of vinegar. Take Persian scientist Ibn Sina's *Al-Qanoon fit Tibb* (*The Canon of Medicine*), completed in 1025 and which carried influence for centuries through the Islamic world, Europe and into India. Included are remedies using vinegar for clotting, healing burns, relieving inflammation and headaches. Vinegar has a very long-standing role in ancient Chinese medicine, too, featuring in Li Shizhen's highly-esteemed mid-sixteenth century *Bencao Gangmu* (*Compendium of Materia Medica*). Amongst its nearly 2,000 entries come recommendations to take vinegar for problems with circulation, jaundice, loss of appetite and for the liver. The Japanese samurai warriors used to take an egg tonic made by sitting a whole egg in vinegar until it dissolved shell-and-all, then drinking a watered dilution of that three times a day. I'm not recommending it, just saying they swore it kept them fit and strong.

You'd think that given how long vinegar has been acclaimed as beneficial for health, a settled position would have been reached on exactly what it does and how. That is not the case. The research I have seen is bound up with conflicts and questions. Core themes do stride through, though – of complaints it may help with and benefits it may bring.

(For particular health benefits of raw unpasteurised and unfiltered vinegars, especially apple cider vinegar, see page 138.)

Dosage

To take vinegar as a daily tonic or with meals, do not drink it neat. It is too acidic. The occasional neat sip to taste is fine, but not for regular consumption, and not for a heavily acidic vinegar. Water it down.

Cholesterol

A pre-dinner dose might also be taken for vinegar's purported ability to help lower cholesterol. It's the apple cider vinegar and the black grain vinegars that are especially of benefit.

Arthritis

The very long list of people who take apple cider vinegar for arthritis and say it has been a wonder includes explorer Sir Ranulph Fiennes, and who am I to argue with a man who at sixty-five years of age climbed Mount Everest.

Healthy hair and skin

Both Helen of Troy and Lucrezia Borgia reputedly bathed in vinegar. It was most likely vinegar added to water, but the point holds true that vinegar is allegedly conditioning for both the hair and skin. Try it as a hair conditioner (dilute one part vinegar to three or four parts water) for a natural way to balance your scalp's pH.

Colds and flu

In Chinese medicinal lore, the steam of boiling vinegar is considered purifying and used to kill flu viruses. (Those of us who have put vinegar into a searingly hot pan and had to stand back in the face of the fumes could well see that working.)

Detoxification

Vinegar is thought to help the body detoxify. Not only are toxins flushed out of the system but the circulation is given a bit of a kick-start. I can vouch for the second part of that as I happily take a nip of the more mildly acidic vinegars if in need of a bit of a morning pick-me-up (especially if what I need to be picked up from has been self-induced).

Blood pressure

The ability to reduce high blood pressure is one of the current health vinegar benefits much touted around. It is believed that it is the acetic acid itself that achieves this, therefore it is potentially a benefit of all vinegars, not just specific ones.

Gut health

Vinegar can work as a prebiotic, to stimulate digestion and help your stomach absorb nutrients.

Blood sugar

It is believed that it is the acetic acid of vinegar that helps reduced high blood pressure, making it potentially a benefit of all vinegars, not just specific ones.

Amino acids

The amino acids present in some vinegars are good for us in varying ways. They are known to help fight fatigue, irritability and the kind of muscle pain or cramping that can be the result of overstrenuous exercise. The vinegars high in amino acids are the Japanese and Chinese black grain vinegars, apple cider vinegar and coconut vinegar. It is very possible that a regular, small-dose intake of these vinegars can help boost our amino acid levels.

Antibacterial

This is probably one of the least controversial claims. From Hippocrates and his ancient Greek physician colleagues in c.400 BC using it to treat wounds, to medieval plagues and World War I, when antibiotics were not widely available and vinegar was one of the most effective ways to prevent soldiers' wounds becoming infected.

Vinegar flavour wheels

Each recipe in this book comes with a flavour wheel for its vinegar, a selection of which is shown below. The wheel is a guide to that vinegar's acidity and also its flavour profile. The 'spokes' show how various characteristics within a vinegar compare and relate to each other – not necessarily how they compare across different vinegar styles. It is true, of course, that not all vinegars within any given vinegar style will necessarily have all of – or the same – flavour profiles shown. So what these wheels really demonstrate are the possibilities of the flavour characteristics in vinegars that you might find. In vinegars that I hope you will find.

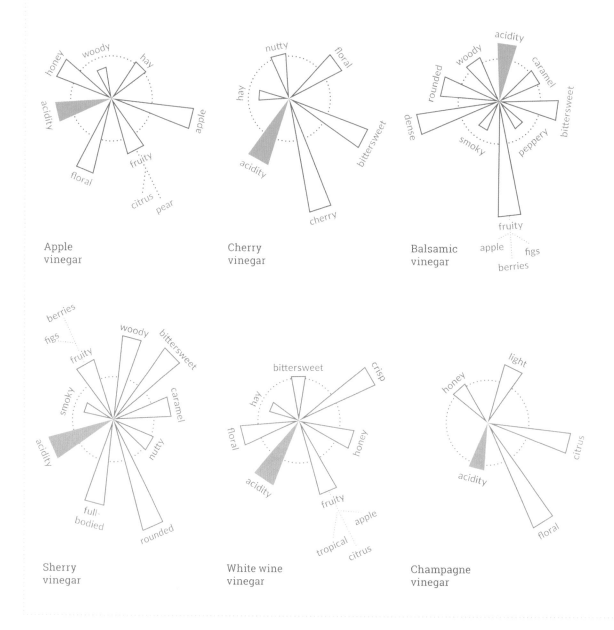

Apple
vinegar

Cherry
vinegar

Balsamic
vinegar

Sherry
vinegar

White wine
vinegar

Champagne
vinegar

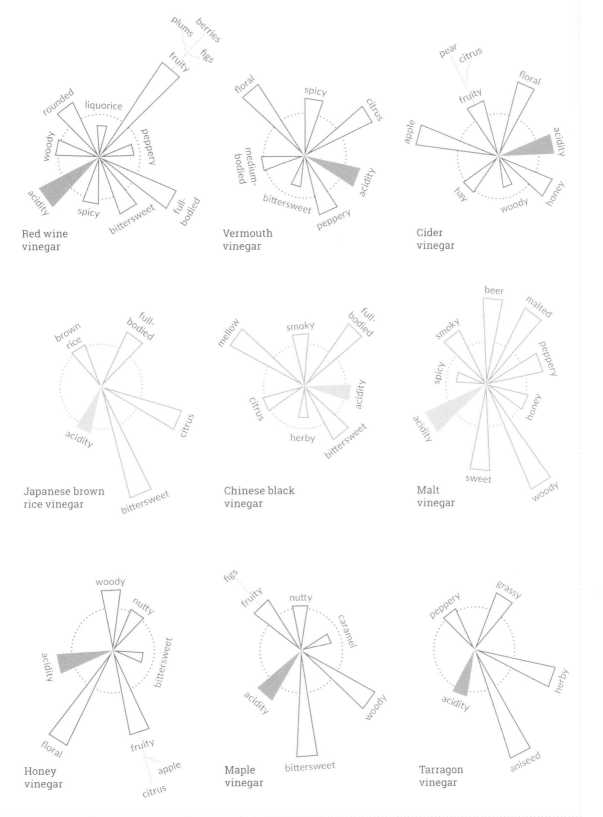

Red wine
vinegar

Vermouth
vinegar

Cider
vinegar

Japanese brown
rice vinegar

Chinese black
vinegar

Malt
vinegar

Honey
vinegar

Maple
vinegar

Tarragon
vinegar

Tasting and Storing Vinegar

The vinegars of the world share so much: their alchemy, wonder, the delicious contrast of sweetness to acidity, the usefulness to the cook of those elements as well as the layers of flavour that some (many) bring.

I hope that this book will be your guide to understanding and gauging vinegars from the label alone or by talking to the seller. But let's not underestimate the judgement to be made by simply tasting the vinegar and seeing if you like it. It's all very well knowing a lot about the heritage and production of a vinegar, but for it to be of any use to us in the kitchen we have to taste it and then decide if that particular vinegar has earned a space in our cupboard. Or, if you've already bought it, help you judge how best to use it.

How to taste vinegar

1. Pour about 2 teaspoons of the vinegar into a coloured glass or cup. It should be coloured so that your perceptions are not affected by the appearance of the vinegar.

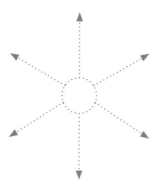

6. If you are tasting several vinegars, take a bit of something neutralising such as apple or bread between tastings.

5. Step back and ponder what you have just experienced. Think how this vinegar might sit within your cooking repertoire, and which other flavours it will marry with and help accentuate.

2. Leave it for a minute to let the smell settle down.

3. Take a gentle sniff. Step back. Let your nose get used to that smell. Then go back for another gentle sniff – you will find you get more from the second go once your senses are attuned.

4. Take a small sip. Let the vinegar sit initially on the front of your tongue as that is particularly sensitive to taste. Then breathe in through your mouth so that the air can develop the vinegar flavour on your palate. You should start to notice the flavours change. Swallow.

There are some key elements to look for when tasting vinegar:

- The balance of acidity to sweetness.
- The vinegar should be smooth, its acidity bright, but not so powerfully acidic that you feel a burn at the back of your throat.
- The flavour and aroma should be connected to whatever its base element is. Cider vinegars should have something of the apple about them; sherry vinegars should connect with whatever sherry variety they are from; and so on.
- Consider the density of the vinegar. See if it coats the inside of a glass or cup, or even just the bottle it's in, when tilted. A thicker balsamic or other vinegar will tend to be used as a condiment, and as a finish to a dish.
- As you taste the vinegar you should find its flavour develops. The initial taste may be dominated by the acidity, but that should then round out as its layers of flavour come through. The 'better' a vinegar, the more layers of flavour there will be. Your vinegar should hopefully have a pleasing aftertaste.

STORING VINEGAR

Vinegar doesn't go 'off' as such. It is, after all, a preservative. Yet opened vinegars can deteriorate in two key ways.

Firstly, in flavour. Exposure to air in the bottle as its liquid level goes down will dull the flavour profile. It's a sad thing to go back to a vinegar bottle that is nearly empty and has been that way for a while, hoping to enjoy its last lingering pleasures, only to find they are a shadow of what they were. My best advice once a bottle is about halfway done is, rather than eek it out, go for it and use it aplenty.

Then there are vinegar eels. Pesky little roundworms that feed on the mother of vinegar in raw, unfiltered vinegars. They are totally harmless but fairly unappealing and another argument in favour of using a vinegar once it is opened.

Store your vinegars as tightly sealed as possible, away from bright light (or in coloured bottles if they are in the light), and away from extremes of temperature.

Vinegar in the kitchen

Pickles

Pickling is one of the most common ways of using vinegar, taking advantage of its acidity to act as a preservative. We can choose whether to use quite plain vinegars for pickling so as to not 'interfere' with the flavours of whatever is being pickled, or go for a more interesting vinegar that can add its own level of flavour too. If chosen well to partner with whatever is being pickled, it can even enhance.

Note that the pickle-juice can be every bit as lovely and useful to the cook as whatever it has pickled. Just as it has given its own elements to that, it has taken others on. The vinegar will, over the pickling time, become imbued with all other flavours it has been sitting with, becoming an even lovelier vinegar or perfect to use as a dressing.

Quick-Pickles

Conventional pickling takes anything from a couple of weeks to a couple of months before being ready for eating. Part of that time is for whatever is being pickled to be penetrated by the pickling liquid, but part of it is to allow time for the flavours to mellow and round out. Try a jar of cucumber pickles just a couple of weeks after doing them and the flavours are pretty full on. After another couple of months, they will be less in your face.

All of which is but a preamble to the joys of quick-pickling. Best done with a mild vinegar – such as Japanese rice vinegar – that does not need time for its edges to be knocked off. It doesn't have any edges. What it does have is mild but effective acidity that in a couple of hours can really bring the flavours out of maybe cucumbers, radishes or onions. Whatever

you use they should be much more finely sliced than for conventional pickling. You want to give the vinegar the best chance of penetrating the pickled ingredient quickly. Note these pickles will not keep in the same way as conventional pickles.

Again, the quick-pickle juice will be useful for making a dressing or maybe using as the base for a drink.

Marinades

Vinegar does a couple of things as a meat marinade: it acts as a tenderiser and it contributes some flavour. I am aware that some science has cast doubts on how technically 'right' the first of those is but I am holding true to my personal experience and that of others over many, many years. Vinegar – like wine, or other acidic marinades such as buttermilk or yoghurt – can help turn a tougher cut into something tenderly fabulous.

For fish, marinating in vinegar crosses with what happens in a ceviche as the acidity 'cooks' the flesh. It helps protect the flavour of the fish much more than cooking over heat and gives a light texture – the added bite of the vinegar is always welcome.

For fruits, the vinegar is drawn into the fruit to balance its natural sweetness; and draws sweetness out of the fruit to balance its own acidity. What a marriage!

Roasting

One of my favourite ways to use vinegar is to toss it around all kinds of things that might get roasted. Be that meats, vegetables or fruits. Being in amongst all the other ingredients at the start of the roasting process allows it to really get melded in deeply with the other flavours, fully harmonising, and doing its absolute vinegar best to bring it all together.

Baking

Vinegar's acidity is put to technical use for baking. It can emulate the reactions of buttermilk and so be used to make pancakes or soda bread loaves. It can raise sponges into a lightness you have to try to fully appreciate. It can help keep meringues chewy on the inside, but crisp on the outside.

In baking – unless you especially want the flavour of the vinegar to come through – it is best to choose a plainer vinegar.

Seasoning

Just as vinegar can act as a lift within sauces, it can do so in its own right, too. We are all comfortable with how a sprinkling of salt helps bring out the best possible elements of a dish. Vinegar does that too. It brightens flavours and makes them the best version of themselves.

To use it as a finishing touch before serving, the trick is how you apply the vinegar. A straightforward 'pour' of vinegar can be too direct. I think a spray is best, allowing a light spritz of finish to be delicately placed across a dish or plate.

Dressings

Using vinegar in salad dressings is probably second in the list of 'usual' uses for vinegar (after pickling). It is indeed a great way to lift a salad, harmonising and balancing flavours. Especially useful if you can use a vinegar that brings its own flavour, too.

Drinks

Drinking vinegar 'shrubs' are a very old way of using vinegar to make drinks and have made a huge comeback in recent years. Vinegar is used to draw out the flavours of all kinds of fresh produce – be that fruits or root veg. It is sweetened and ready to use as a soft drink cordial, where its acidity and depth goes some way to replicating the pleasures of an alcoholic drink. Hence its modern revival as part of the low/no alcohol movement.

Which isn't to say it doesn't have its place in alcoholic drinks, too. Shrubs are great mixed into cocktails, as is just a dash of vinegar. The mixologists amongst us can play around with flavour matches that take advantage of the extra depth the vinegar brings. Again, it lifts and balances.

Away from shrubs, a simple dash or two of vinegar into a gin and tonic, a glass of sparkling wine or a cocktail can add depth, some welcome acidity and cut through any sweetness. The same is true with adding vinegar to soft drinks.

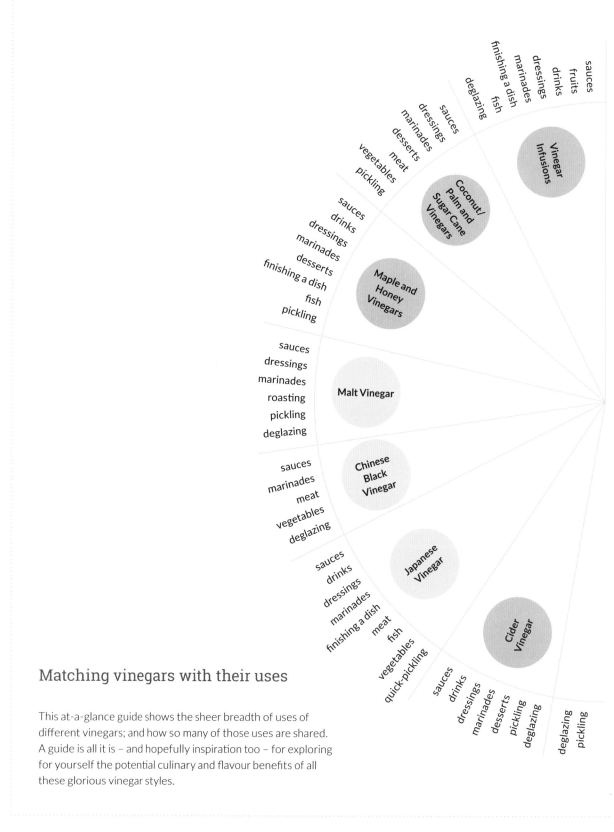

Vinegar Infusions
- sauces
- fruits
- drinks
- dressings
- marinades
- finishing a dish
- fish
- deglazing

Coconut/ Palm and Sugar Cane Vinegars
- sauces
- dressings
- marinades
- desserts
- meat
- vegetables
- pickling

Maple and Honey Vinegars
- sauces
- drinks
- dressings
- marinades
- desserts
- finishing a dish
- fish
- pickling

Malt Vinegar
- sauces
- dressings
- marinades
- roasting
- pickling
- deglazing

Chinese Black Vinegar
- sauces
- marinades
- meat
- vegetables
- deglazing

Japanese Vinegar
- sauces
- drinks
- dressings
- marinades
- finishing a dish
- meat
- fish
- vegetables
- quick-pickling

Cider Vinegar
- sauces
- drinks
- dressings
- marinades
- desserts
- pickling
- deglazing

- deglazing
- pickling

Matching vinegars with their uses

This at-a-glance guide shows the sheer breadth of uses of
different vinegars; and how so many of those uses are shared.
A guide is all it is – and hopefully inspiration too – for exploring
for yourself the potential culinary and flavour benefits of all
these glorious vinegar styles.

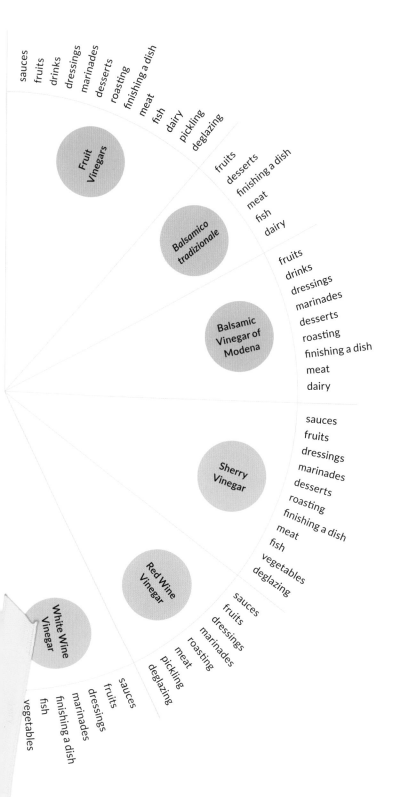

Fruit Vinegars
- sauces
- fruits
- drinks
- dressings
- marinades
- desserts
- roasting
- finishing a dish
- meat
- fish
- dairy
- pickling
- deglazing

Balsamico tradizionale
- fruits
- desserts
- finishing a dish
- meat
- fish
- dairy

Balsamic Vinegar of Modena
- fruits
- drinks
- dressings
- marinades
- desserts
- roasting
- finishing a dish
- meat
- dairy

Sherry Vinegar
- sauces
- fruits
- dressings
- marinades
- desserts
- roasting
- finishing a dish
- meat
- fish
- vegetables
- deglazing

Red Wine Vinegar
- sauces
- fruits
- dressings
- marinades
- roasting
- meat
- pickling
- deglazing

White Wine Vinegar
- sauces
- fruits
- dressings
- marinades
- finishing a dish
- fish
- vegetables

Sauces and Finishing a Dish

Here are some of the basic ways in which a variety of vinegars can be used to help bring a dish together. They are all so useful for cooking so many different meals, and their real glory is that the choice of vinegar rests entirely with the cook as to what feels right and what will best complement the whole.

Salad dressings are first. A fitting place to start when, for many people, using vinegar to dress a salad is both the beginning and end of what they use it for. While I hope to significantly expand this idea in the course of the recipes that follow, never let it be said that vinegar is anything but exceptional – essential – for dressing a salad. The right vinegar with the right oil and a little seasoning is hard to beat (although ideas are given here for how you can). Put as much thought – or more – into your vinegar as your oil and your dressing will sing with vibrancy and flavour. It will lift your salad and therefore the whole meal.

Simple sauces also work a similar magic. Here are béarnaise, beurre noir and beurre blanc (black and white butter) sauces and mayonnaise. Being French, these sauces are buttery, and being buttery they need something to cut through the fattiness. Step forward the clear, sharp notes of vinegar to do just that. In all of these sauces a wine vinegar (the classic French vinegar) would be the natural first choice, but I hope you will see that fruit or herb vinegars, cider vinegar, sherry vinegar, or even the grain vinegars have a right to be in these recipes, too.

From French sauces to the traditional accompaniments for a British roast, and more possibilities for mixing things up with your vinegar choice. How about cranberry sauce made with sherry vinegar or a blackcurrant vinegar; or mint sauce with a little hint of fig vinegar? The flavour notes will lie in the layers of how you enjoy the meal, giving almost unidentifiable depth.

Here too is a note about using vinegar in gravy. There is the kind of gravy made from all the good stuff left behind in the tray after roasting, but I know this is not how all gravies begin their life, so I have also included a basic no-roasting-tin gravy recipe. (For fantastic onion gravy that is the star turn with sausages and mash or toad in the hole, see page 224 where it accompanies meatballs.)

After all these come some simpler ways to round off a dish by deglazing the stove-top pan it was cooked in with a little of the vinegar of your choice. Maybe a cherry or red wine vinegar sizzled down in the steak pan to become just a smidge of sauce that can be drizzled over for a burst of flavour and acidity, cutting through the richness of the meat. It's a principle you can use whenever pan-cooking meats, game, poultry or fish.

The last word on using vinegar to finish a dish, to bring it all together, goes to the simplest way of all: a spritz of vinegar. Literally a spray of it, so that its mist will lie oh-so-delicately over the plate. I first came across this way of using vinegar to season a dish at its end with Gölles fruit vinegars in Austria. I still use these, and have decanted others into small spray bottles for the purpose. There is a whole repertoire of flavours – cucumber vinegar, black-cherry vinegar, vermouth vinegar and more – that with the lightest of spritzes are the perfect finishing touch.

SALAD DRESSINGS

The importance of vinegar in a salad dressing is somewhat given away by the name 'vinaigrette', which at its most basic is a mix of oil with vinegar and seasoning.

The standard ratio is two or three parts oil to one part vinegar. The final decision on that balance will be affected by the strength of the oil, the strength of the vinegar, what you are using it for and your own personal taste preference. For example, I – unsurprisingly, perhaps – will always favour a vinegar-heavy dressing.

The starting point should be thinking about what your vinaigrette is dressing, or what the dressed salad will be served with. Then just translate what you know about ingredient and flavour partnerships in the rest of your cooking and apply those to constructing the perfect vinaigrette. (A note for making salads that contain petals of flowers such as marigold, borage and nasturtium: the vinegar in a dressing can change their colour, so be sure to dress the petals at the last minute. The same rule applies to most leaf-based salads, to avoid them going sadly limp.)

Your salad dressing choices are infinite. Over the next couple of pages are a few ideas to get your creative juices going.

The building blocks to your dressing

Choose the vinegar you think will partner best with what it is dressing, or what the dressed salad will be served with.

Choose your oil with both the final dish and your vinegar choice in mind.

Remember to season it well with salt (and a little less well with pepper).

Then consider the following:

Does it need sweetening with sugar or honey? (If using a sweet vinegar like Moscatel or balsamic it will probably be sweet enough as it is.)

Do you want to add an emulsifier such as mustard or tahini to help stop the vinegar and oil separating – your choice of which will also add another layer of flavour?

Do you want other flavours/textures in there too, such as chopped shallot, chopped herbs, cayenne, caraway seeds, garlic?

OIL-FREE DRESSINGS

Not all salad dressings require oil, much as it is an almost Pavlovian response to reach for the oil when making them. Sherry vinegar mixed with honey and chilli flakes makes a delicious dressing to toss through tomatoes, herbs and walnuts. Or how about a mix of wine vinegar, lemon juice, Madeira wine, salt and chopped spring onions for a cucumber salad?

BASIC VINAIGRETTE

**3 tablespoons
  Moscatel vinegar**
6 tablespoons extra virgin
  olive oil
½ teaspoon English mustard
a good pinch of salt

Whisk everything together, then taste to see what it
needs more of.

RED WINE VINEGAR WITH HERBS

**3 tablespoons red
  wine vinegar**
6 tablespoons mild extra virgin
  olive oil or groundnut oil
2 teaspoons Dijon mustard
2 tablespoons finely
  chopped shallot
1 teaspoon capers,
  finely chopped
2 tablespoons finely chopped
  herb leaves – try parsley,
  wild garlic, dill, chervil
a pinch of caster sugar
  (optional)
salt and freshly ground
  black pepper

Whisk together the vinegar, oil and mustard to emulsify. Add
the other ingredients, season, taste and see if it needs more salt
or a pinch of sugar.

GOOD WITH
Salads of strong leaves, such as radicchio or chicory.

MUSTARD VINAIGRETTE FOR POTATO SALAD

150ml chicken or
  vegetable stock
½ red onion, finely chopped
4 teaspoons English mustard
**25ml white wine vinegar
  or cider vinegar**
75ml extra virgin olive oil
½ teaspoon caster sugar
salt and freshly ground
  black pepper

There are all kinds of variations on dressings for potato salad.
You could use a basic vinaigrette, or a mayonnaise, but my
preference is this mustard-rich vibrant vinaigrette. It is essential
to add it to the potatoes while they are still warm so they can fully
take on board the flavours. Then finish with some fresh tarragon
and parsley.

Bring the stock to the boil in a small saucepan, tip in the
chopped onion and return to the boil for 2 minutes. Strain the
onions out (keeping the liquid) and rinse the onions under cold
water through a sieve to refresh. Set them aside to drain.

In a large bowl, whisk together the mustard, vinegar, oil and
sugar. Whisk into that 75ml of the reserved stock, which should
by now have cooled, and season well. Stir through freshly-
cooked, still-warm potatoes.

TARRAGON AND NUTMEG

2 tablespoons
   tarragon vinegar
6 tablespoons walnut oil
¼ teaspoon English mustard
whole nutmeg
salt and freshly ground
   black pepper

Whisk together the vinegar, oil and mustard. Season, add a few gratings of nutmeg and taste.

SHERRY VINEGAR AND HAZELNUT

40g hazelnut kernels
2 tablespoons sherry vinegar
3 tablespoons extra virgin
   olive oil
3 tablespoons sunflower oil
2 teaspoons Dijon mustard
salt and freshly ground
   black pepper

In a spice or coffee grinder, grind the hazelnuts.

Whisk together the vinegar, oils and mustard. Whisk in 2 tablespoons of the hazelnuts, season and taste.

GOOD WITH
Pear or blue cheese salad.

CIDER AND HONEY

3 tablespoons cider vinegar
6 tablespoons groundnut oil
2 teaspoons mild honey
a pinch of ground cinnamon
salt and freshly ground
   black pepper

Whisk together the vinegar, oil and honey. Add the cinnamon, season and taste.

GOOD WITH
Beetroot or goat's cheese salads.

RICE VINEGAR AND TAHINI

3 tablespoons rice vinegar
   (or a dashi rice vinegar*
   for deeper flavour)
6 tablespoons groundnut oil
1 teaspoon tahini
salt and freshly ground
   black pepper

Whisk together the vinegar, oil and tahini. Season and taste.

* To make dashi rice vinegar: gently simmer 15g of kombu in 250ml rice vinegar for 3 minutes. Take it off the heat and stir in 1 tablespoon of bonito flakes. Leave it for 2 minutes then strain the solids out. Any unused dashi vinegar will keep for several months. It's great to have a stash of this for vinaigrette, it can be used to add a dash of Japanese-influenced depth to so many dishes – including the gomazu sauce on page 193.

Calling this 'black butter' is worryingly misleading as it sounds as if the plan is for the butter to go black. It isn't. If it does, the butter will have burnt and be horribly acrid. We want the butter to be heated to become a gorgeous deep mahogany brown, at which point vinegar is added to give it much-needed bite and to cut through the fat.

Herbs are often added, and chopped capers are the classic addition in the well-known pairing of skate with black butter. From there, think about serving beurre noir with any other mild fish; with bitter vegetables such as endive or radicchio; drizzle some over to finish a bowl of filled pasta; or use with a little sugar to sauté fruits such as plums or peaches.

Beurre Noir (Black Butter)

150g unsalted butter, cut into
    even-sized small pieces
**3 tablespoons white wine
    vinegar, or another vinegar
    of your choice**
chopped fresh herbs or capers
    (optional)
salt and freshly ground
    black pepper

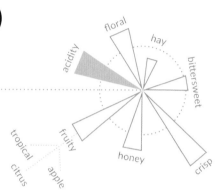

serves 4

Begin by clarifying the butter: heat the butter in a pan until just melted and the white milk solids separate off. Leave to cool a little, strain to remove the white solids, and you have clarified butter.

Pour the clarified butter into a pan set over a moderate heat. Use a wide-based pan for this if you can as that will allow you to see clearly the colour of the butter as it changes at the base of the pan (below the milk solids that rise to the top).

Gently whisk as the butter changes colour from golden to nutty to a rich, deep brown. When the butter stops sizzling it is on its way to browning. Do not wander, or even let your mind wander from the task. Once the butter starts browning it can burn fast. At the exact moment it reaches a mahogany colour, pour the butter into jug or another pan.

Return the now-empty pan to the heat and pour in the vinegar. Let it bubble for a minute over the heat to reduce by about half. Whisk the reduced vinegar into the butter, season and now is also the time to whisk in any other ingredients, such as herbs or capers, that you are adding to the sauce. Use straight away.

VINEGAR VARIATION

The vinegar should be chosen according to what you are serving it with. For example, a full-bodied red wine vinegar or balsamic vinegar would go well with scallops, while a fruit vinegar beurre noir makes a great glaze for a fruit tart.

Another rich, buttery French sauce that needs a hit of vinegar to save it from itself. This sauce is fabulous with poultry, fish and scallops. As ever, think about the choice of vinegar in relation to what you are serving. I like a champagne vinegar with scallops, for example.

Beurre Blanc (White Butter)

2 shallots, finely chopped
75ml white wine vinegar
75ml dry white wine
300g unsalted butter, cut into
    even-sized small pieces
chopped fresh herbs such as
    tarragon, chervil, oregano,
    dill (optional)
salt and freshly ground
    black pepper

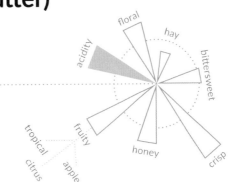

serves 4

Put the shallots, vinegar and wine into a pan over a low heat and reduce until you have just a couple of tablespoons of liquid left. Now whisk in the butter, piece by piece. Keep the heat low to avoid the sauce overheating and separating. It is done when smooth and the consistency of custard. Season and add any chopped herbs, if you fancy. Serve warm.

Béarnaise is a bit like hollandaise in that it is a gorgeously smooth, cashmere jumper of a buttery sauce, but different in that hollandaise's acidity typically comes from lemon juice, whereas vinegar is used for béarnaise. That gives much more potential for layers of flavour within the sauce. Béarnaise sauce is best served lukewarm (too hot and it will split), and is fabulous over steak, any grilled meats or fish.

Béarnaise Sauce

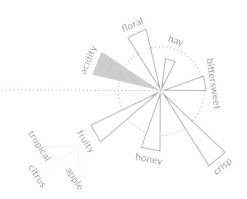

1 tablespoon finely
   chopped shallot
4 tablespoons finely chopped
   tarragon, or half-and-half
   tarragon and chervil
a sprig of thyme
**4 tablespoons white
   wine vinegar**
2 large egg yolks, at
   room temperature
175g unsalted butter, cut into
   small pieces
salt and freshly ground
   black pepper

serves 4

Put the shallots, half the tarragon, the thyme sprig and vinegar into a heavy-based saucepan and season. Sit it over a high heat for barely a couple of minutes until the liquid has reduced by half. Strain and set aside to cool.

Mix the egg yolks with 1 tablespoon of cold water in a glass bowl that can be set over a pan of water without the water touching the base of the bowl. Bring the water in the pan to a gentle simmer, set the bowl over it and whisk in the strained vinegar liquid. As it starts to thicken, add the butter piece by small piece, whisking all the time, until all the butter is incorporated.

Season, taste, season again if needed, and add the rest of the herbs. If you need to keep your béarnaise warm before serving, the bowl of sauce can continue to sit over the warm water for a while.

A more technically correct method of making this sauce is to clarify the butter before using. Not much of a faff, but I rather think it doesn't make too much difference to the end result. If you do want to go this route, heat the butter in a pan until just melted and the white milk solids separate off. Leave to cool a little, strain to remove the white solids, and you have clarified butter ready to use in the recipe above.

VINEGAR VARIATION

Tarragon or any herb-
infused vinegar would make
a great alternative, as would
cider vinegar.

I grew up loathing mayonnaise in about the same proportion to which I now love it. It was only in my mid-twenties that I realised that what I was actually loathing was the manufactured icky white gloop that is sold as mayonnaise – rather than the lustrous, glossy, deeply flavoured heaven that is 'real' mayonnaise. So while I still look suspiciously at any sandwiches and salads I don't make myself to check for any signs of the evil condiment, it is a whole different story when whipping up a mayo myself.

Making mayonnaise is insanely easy and delicious, and a world of creative options are available for any vinegar lover: malt vinegar mayonnaise with steak and chips for essential chip dunking; a quince vinegar mayonnaise with freshly griddled asparagus spears for more dunking opportunities; or any of the vinegar/mayonnaise combinations as noted in the Vinegar Variation below.

Mayonnaise

2 large egg yolks, at room
    temperature
1 tablespoon vinegar
    of your choice
½ teaspoon mustard powder
250ml groundnut or
    sunflower oil
50ml mild olive oil
salt and freshly ground
    black pepper

serves 4, generously

Rinse a mixing bowl with warm water, dry it thoroughly, then add the egg yolks and season. Whisk in the vinegar and mustard powder, then – very gradually – whisk in the oils. You can speed up the addition of the oils as you go, once the mixture is no longer in danger of splitting. Whisk vigorously all the time to create a lusciously thick mayonnaise. Taste at the end to see what it needs more of, if anything – salt, pepper, maybe even more vinegar. In the unlikely event that the mayonnaise isn't used all at once, it can be stored in the fridge for up to 3 days.

VINEGAR VARIATION
- For chicken: tarragon, elderflower, cucumber, lavender or Zinfandel white wine vinegar.
- For fish: cider, fennel, dill, tarragon, chive flower, nasturtium or cucumber vinegar.
- For seafood: champagne, vermouth or a light Japanese rice wine vinegar.
- For burgers: a mixed herb, basil, sage or horseradish vinegar.

These are sauces that traditionally accompany a British roast, but are also worthy of broader use in the sauce-making cook's repertoire. For each, the intensity of the lead ingredient is beautifully balanced by the vinegar. When making these, think about what the sauce is to go with (e.g. beef or salmon); what the sauce's lead ingredient is (e.g. horseradish or dill); and then what characteristic of vinegar is going to be the supreme flavour bridge between those things.

Sauces for a Roast

CRANBERRY SAUCE

250g cranberries
2 tablespoons soft brown sugar
**2 tablespoons balsamic
vinegar, sherry vinegar,
or a fruit vinegar such as
raspberry or blackcurrant**
zest and juice of ½ orange
a pinch of ground allspice

For turkey, of course, whether at Christmas, Thanksgiving or any other time. Boxing Day's turkey-leftover-sandwiches (and the tired-out family eating them) will get a pep-up from this cranberry sauce's fruity bite. Also good with game meats, especially venison and duck; sausages; or with salmon.

serves 6

Put all the ingredients into a pan and stir over a medium heat for 10 minutes or so, until the berries have burst. Allow to cool, then taste in case it might need a little more sugar, vinegar or spice. Store in the fridge for up to 1 week, or freeze.

MINT SAUCE

**2 tablespoons white
wine vinegar**
2 tablespoons caster sugar
3 handfuls of mint,
finely chopped

The classic partner for lamb. A simple white wine vinegar is the standard choice here, or swap it for cider vinegar, red wine vinegar or a two-thirds/one-third split of red wine vinegar and fig vinegar.

serves 6

Heat the vinegar and sugar in a pan with 1 tablespoon of boiling water, just until the sugar has dissolved. Take off the heat and stir through the mint. If you can, leave it for an hour or so to let the flavours mellow and get to know each other. It will keep for a week in the fridge, but be wary as the longer you leave it, the more the vibrant green will be tarnished by the vinegar.

DILL SAUCE

3 tablespoons mustard
**3 tablespoons white wine
    vinegar, or cider vinegar**
3 tablespoons brown sugar
½ teaspoon fine salt
4 tablespoons groundnut
    or sunflower oil
20g dill, finely chopped
freshly ground black pepper

A lovely partner to smoked or baked salmon, or indeed any baked fish. I'd also go for this with anything pork-related. The oil can be swapped for crème fraîche.

serves 6

Mix together the mustard, vinegar, sugar and salt. Slowly whisk in the oil, so it thickens as you go. Stir through the dill, season, then taste to see what it needs more of, if anything. (Or just whizz everything together in a blender.)

HORSERADISH SAUCE

3 tablespoons peeled and finely
    grated fresh horseradish root
**1 tablepoon cider vinegar, or
    white wine vinegar**
½ teaspoon caster sugar
150ml crème fraîche
1 teaspoon wholegrain
    mustard (optional)
salt

What would oh-so-British roast beef be without its horseradish sauce? A wonderful partner for beef casseroles, too, and think about Scandi-influences, with smoked fish or mackerel.

serves 6

Combine all the ingredients with a pinch of salt (and an optional teaspoon of wholegrain mustard). Use within a day or so of making.

As you take the joint out to rest and consider how to turn the sticky stuff left behind in the roasting tray into gravy, consider too what vinegar you might like to use. You'll be gravy-ing it up by adding some wine and/or stock to bubble away in the tray's deliciousness, and a tablespoon of vinegar in there will be a treat. It could be sherry vinegar, a deeply fruited one, cider vinegar or one of the Japanese or Chinese grain vinegars (though probably only if duck). Any of them – and others that may take your fancy – will give your gravy sweet and sour depth.

Otherwise, for a quick gravy made without the remnants of a roast in its tin, you can use the recipe below. Again, think about what vinegar might marry best with the flavours of the roast itself.

Roasting Tin Gravy

2 tablespoons olive oil
2 carrots, roughly chopped
1 medium onion,
    roughly chopped
1 bay leaf
1 teaspoon caster sugar
250ml red wine
250ml stock of your choice
75ml vinegar of your choice
20g butter
salt and freshly ground
    black pepper

serves 6

Heat the oil in a saucepan and sauté the carrots and onions with a pinch of salt until softened. Add the bay leaf, sugar, red wine, stock and vinegar. Bring to the boil, then reduce to a high simmer for approx. 12 minutes, or until reduced to a good gravy consistency. Strain out the solids, whisk in the butter, check the seasoning and serve.

Deglazing a pan after cooking steaks or chops or the like is the simplest of ways to create a quick sauce from the juices left behind. Vinegar goes to work with the very essence of whatever meat or fish has cooked in the pan to make that better than it would otherwise be. It is barely a recipe at all, more just a way of knowing how to bring balance and freshness to this kind of cooking.

This basic deglazing below can be built on by adding 50ml or so of stock or wine at the same time as the vinegar. You could also try adding a couple of anchovies, or whisking in a little cream to thicken.

Pan Deglazes

100ml vinegar of your choice
knob of butter, optional

serves 4

Lift out of the pan whatever you have been cooking and set aside to rest/keep warm, as appropriate. Into the same pan pour 100ml of the vinegar of your choice. Set the pan over a high heat and let it bubble for a minute or two to reduce by about half (stand back as there will be intense vinegar fumes). Season, and serve over whatever this is accompanying. That's it. You could add a knob of butter for a slightly richer version.

VINEGAR VARIATION
For red meats, go for a red wine vinegar, sherry vinegar, a good malt vinegar or an intensely fruity one. For white meat, the same vinegars apply, plus white wine vinegar or a cider vinegar. For fish, try a delicate fruited vinegar, a light white wine vinegar, a herb infusion or honey vinegar.

This sauce was popular in recipe books of the eighteenth and nineteenth centuries, but has rather fallen out of favour – or at least out of use. It's a shame as it has a lovely rich flavour to accompany roast pork, game, sausages or some really full-on langoustines. I think its revival is timely as more and more of us like to make our own elderflower drinks in the summer. If that includes you, you will know where to find the elderberries in the autumn for making this. (Important health and safety note: do not be in any way tempted to eat the elderberries without cooking them first.)

The recipe from Florence White's cookbook *Good Things in England* suggests storing pontac sauce for seven years before using. I don't think we need to worry about doing that, but try to give it seven days or so for the flavours to get acquainted.

Elderberry Pontac (or 'Pontack') Sauce

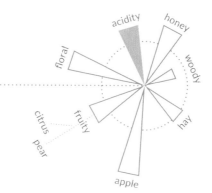

500g elderberries (use a fork
    to lift them off the stalks)
350ml cider vinegar
100g caster sugar
5 filleted anchovies, rinsed
    of their oil or salt
4 shallots, finely chopped
5 allspice berries
5 cloves
a blade of mace, or a good
    grating of fresh nutmeg
3cm piece of fresh ginger,
    peeled and grated
1 tablespoon black peppercorns
salt

makes 350ml

Preheat the oven to 120°C/100°C Fan/Gas Mark ½.

Put the elderberries, vinegar and sugar in an ovenproof dish suitable for use on the hob, and heat on the hob, just until the sugar has dissolved. Remove from the heat.

Add the remaining ingredients and a good pinch of salt. Cover the dish and sit it in the oven overnight, or for a minimum of 8 hours.

Strain the sauce through a sieve, pushing at the berries to get as much of their juice out as you can. Store the strained sauce in a sterilised jar and keep for 7 days before using. Once opened, store in the fridge. It will certainly keep for a good while, but I cannot vouch for 7 years.

VINEGAR VARIATIONS
You could use red or white wine vinegars, honey vinegar, or any herb-infused vinegar instead.

FRUIT AND BALSAMIC VINEGARS

Fruit Vinegars

It is a rather small limb for me to go out on to say that (probably) the very first, the very oldest types of vinegar are those made from fruits. The natural sugars present in fruit juices make them literally ripe for yeasts in the air to turn them into alcohol. From there it would have been only a matter of extra exposure to the atmosphere and the right kind of naturally occurring bacteria for them to become vinegar.

Historians believe that in ancient Egypt, and the ancient Babylonian and Sumerian regions of modern-day Iraq, there were types of vinegar being made from grains and fruits. Which means that from around 3000 BC we start to see evidence that give credence to figs, dates and grapes being pressed and the juice becoming a vinegar that was then used as a medicine, a preservative and to cook with. It is very probable that the Chinese vinegars we now associate with being primarily grain vinegars actually began as fruit ferment vinegars.

Just as rice vinegar is found where rice crops abound, and likewise wine vinegars appear where there are grape vines, so it is with the different fruit vinegars. They were traditionally made, and used, and have knitted themselves into their region's local cuisine wherever the crops are plentiful. We worry about waste these days, but for our agricultural and culinary ancestors waste was not an option. When fruits could not be preserved by the modern chilling technologies we have now, and the seasons meant the seasons with no jiggery-pokery of year-round crops, fruit harvests had to be maximised and made into all kinds of different things. Vinegar would be prime for that – especially as it could be used to preserve other produce.

Take, for example, the gooseberry, a very popular fruit in England in Victorian times. Recipes for its vinegar appear in many nineteenth-century domestic household management books, and I was thrilled to also find a recipe for making gooseberry vinegar in the *Vintner's, Brewer's, Spirit Merchant's and Licensed Victualler's Guide* of London in 1838 that was primarily aimed at the professions in the title. This is vinegar-making at its most hands off – the pressed gooseberry is fermented with yeast into alcohol, then simply left to stand and become vinegar – but its author reassures that this will 'render it an admired vinegar', and I bet it did. Would that we had more opportunities these days to enjoy a good gooseberry vinegar from a bar or spirits shop. Just the thing for a gin and tonic.

Modern fruit vinegar is still, at its most simple, the fruit juice or the 'must' of the fruit that is fermented into alcohol and from there to vinegar. 'Must' is usually talked about in balsamic-making as what you get when you press the fruit (juice, skins and all), but can apply to other fruit vinegars too. On which basis, raspberry vinegar is made from raspberries that have been fermented into alcohol, then in turn fermented into vinegar. And yet the words 'raspberry vinegar' on the label of your vinegar could mean something quite different. Not bad necessarily, just different. It could be another vinegar – distilled, rice, balsamic, wine or cider vinegar – that has had raspberry-ness added to it via an infusion, or an extract of the fruit, or maybe by heating the vinegar with the fruit. Modern vinegar-makers are developing lots of new, clever ways of getting the maximum fruit flavour in there. And some of them are good.

must

the pressings of fruit to extract for use the juice, skin and seeds. Usually grapes but also apples and other fruits.

Adding a non-vinegar fruit element to a vinegar obviously weakens the overall acidity. Only a base vinegar that is high in acidity can handle being blended with a non-vinegar fruit ingredient, and still be acidic enough for cooking tasks where high acidity is required (such as pickling or sousing), so then the challenge is in knocking off the base vinegar's harsh edges. A close look on the vinegar-product shelf in Taiwan would reveal that many or even most of its mass of fruit vinegars are actually grain vinegars with fruit juice added. Not that the label itself would reveal that to me and my non-existent Mandarin. It is the low (below 5%) vinegar acidity that is the clue. These are usually used as drinking vinegars and so the low acidity doesn't matter in a cooking sense. You may also find low-acidity fruit vinegar blends sometimes labelled as 'condiment' vinegars.

The point is about knowing what it is we are getting, and how it has been made. Then we can make an informed choice. On the label there should clearly be a distinction made between whether 'raspberry vinegar' (or whatever, I don't mean to pick on raspberries here) means twice-fermented raspberries; or means another base vinegar with raspberry added to it somehow. When all is said and done, what matters most – as well as knowing what it is you are buying and using – is that the end-result vinegar is packed with well-balanced flavour. Because that is the reason fruits have been used as vinegars for millennia right across the world.

Japan deserves its own special mention for fruit vinegars. Vinegar is seriously trendy in Japan. In Tokyo Station there is an 'Expre-su Bar' (the suffix 'su' meaning vinegar), where in the morning you see locals queuing for their morning vinegar hit, just as in London you see folks queuing for coffee. Come the afternoon, that same bar switches to selling ice cream with vinegar drizzled over it. Much of this fashion is for fruit vinegars.

Then there is Mexico, where pineapples are one of its most important crops and where you might find local dishes using *vinagre de piña*. Date vinegars are still mainly produced in the Middle East.

There are so many international fruit vinegars, and so many of them are excitingly – if slightly frustratingly – contained at a regional level and are not being made or exported commercially. In our age of globalisation, I rather love that there are wonderful, intriguing vinegars in kitchens around the world that are really only known to, made by or used by the locals. It is curiously heartening.

Categorising fruit is a tricky business, and not one I am in, so the distinctions that follow of berry fruits, stone fruits, pomme fruits and tropical fruits are made only where helpful for the purposes of considering fruit vinegars. Specific 'cooking with' ideas are given with each vinegar, but here are a few suggestions as to how fruit vinegars might be used: ················

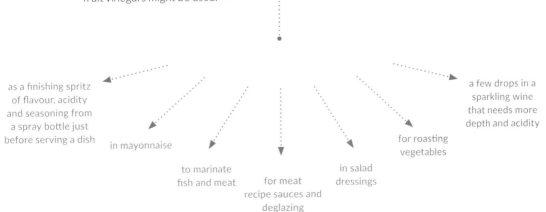

as a finishing spritz of flavour, acidity and seasoning from a spray bottle just before serving a dish

in mayonnaise

to marinate fish and meat

for meat recipe sauces and deglazing

in salad dressings

for roasting vegetables

a few drops in a sparkling wine that needs more depth and acidity

Pomme fruits

Apple

Most apple vinegars are to be found as apple cider vinegar. But sometimes apples are given their own focus, where the onus is on the fruit rather than the cider which is the apple vinegar's middle stage of alcoholic fermentation. Meaning: where it is made in non-cider regions, it would more typically be called apple vinegar, and possibly made with dessert (not cider) apples.

It is a common feature of Korean cooking, used to stand up to and balance out strong flavours, and proving once again that where a nation has a culture of growing and enjoying particular crops, these tend to be what emerge as their most-used vinegars too.

Try: partnered with pumpkin seed oil in cabbage and pork dishes; in a vinaigrette to dress asparagus; added to a beer as the Japanese might have it; with roasted vegetables; in Korean dishes.

(For apple 'balsamics' – quotation marks necessary or not dependent on your view of the absolute right of protection the Italians have over any use of the word balsamic outside of their designated regions – see page 63.)

Pear

The deep flavour of pears makes them even more suited to being vinegared than apples, I think. A good pear vinegar has the same lovely fragrance that the fruit's tannin-rich skins hold.

Try: as a marinade for meat; in duck and game recipes, or to finish them; in Asian cooking, especially vegetables and fish; as a drinking vinegar; in salad dressings; a few drops into sparkling wine.

Quince

Quinces not only have a short season but also a short larder life, so making them into vinegar is a wonderful way of preserving their heavy, musky fragrance and flavour for year-round culinary pleasure. A good quince vinegar is almost honey-sweet, but with finely balanced acidity.

Try: in Asian cooking; mayonnaise and hollandaise; for marinading, cooking or dressing chicken; into sauces; to dress raw fish; over hard or soft cheese; over roasted fruit.

Tropical fruits

Banana

Not the most common of vinegars outside the banana-growing nations, of which India and South and Central America are the most significant. Historically, banana vinegar was made because bananas would go off quickly, so it was a good way of using and preserving them. Typically it is made from fermenting pressed banana flesh, although it can also be made using the skins.

Try: think about using it whenever making the food of banana-producing regions, so that includes India, China, South and Central America and the Philippines; also very good for ceviches.

Kachampuli

This non-vinegar is worth mentioning here because kachampuli is popular in south-west India and confusingly referred to as 'vinegar'. It is the concentrated, slightly fermented juice of the gummi-gutta fruit, and widely used for dressing salads or cooking meat. But actual alcohol- and acetic-fermented vinegar it is not.

Persimmon

Made with the South Korean *meoksi* variety of persimmon, this is a vinegar with a very long heritage in Korea. So much so that it was entered as the 2,000th product in the 'Ark of Taste' catalogue of heritage foods. It used to be a key ingredient in Korean cooking, but is sadly rather harder to find these days. Its heritage of use as a medicinal tonic – especially for controlling cholesterol and liver function – is as long as its pedigree in the kitchen.

Try: in Korean cooking; in salad dressings; in fruit salads.

Pineapple

This is a favourite vinegar in Honduras, where pineapples are grown aplenty and every part of the fruit is used, from the prickly skins to the core. In the Philippines, where pineapple vinegar is one of the more expensive of the locally produced vinegars, the commercial producers make use of the off-cut trimmings of canning the fruit to make the vinegar.

Pineapple vinegars in Taiwan – another area of mass pineapple production – tend to be a blend of pineapple juice with grain vinegar, as mentioned earlier. In summary: wherever there are pineapples grown – or more pertinently, wherever they are grown and then prepared for commercial sale – there will be pineapple vinegars made in varying ways to suit the local economy.

Try: as an alternative to Japanese rice vinegars; in salad dressings; as a marinade for meat or fish; over starfruit; over pineapple slices baked with butter and sugar to caramelise; in the cuisine of any pineapple-growing region, such as the Philippines, Taiwan, Honduras and Mexico.

Berry fruits*

*for simplicity, including those that
are called berries even if they are not
actually botanically so

Aronia berries/
Chokeberries

These shrubs are commonly found in Eastern Europe and North America, with their sour, dark-skinned berries high in the good-for-you antioxidants and polyphenols. They are used in wines, jams, juices and – of course – vinegars.

Try: as a marinade for fish and meat; for meat recipe sauces and deglazing; into sparkling wine; over ice cream.

Bokbunja/
Black raspberry

This wild berry is hugely popular in Korea, China and Japan, where it often crops up as a vinegar that is high in antioxidants, just as the fruit is in its natural state.

Try: in duck and other game dishes, or as a deglaze, or to finish a dish; drizzled over hard or soft cheeses, fruit salads or ice cream; into cocktails; made into a drinking vinegar.

Cucumber

So many cucumbers barely taste of anything that you might imagine a cucumber vinegar would barely taste of anything either. Not so. Cucumber vinegar tastes like my memory of the best cucumber I ever had, given to me by a gardener straight off its vine. It is the taste of a British summer (with notes that are familiar to anyone partial to a Hendrick's gin).

Try: for pickling cucumbers; to finish gazpacho; a spritz over light summer salads, crab or salmon;

in Asian dishes in place of, or as well as, the lighter rice vinegars; as a marinade for fish, mixed with light oil, grated ginger and black mustard seeds; into a gin cocktail or G&T.

Elderberry

Recipes for elderberry vinegars crop up frequently in old British cookbooks of the 1700s and 1800s.
These berries can't be eaten raw, so turning them into vinegar was a savvy way of making them useful, and I think their popularity back then makes them well worth a look now, too. Elderberry vinegar tends to be sweet, thick and full of flavour.

Try: in salad dressings; over apple slices (especially in a pie or crumble); drizzled onto hard cheese; as a marinade for fish and meat; for meat recipe sauces and deglazing; over ice cream, chocolate cakes or brownies.

Fig

Fleshy, aromatic figs make for an intense, sweet vinegar that is one of the very oldest vinegars we know of. As well as vinegars in which the figs have been double-fermented, this is one fruit that has especially excellent vinegar blends. Look out for rice vinegars suffused with fig, or wine vinegars macerated with dried figs.

Try: drizzled onto hard or soft cheese; for carpaccio; as a marinade for fish and meat; for meat recipe sauces and deglazing; in game dishes, or to finish them; with roasted vegetables; over ice cream, chocolate cakes or brownies; over roasted fruits.

Gooseberry

Another vinegar that seems
to always crop up in old recipe
books and, happily, is now being
revived. With their natural
balance of sweet and sharp, gooseberries make
for an entrancingly fragrant vinegar.

*Try: for dressing savoury and fruit salads; in
mayonnaise; as a marinade for fish; over pancakes;
into a G&T; a few drops into sparkling wine; over ice
cream; into elderflower cordial.*

Melon

The juice of sweet, ripe
melons is perfect for
creating a light, zesty vinegar or balsamic blend.

*Try: as a marinade for fish, or in a fish carpaccio; on
melon sorbet; on slices of fresh melon with cracked
black pepper; with prosciutto.*

Pomegranate

Another ancient vinegar,
which has lots of fabulous
modern uses and often
crops up as a blend with
balsamic vinegar.

The pomegranate's credentials as a
'superfood' are interesting in vinegar terms.
Just as apple vinegars concentrate the
polyphenols of apples, so with pomegranate
vinegar. A recent study of the 'mother' (the
name for the film of cellulose that binds
together the bacteria that make the vinegar) in
apple cider vinegar compared it to the mother
from pomegranate vinegar, and interestingly it
was the pomegranate mother that came out
as having a higher concentration of some
beneficial polyphenols.

*Try: as a marinade for fish; for meat recipe sauces
and deglazing; in game dishes or to finish them;*

*a few drops into sparkling wine; over ice cream,
chocolate cakes or brownies; over smoked duck;
over fruit salad and pancakes.*

Raspberry, strawberry, blackberry, blackcurrant

The punch of rich red
fruitiness makes these an
excellent option instead of –
or in tandem with – red wine
vinegar for marinades and salads.

Raspberry vinegar is traditionally drizzled
over Yorkshire puddings for good reason. It is
a sensationally delicious combination, and one
worth remembering for other batter recipes
such as pancakes. Yet raspberry vinegar is
reputedly difficult to produce in marketable
quantities while consistently retaining flavour.
You may have to hunt around for one with
enough 'raspberry' to it, or go for an infused/
extracted version.

When I first tried a really good blackcurrant
vinegar (by the Austrian maker Gegenbauer), it
was like a blackcurrant flavour explosion. Not
very sweet at all, but then blackcurrants tend
not to be. Sensational.

*Try: drizzled onto hard cheese; as a marinade
for fish and meat; for meat recipe sauces and
deglazing; in game dishes or to finish them; over
smoked duck; for roasting vegetables; a few drops
into sparkling wine; over ice cream, chocolate
cakes or brownies; over roasted fruits; blackcurrant
vinegar on slices of fresh apple with some cracked
black pepper.*

Tomato

Sweet, juicy tomatoes are
perfect for a vinegar that has
something of the air of sun-
dried tomatoes about it. Use sparingly.

*Try: on goat's cheese; in tomato salads and sauces;
in Asian cooking; into a Bloody Mary.*

Stone fruits

Apricot

It is not easy to protect the special fragrance of ripe apricots when they are made into vinegar, so where that is achieved the vinegar is a very special prize indeed. The gorgeous combination of the sweetness of the fruit with the acidity of vinegar makes for a surprisingly powerful vinegar that can hold its own with strong flavours and works gorgeously as a spritz finish.

Try: in Asian sweet-and-sour dishes; as a spritz over salmon; with seafood and crustaceans; partnered with ginger or cardamom; drizzled over goat's cheese with cracked black pepper; as a Korean-style dressing with sesame oil, black sesame seeds, cayenne pepper, a little grated ginger and chopped coriander leaves; for marinating, cooking or dressing chicken; in meringue; whipped into cream.

Cherry

These vinegars are sometimes made with sour cherries, and sometimes with sweet cherries. Whichever you choose, this should be a burst of sweet, fruity acidity, and another very broadly usable fruit vinegar. It is as happy in salad dressings as in Asian dishes or garnishing a European peasant soup. Some cherry vinegars have a very pleasing almond note to them, too.

Try: as a marinade for meat; for deglazing meat pans; in duck and game dishes, or to finish them;

in Asian cooking, especially vegetables and fish; as a drinking vinegar; with beetroot; drizzled over goat's cheese; for dressing dark leaves.

Mango

World production of mangoes centres on Asia and India in particular. As the global demand for the fruit increases, there are – maybe slightly perversely – increasing volumes of mangoes that don't make the cut for more typical usage, and so are made into by-products such as mango vinegar. To be found in mango-producing nations across Asia, Africa, South and Central America. It is typically made by diluting and filtering the mango pulp, adding sugar so that it can be turned into alcohol, and from there made into vinegar. As mangoes have grown in global popularity, mango-buying (rather than producing) nations can have a crack at making mango vinegar, too, adding to the international spread of use of this vinegar. These are vinegars full of lush fruitiness.

Try: when cooking dishes from those regions where mangoes – and mango vinegars – can be found; for fish ceviche; with seafood; over fruit salads and ice cream.

Plum

Plums make for marvellous vinegar – fruitily, muskily intense and sweet. This is one of my favourites, and exceptionally versatile as it can be used in place of red wine vinegars and partners well with sweet and savoury flavours.

Note that if you come across the Japanese *ume* plum vinegar (which is typically used to pickle the nation's magnificent *sakura* cherry blossom ahead of them being dried and salted), it is not technically a vinegar but is the brine that results from salting the *ume* into *umeboshi*.

Try: in Asian dishes; drizzled onto hard cheese or goat's cheese; over ice cream; as a marinade for fish; for meat recipe sauces and deglazing; in game dishes or to finish them; over smoked duck; with beetroot or red cabbage; over roasted fruits; a few drops into sparkling wine.

Prune

It is interesting just how different the vinegar made from dried plums is from that made from fresh plums – it is even more intense.

Try: to season pork, game or offal (especially liver) dishes; in pâtés; over ice cream.

Walnut

This is one where the fruit – in this case walnuts – is not doubled fermented into vinegar, but where walnut-ness is added to another vinegar. The base is often a white wine vinegar, with champagne vinegar an especially popular choice for its own subtlety that allows the walnut through. Walnut vinegar is more rounded than walnut oils, making it a good choice for dishes that will benefit from the nutty edge.

Try: drizzled onto hard cheese or goat's cheese; over fruits such as peaches, melon or strawberries; as a salad dressing; as a glaze or finishing spritz to meat.

The breadth of fruit vinegars uses and pairings

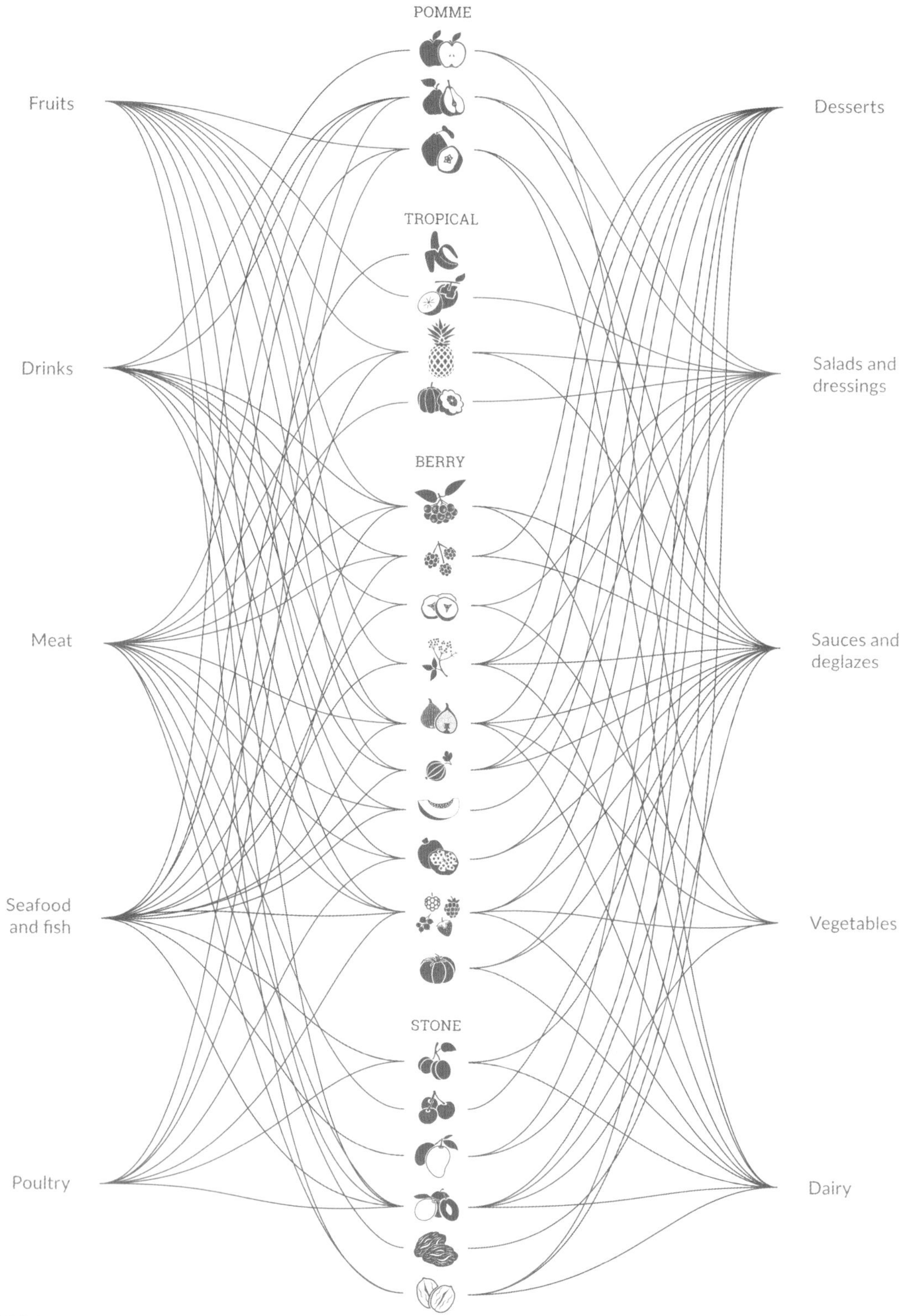

POMME

TROPICAL

BERRY

STONE

Fruits

Drinks

Meat

Seafood and fish

Poultry

Desserts

Salads and dressings

Sauces and deglazes

Vegetables

Dairy

Balsamic Vinegars

FRUIT BALSAMIC VINEGARS

The most famous fruit balsamic vinegar is, of course, the Italian balsamic vinegar made using fermented grape must, or grape must with wine vinegar. It is not the only fruit balsamic vinegar around, though – whatever the Modenese people who produce that iconic balsamic may think. In 2009, when Balsamic Vinegar of Modena was applying for its protected EU IGP/PGI status (see page 69), there were question marks raised by Germany and Greece. Germany was worried that it would damage their ability to produce and sell its *Balsamessig*, and Greece was similarly concerned about its *balsamico* or *balsamon*; both had been making their products long enough for their concerns to be legitimate. The ruling was that the Modenese way is indeed especially worthy of protection, covering any balsamics claiming to be made like that, or in Modena. Crucially, though, it was not a ban on balsamics everywhere. I know some balsamic producers in Modena would love to own the word completely, but others have no intellectual or commercial problem where the risk of confusion is very small – for example, if the fruit being balsamic-ed is not giving the illusion of being a Modena grape balsamic.

All of which leads the way to the glorious fruit balsamic vinegars produced in many countries, and possibly best of all in Germany and Austria. I am thinking of their apple balsamic, pear balsamic and fig balsamic. Such beautifully rich, fragrant, delicious, musky and dense vinegars that bear the hallmarks of traditional balsamic-making: the fruit is pressed to produce a must, then fermented and aged in wooden barrels that decrease in size as the vinegar ages. Over time, water evaporates through the wood of the barrels to intensify the vinegar and cause it to become denser. It is the way of vinegar-ageing that is familiar in sherry vinegar in Andalucía, and, yes, balsamic vinegar in Modena.

Such fruit balsamics are wonderful as a sauce or dressing, for dipping bread or vegetables into or for finishing a dish. Their inherent sweetness also makes them a terrific option for a drinking vinegar – just pour over ice, dilute with sparkling water and be immediately refreshed.

Just as with the balsamic of Modena, there are other fruit balsamics being produced by mixing fruit must with wine vinegar. The same logic applies as to Modena balsamic: if the lead ingredient on the bottle's label is wine vinegar rather than fruit, you are buying a vinegar that is mainly wine vinegar. That can be fine and perfectly lovely in its own right, but it may be less dense and so more suited to cooking or making dressings, than as a dish finisher. Many aspects of the choosing guide on page 76 apply here.

Then there are the blends: balsamic vinegar mixed with raspberries, cherries or tomatoes, for example. The makers of these have taken quite a large stride away from classic balsamic, and in so doing are striving to achieve a cohesion of flavours, sweetness (often very high), acidity (often very low) and density. Get a good one and its flavour could be wonderful. Some of these are thick enough to be used as a savoury glaze or sweet sauce, which is handy – but the flip-side is that they can be oversweet and cloying. I think it is far better to make your own reduction of fruit balsamic in the same way as a reduction of a Modenese balsamic (see page 72).

Leading us seamlessly onto the big-gun in the balsamic world…

THE BALSAMIC VINEGARS OF EMILIA-ROMAGNA

Most mentions of 'balsamic vinegar' do not, broadly speaking, mean one of the fig or apple or other fruit versions of page 63. If that is what is meant it will be explicitly said. What is generally meant is the wonderful but slightly confusing world of balsamic vinegars that hail from the iconic grape balsamics of northern Italy. So this section is concerned with ironing-out our understanding of which of those are truly wonderful, and which are only trying to appear so. Because choosing one of these balsamic vinegars can be a perplexing business. Bottles of varying shapes and sizes, lined up against each other, all carrying the word 'balsamic' but with prices that vary enormously and not necessarily any particularly clear indication as to why. (Later in this chapter comes a guide to choosing that will hopefully help you quickly decipher what those bottles of balsamic on the shelf actually are.)

From the balsamic *Tradizionale* at the top end, through the many other balsamics vinegars which are a commercial reaction to *Tradizionale*'s huge popularity, the key to knowing how to choose – or how to use – each of them lies in understanding more about what they are, where they have come from and how they are made.

Each section on the particular versions of balsamic has its own 'in the kitchen' ideas for using. They stretch beyond the salad dressing convention that causes those two bottles of olive oil and balsamic to be such a familiar sight on so many café tables. Theirs is something of an incongruous partnership given that the north of Italy, from where balsamic originates, is not really olive oil country. Food-writer Anne del Conte has called it the 'butter line' across Italy. South of it is olive oil while in the north the Roman olive groves were given over to grapes, and for centuries the locals instead got their fats for cooking from the animals they farmed. In the balsamic region that wasn't so much butter as delicious pork fat. There is olive oil there now, of course, but I am still unconvinced by the happiness of its relationship with balsamic. My preference would be to use another wine vinegar for a salad dressing. After all, it's not as though we are short of ways of using balsamic – as I hope you will discover.

EU certifications of the origins, geographical location and traditional character of foods

Denominazione di Origine Protetta (DOP)
Protected Designation Origin (PDO)

.... The highest level of classification, given to products with the strongest links to where they are made. Every stage of producing it must take place in the specific region, area or country. Their qualities are intrinsically connected to that geographical environment.

Indicazione Geografica Protetta (IGP)
Protected Geographical Indication (PGI)

.... Classification given to products with links to a geographical region that impact upon the quality or reputation of the product. At least one stage of producing it must take place in the specific region, area or country.

Overview of balsamic vinegar styles

Aceto Balsamico Tradizionale di Modena (DOP)
Traditional Balsamic of Modena (PDO)

Aceto Balsamico Tradizionale di Reggio Emilia (DOP)
Traditional Balsamic of Reggio Emilia (PDO)

This is the authentic, legendary balsamic vinegar that is made only in northern Italy's regions of Modena and neighbouring Reggio Emilia. Its only ingredient is grape must. It is produced in very particular ways, is strictly assessed for quality, is distinctively bottled and labelled and is far more expensive than other balsamics due to how it is made and its limited supply versus extensive demand.

Aceto Balsamic di Modena (IGP)
Balsamic Vinegar of Modena (PGI)

This is what most recipes mean when they refer to 'balsamic vinegar'. It is certainly what I mean. Ingredients are grape must blended with wine vinegar. There are also controls about where it is made and how, but they allow real variance in production and therefore quality. Labelling interpretation skills are required.

Condimento/condiment

An all-embracing term, sometimes used to describe balsamic vinegars that may have some of the attributes of *Tradizionale* or Balsamic Vinegar of Modena, but do not have the classification. Or it is a name sometimes used for pseudo-balsamics that are a rather long way away from the real McCoy. When they are good they are very, very good, but when they are bad... Again – when buying these, some basic balsamic label-interpreting skills will be a help.

'Variations on a balsamic theme'

This is my phrase rather than an official classification, and it includes white balsamic and balsamic pearls.

ACETO BALSAMICO TRADIZIONALE DI MODENA AND *ACETO BALSAMICO TRADIZIONALE DI REGGIO EMILIA*

In the northern Italian region of Emilia-Romagna sit two cities with huge international vinegar impact. They are the well-known balsamic-bottle words of 'Modena' and 'Reggio Emilia'. The balsamic vinegars produced in these provinces in the traditional style – the *Aceto Balsamico Tradizionale di Modena* and *Aceto Balsamico Tradizionale di Reggio Emilia* – are the elite of balsamic vinegars.

To understand *Tradizionale* (in my shorthand) is to understand how balsamic vinegar achieved its status, and why producers go to great lengths to replicate it more cheaply. It is the key to everything else there is to know about balsamic. So if all this seems like a lengthy description for something you may never have, please bear with it.

The facts about the origins of balsamic are a little thin. It could have originated in Modena or Reggio Emilia, or it could have been in another town in the region. What seems likely is that this is another story of vinegar created by accident. *Saba* is the syrup made from cooked grape must that has long been used in the area for cooking. 'Must' is what you get from pressing grapes: juice, skin, seeds, stems – the lot. Balsamic vinegar may have begun with some *saba* being left exposed, fermenting in the natural yeasts and bacteria in the air, so that by the time it was found again it had taken on a very pleasing sweet-and-sour flavour. Could it really be that from the simplicity of such sheer chance was born the vinegar prized for centuries beyond all others by generations of locals, and more recently by the world? I rather hope so, and don't really mind not knowing for sure. It all adds to the lure.

As does the lore that surrounds the first mentions of balsamic vinegar in poetry, or in the ancient records of local families and the dukes that historically ruled the region. I am not going to dwell too much on that here. I worry how much of it is actual fact, and how much has just been repeated so often by those who tell the story of balsamic that they now just sound like facts. What is safe to say is that from around the eleventh century onwards, families in the Modena and Reggio Emilia regions were producing their own limited supplies of cooked grape-must vinegar.

The process used then is recognisable from that of today: grape must was cooked to reduce it and intensify its fruity sweetness; it was double-fermented to acidity, and aged through sequences of ever-smaller wooden barrels of different woods. The barrels would often be kept in airy attics to be exposed to variations in temperature. Through warm summers the vinegar would evaporate through the wood, then in cold winters it would rest. As time went on the vinegar became darker. It intensified in flavour and texture as it naturally evaporated through the wood.

The end result was that this balsamic vinegar, with its distinctive characteristics, produced in small batches and over many years, began to take on value. It could not be bought but would be given as a gift of status beyond its own region, thus spreading its fame. One of the stories often told about balsamic dates to 1046, when the feudal leaders of Tuscany (not very far from Emilia Romagna) presented the German king Henry III, who was to become Roman Emperor, with the vinegar as a gift. Very definitely the kind of gift you only give to impress.

The nub of all this is that historically the *Tradizionale* balsamic vinegar was not a commercial product. It was made by families for their own use, with the barrels of balsamic being handed down through the generations. I have spoken to Modena locals in their fifties or so who remember travelling not all that far outside the region when they were younger, and being surprised to realise that the balsamic vinegar they knew and loved – and maybe took for granted – was simply not to be found. Those other towns enjoyed their own mono-varietal wine vinegars such as Chianti or Barolo, but balsamic vinegar was a local product for local consumption. Local families still today very much prize their stocks of *Tradizionale*, and the good stuff will always come out for special occasions such as weddings.

The second half of the twentieth century brought increasing interest in travelling and exploring different food cultures. That would come to mean more tourists travelling to Italy and discovering its many culinary charms. At the same time,

Italians who had moved elsewhere were becoming increasingly proud of how others revered their coffee, their food ... ok, maybe not their vinegar – yet – but perhaps the balsamic producers had a feeling for what was happening. In 1969 a Coterie was set up in Modena of *Tradizionale* producers, with the stated aims of protecting and promoting their vinegar. With hindsight we can see they were potentially conflicting goals.

The late 1970s is when the first balsamic vinegars were exported to the US. To say they caught on is a bit of an understatement. Through the 1980s and 1990s balsamic vinegars became hugely fashionable and desirable – chefs were drizzling them over everything. What ensued was a conflict between considerable demand, *Tradizionale*'s limited supply, and price.

Remember, *Tradizionale* is not – was not – intended to be produced on a significantly commercial scale. Its process does not allow for that. It just takes too long. So the vinegar-makers' response was to produce and market another incarnation of balsamic vinegar. (To discover the commercial development of *Aceto Balsamico di Modena* – which is notably not *Tradizionale* – see page 69).

The *Aceto Balsamico Tradizionale di Modena* and *Aceto Balsamico Tradizionale di Reggio Emilia* are still being produced, of course. It is a minuscule amount of the total balsamic vinegar made each year, but the fact of its continuing existence gives credibility to the non-*Tradizionale* balsamic. For as long as consumers can read about ancient Italian dukes, see pictures of wooden barrels and hear about years of ageing, they will continue to associate the (relatively) cheap balsamic vinegar they buy with *Tradizionale*'s glorious elixir.

Modern *Tradizionale* is produced under very strict guidelines that are set out and enforced by the governing Consortia that evolved out of the Coterie. Since gaining EU DOP/PDO (*Denominazione di Origine Protetta*/Protected Designation of Origin) status, the specific criteria of its production are further regulated and protected. The rules can seem complicated but for the most part are there to protect the very simplicity of how the *Tradizionale* has long been made. The basic process is as it has ever been.

The grapes: any variety can be used as long as they are from the region. That could be Trebbiano, Lambrusco, Pignoletto, Sauvignon or others. They are harvested in autumn, then pressed to produce the grape must.

Cooking: the grape must is cooked in a large open vessel at approximately 80°C for several hours, or as long as it takes to achieve the concentrated sweetness the producer is after. As the must cooks it begins to take on the characteristic balsamic elements of colour, flavour and smell. Known as *mosto cotto*, it can be used at this point as a sweet syrup.

Fermentation and ageing: the cooked grape must sits in a wooden barrel for the winter to naturally go through its initial fermentation. Then in the spring it will begin its long journey through the 'battery' of half a dozen or so wooden barrels that decrease in size as they progress.

Every year some of the 'ready' balsamic *Tradizionale* is removed from the smallest barrel in the battery. That is then replenished (but not filled, as there needs to be room for air) by the next largest barrel, and so on and so on until the vinegar-maker draws upon the cooked must that has been fermenting in its larger barrel but not yet joined the battery. This *rincalzo* process means that generations of vinegar flow together to form the resulting *Tradizionale*. It is very similar to the *solera* system used in Andalucía for sherry vinegar (see page 115), but I would not – could not – lay a bet on which came first.

What is happening while the vinegar is in the barrels is natural acetic fermentation and evaporation. Water in the vinegar passes through the wood, drawn out by the heat. And just as the wood allows elements out, it adds elements in. The types of wood used – maybe oak, mulberry, chestnut, cherry, acacia or juniper – give different characteristics to the vinegar. It is a wonderful thing to see a room of barrel batteries, all the different sizes lined up regimentally, always on their sides, with a bunghole covered by a simple scrap of cotton.

Assessing, bottling, labelling: assessing the age of the vinegar is complicated given how it flows through the battery, with one generation of must mingling with another. The Consortia are the arbiters of how ageing is assessed and the minimum age categorisation on the bottles is twelve years. When a producer thinks he or she has some *Tradizionale* that is 'ready', it is drawn out of the barrel and taken to one of the regularly held tasting panels, where qualified testers use a points system to assess all the sensorial elements of the vinegar to see if it is up to scratch. If the vinegar passes, the Consortia bottle the vinegar for the producer, in the officially regulated bottle, with the officially regulated labelling for its age, and a number that identifies that vinegar with its producer.

All these steps are intended to protect the integrity of the balsamic vinegar for the buyer. Buy a DOP/PDO *Tradizionale* balsamic that is marked as such, bottled and labelled by the Consortia according to their classifications, and you will be assured a top-quality, lustrous, deeply flavoured, sweetly sour balsamic treat.

It is the very balsamic that everything else that uses the word is trying in some way to emulate, whether that is in flavour, colour, usage, perception or status.

IN THE KITCHEN
Aceto Balsamico Tradizionale di Modena/Reggio Emilia

This is balsamic for treasuring and enjoying in the simplest of ways that allow its characteristics to shine through – which means using it to finish a dish. This vinegar is too good for cooking with. Heat would only damage the very characteristics of flavour and aroma that are so prized and have taken years to develop.

Add a few drops on food just before serving. It could be on chunks of the Parmesan cheese that is produced from the same region; scallops; grilled meats; sweet-and-sour *agrodolce* onions; seafood; or the *bollito misto* stew of an eclectic range of meat cuts that is another local delicacy.

Tradizionale, with its perfect balance of relatively mild acidity, its sweetness, density and flavour, is also wonderful over sweet food. Macerating strawberries in balsamic is a classic combination, but think also about a few drops on other berries or over any rich chocolate dessert, or about using it as a finish for panna cotta, zabaglione or ice cream. It will cut through their richness like a dream.

Or make like the Modenese and take a spoonful of *Tradizionale* as an aperitif or digestif.

BALSAMIC VINEGAR OF MODENA

Balsamic Vinegar of Modena IGP is not the same thing as the *Aceto Balsamico Tradizionale di Modena* or *Aceto Balsamico Tradizionale di Reggio Emilia* with its higher DOP status. The clue is in the name, with the loss of the word 'traditional' all-important in drawing the distinction between the two. At its simplest it is a mix of grape must with wine vinegar. Yet from such a simple sentence comes significant variance in vinegars, all within the boundaries of protected EU IGP/PGI (*Indicazione Geografica Protetta*/Protected Geographical Indication) status.

As you will know from the section on *Tradizionale*, that takes many years to be produced. It was never intended as a commercial product, yet by the mid-1980s balsamic vinegar found itself at the heart of a surge of interest in international ingredients. It stretched its legs well beyond its own corner of northern Italy and began to be exported internationally.

Demand increased very fast as balsamic caught a mood of food-fashion. Supply had to keep up and a push towards ever-cheaper balsamics was inevitable. As luck would have it there was an alternative already being produced in Modena with just enough shared history and character with *Tradizionale* to satisfy the balsamic cravings of the world.

Records from the kitchens of the ducal family of the Modena region in the seventeenth and eighteenth centuries mention three types of vinegar: wine vinegar, *balsamico fine* (the equivalent of our *Tradizionale*) and *mezzo balsamico*. That idea of *mezzo balsamico* – meaning 'half balsamic' – is very important. It tells us that there has long been a need to produce an everyday version of balsamic vinegar that is suitable for cooking. After all, lustrous *Tradizionale* is for enjoying on its own or as a condiment to finish a dish, not for cooking with.

This *mezzo balsamico*, which shares its heritage and identity with *Tradizionale*, has its equivalent in our modern Balsamic Vinegar of Modena, the name which encompasses production in both Modena and Reggio Emilia. In 1980 there were just four companies making it. Now there are close to 300 businesses with a stake in the varying stages of production – be that harvesting grapes or cooking must, packaging and so on.

The rapid explosion in balsamic vinegar demand had another impact too: knock-offs. All kinds of 'balsamic' vinegars were made in all kinds of places, with heaven knows what done to them to try to emulate authentic balsamic. The price inevitably reduced, but so did the quality. The Modena producers collectively put their foot down in the face of these bastardisations of 'their' product. The Consortia stepped up to monitor for counterfeits, to protect Balsamic Vinegar of Modena and make sure that all its producers abided by the laws around its regionality, its methods of production and quality. Since 2009, this vinegar has been protected by EU IGP status.

So that is all simple then, isn't it? There is DOP status *Aceto Balsamico Tradizionale*, made in carefully controlled ways with labelling that says so; and there is Balsamic Vinegar of Modena IGP, which we know is different because it doesn't have the word 'traditional' in there, but is also controlled in how it is made and sold. Two types of balsamic, each lovely but different. Perfectly clear.

Except... There is a lot of breadth (I would say too much) in the rules of how Balsamic Vinegar of Modena IGP is made. They are minimum standards, which are incredibly useful to have. Some producers are making and selling at that minimum standard, but the problem (if it can be called that) is that others are going far beyond to try to make a 'better' balsamic, and it is often not at all clear from the bottle what those differences are. We can see them in the price sure enough, but what lies behind that can be confusing.

The grapes: producers have to use grapes typical of the region (Lambrusco, Trebbiano, etc), but they can come from anywhere. The demand for Balsamic Vinegar of Modena is so high that it is not feasible for all producers to use grapes only grown in the area – although producers who want to embrace the flavours of the *terroir* will source locally.

The must: the pressings of the grape juice, skin and seeds are the must that are at the heart of balsamic. 'Cooked' grape must means that the must has been heated over time to reduce, and to develop its sweetness, colour and texture (similar to *Tradizionale*). The longer the must cooks, the more expensive the vinegar is to produce. This step can be made quicker and cheaper by cutting the cooking time and compensating with the addition of caramel.

Cheaper still – and also allowed under the regulations – is 'concentrated' grape must, which means the must has been rapidly subjected to heat to get done in a minute or two what would otherwise take hours. Less time means less cost, but also less flavour.

The blend: the cooked or concentrated grape must is mixed with wine vinegar. Some producers will strive to use a local wine vinegar to balance the elements of the region within the balsamic, but they certainly don't have to. The rules then stipulate the addition of a vinegar that is at least ten years old. How much and what type of aged vinegar is down to the producer. Some add *Tradizionale* as the something old, and you can just imagine what that does to the end result.

The blend of vinegar with the cooked/concentrated grape must needs to achieve 6% acidity. Within that, the ratio of ingredients is down to the producer. Given that it is the grape must that gives balsamic its defining character, the better balsamics are certainly those that have more rather than less must.

'Ageing': those inverted commas may tell you that I head into this area with a raised eyebrow of worry. The minimum requirement for Balsamic Vinegar of Modena is that once blended it is kept in wooden barrels for sixty days before bottling. Sounds good, doesn't it? The reality can be rather less inspiring. 'Tanks' may be a better word to describe what is often used because while they are wooden, they are also usually huge. The volume of balsamic to the amount of wood and the very brief time it is in there (even if some producers decide to go for a more impressive-sounding six months or so) means little if anything interesting will happen to the vinegar. If the intention is for the balsamic to emulate *Tradizionale* and evaporate through the wood to reduce and intensify, while taking on some elements of the character of the wood, that is just not realistic in these huge containers. A bottle of Balsamic Vinegar of Modena that says it is *invecchiato* or 'aged' means it has been kept for a minimum of three years. There is no distinction made of how it is kept; it could still be in huge tanks doing very little. That said, it having aged at all is probably preferable to it not having aged.

Density: *Tradizionale* is naturally dense from its years of ageing and evaporation, so the theory goes that a denser Balsamic Vinegar of Modena is closer to the desired quality. Some producers of Balsamic Vinegar of Modena add thickener to achieve the effect, while some subject it to rapid heat evaporation, although the latter can end up with a slightly bitter, almost burnt-tasting balsamic that has to be tempered with sweetener. The more grape must there is in the balsamic the denser it will be, and an (expensive) way to do it is to give the vinegar some time in *Tradizionale*-style barrels to naturally evaporate and develop. That's the cream of the crop option.

Producers sometimes talk about the difference between the density and viscosity of balsamic. For the vinegar-maker it is an important distinction: density is the measurement of molecular weight; viscosity is resistance to flow. As a cook rather than a chemist, the intricacies of that distinction are slightly lost on me. But I know it when I see it, and you will too, and will be able to make an overall judgement on the texture and 'thickness' of the balsamic. (See page 77 for more on density and how to choose balsamic.)

Labelling: the IGP and Consortia rules are tightly controlled so that only balsamic made to their criteria can be sold as Balsamic Vinegar of Modena IGP. The label will show the official stamp designating that it is IGP balsamic, its acidity and the ingredients. Nothing is allowed to be said about the detail of how it has been produced – a ruling that was introduced to help stop false claims. The problem is that it does not allow true claims either. Some producers are trying to find ways to add information to the label about the vinegar's density as one way of distinguishing themselves from the sheer volume of Balsamic Vinegar of Modena out there. This is being done by a leaf grading or number. The more leaves or the higher the number, the denser the balsamic.

All of which brings us back to price. 'You get what you pay for' is a fallible mantra, but I think in the world of Balsamic Vinegar of Modena it is broadly true. I asked a producer if she thought balsamics were inflated in price to give an illusion of quality to a cheaply made product. My question seemed so off the mark that it confused her. This is an industry driven by keeping price down. Given that some ways of making Balsamic Vinegar of Modena are clearly more expensive than others, it is not unreasonable for that to be reflected in the price.

IN THE KITCHEN
Balsamic Vinegar of Modena

For all the recipes in this book, when the ingredients list says 'balsamic vinegar' this is the type it means and it should be chosen as cleverly as you can. At 6% Balsamic Vinegar of Modena is more acidic than *Tradizionale*, and that brings benefits when cooking with it. The sheer range of non-*Tradizionale* balsamics means there is quite a breadth of vinegars you could cook with. Consider the attributes of colour, flavour, acidity, sweetness and density when deciding how to use them.

The earlier on in the cooking process that you use the balsamic, the more places it has to hide. So if I were to add it to a ragu, perhaps, or a stew, or to marinate meat, it would not need to be an especially wondrous balsamic.

For finishing a dish – so where the balsamic is added closer to the food being eaten – it will be more to the fore, so needs to be better.

While in Modena I picked up a pamphlet produced by the balsamic Consortia, which includes ideas for using the vinegar, and says in capital letters at the end: 'ALL BOILED OR RAW VEGETABLES MAY BE SEASONED WITH AN ADDITION OF BALSAMIC VINEGAR'.

Words to heed and then look beyond. A good balsamic can be used for so many things:

- as a salad dressing with olive oil (but see note on page 64)
- to finish a soup
- to marinate meat cutlets
- to pickle eggs
- to drizzle over slices of fruit such apple or melon
- as a serving garnish and seasoning over tomatoes, omelettes, steaks, offal and all manner of roasted vegetables
- for roasting meat, fish, shellfish, vegetables or fruits where it can really add its own depth and bring out the flavour of whatever you are roasting
- to make a balsamic reduction by gently heating the balsamic vinegar in a pan with sugar to taste. Go slowly so that the vinegar doesn't burn, and just until you get the thickness you want it to be. Then use as a syrup for all kinds of desserts.

CONDIMENTO

You might come across a bottle of balsamic labelled as *condimento* or condiment, without reference to it being a IGP or DOP balsamic. What we are dealing with here is non-DOP, non-IGP, therefore non-official balsamic. And it's a bit of a balsamic wild-west.

As soon as you enter a world where balsamic production is uncontrolled, the wheels can come off quite quickly. The producers of these 'balsamics' (note the inverted commas of my concern) can do what they like – and for the consumer, that is unnerving.

That said, some non-DOP, non-IGP *condimento* balsamics are pretty darn good. There can be quite legitimate reasons (in consumers' eyes, if not those of the balsamic governing Consortia) for not having its official status on the label. So how do you spot the difference? The price in conjunction with the section on how to choose balsamic (see page 76) should help you navigate your way through deciding how close a *condimento* is to a real balsamic, and how suited or not it might be to how you want to use it.

If you find a fairly pricey *condimento*, from a reputable source, with only grape must listed as its ingredient, you could possibly – possibly – have in your hands a nearly-*Tradizionale*. Maybe its lack of official accreditation is just a question of not having been aged for quite as long as required, but it may still have been long enough to achieve a good result.

Or maybe it is a question of bottling. Balsamic Vinegar of Modena IGP is not allowed to be sold in 100ml bottles because that is the size in which *Tradizionale* is sold. So if a legitimate producer wants to bottle their approved balsamic in 100ml handy-for-air-travel bottles, it can only do so by losing the IGP label for that bottle. The choice then is to go with *condimento* as the description.

The difficulty comes when *condimento* 'balsamic' is barely worth the word. These do not have official accreditation maybe because they are produced far away from Modena, maybe because they do not contain the right ingredients or maybe they are of too low quality. There could be all kinds of reasons.

Often, *condimento* balsamics are thick, sweet glazes and reductions that are used purely as a dressing, and accordingly have such low acidity that they could not hit the criteria on that front even if on others. They do not have the depth of flavour, or the required balance of sweetness to acidity, and a first taste will tell you so.

IN THE KITCHEN
Condimento

Where you can see that a *Condimento* balsamic has an affinity with Balsamic Vinegar of Modena in terms of its acidity, density and flavour then use it in similar ways to how you would that. But where the *Condimento*'s acidity is shown as being around 4% – lower than the legal minimums for *Tradizionale* and Balsamic Vinegar of Modena – that is reflected in the taste. It is sweeter and less acidic, thus leaning towards use as a glaze or literally as a condiment. Condiment balsamics are often quite dense which makes them especially useful as a sauce for ice cream and desserts.

VARIATIONS ON A BALSAMIC THEME

Here lie the good, the questionable and the unexpected products that carry the word 'balsamic', and with it the associations of sweetness, flavour and – of course – prestige.

White balsamic tries to get the balance of sweetness to acidity of a conventional balsamic, but without the colour. It is a choice to be made purely for aesthetic reasons of wanting a pale colour. Real balsamic is made by cooking grape must to reduce it, which inevitably darkens it. So a white balsamic will either have very little cooked must in relation to white wine vinegar, or it will be concentrate. Any ageing will be in stainless steel tanks rather than wood for the same reason. White balsamic is not regulated by the DOP, IGP and balsamic Consortia. Your judgement on it will be down to price and the clues on the label about the ingredients (see page 76).

Balsamic syrups and glazes are thickened versions of balsamic to be used as a dressing or sauce. Similar to some condiment balsamics.

Balsamic pearls are little balls of balsamic in a jelly coating that can be used as a garnish for salads or other dishes. Bite into them for a burst of balsamic.

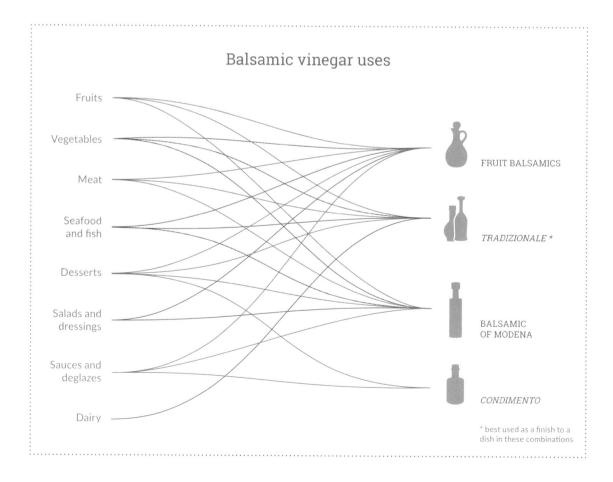

Balsamic vinegar uses

Fruits
Vegetables
Meat
Seafood and fish
Desserts
Salads and dressings
Sauces and deglazes
Dairy

FRUIT BALSAMICS

TRADIZIONALE *

BALSAMIC OF MODENA

CONDIMENTO

* best used as a finish to a dish in these combinations

A BALSAMIC CALL TO ARMS

Marina Spaggiari is a long-standing maker of *Tradizionale*, initially within her family, and then for the Nero Modena business. I asked her why she still makes it when there is so little commercial value in it relative to the IGP balsamic they also make. Her answer, an immediate and ecstatic, 'Because I love it!'

In a nutshell, that is the key to the whole balsamic industry that flows through and from *Tradizionale* at the top. It is beloved by its locals and the rest of the world. Balsamic in its various forms dominates sales of vinegars and dressings. Yet I wonder and worry about just how long it can retain its status in the dual face of lower-quality products seeping into the market thereby tarnishing its reputation, and other vinegars gaining momentum.

I think it is a worry the Italians may share (if they don't – they should). Why else would they put up such significant resistance to Spain's Montilla-Moriles vinegar being given its PDO status? With three protected status vinegars – compared to Italy's two – Spain may be a real threat. For now, Montilla-Moriles is hard to get hold of outside of Spain, but that could change. Certainly Spain's sherry vinegars are easily attainable, and you will see in these recipes that I will often suggest one of those as a variation to balsamic. They share properties of sweet-and-sour, with depth of flavour and colour. Sherry vinegar lacks the density of balsamic, but for cooking purposes that rarely matters – or it can be reduced. Mostly I make or suggest the swap because there is less variation in quality in a sherry vinegar than a balsamic. And that – I believe – is the crux on which balsamic's future will be settled.

In my view, balsamic can only continue to be loved around the world as a vinegar of prestige if the general quality is more consistent. Producers in Modena may understandably feel there are already quite enough controls put in place on production, and I can see that the idea of more controls isn't popular. But how about different controls? Ones that create greater consistency and clarity for the consumer as to who is producing really good Balsamic Vinegar of Modena and what the varying grades of it are.

That change will only happen if the producers – and their controlling Consortia – stop taking for granted our worldwide affection towards balsamic, and our ignorance. I had a lunch in Modena at which the balsamic on the table was awful: barely acidic, no balance, no depth. I found it slightly heartbreaking that in Modena of all places that would be what was served. I asked my host why, and his answer – depressingly – was that the tourists don't know the difference.

Well, I hope we all come to know the difference. That we make more informed choices on the balsamics we buy. If the last thirty years of the rise of balsamic vinegar tells us anything it is that its production adapts swiftly to market demands. So let's do that again – let's buy more cleverly, and make sure more of the balsamic on the shelves is worthy of that illustrious name.

HOW TO CHOOSE BALSAMIC

Balsamic is loved for its deep colour, deep flavour, enticing smell, dense texture, delicious balance of sweetness to acidity and prestige. Every balsamic vinegar has its merits and issues along the spectrums of those criteria. When choosing which balsamic to go for, it is always a balance of how it has been made, what you want to do with it and price.

The following should help you understand how to strike that balance.

Aceto Balsamico Tradizionale di Modena/Reggio Emilia (DOP)
Traditional Balsamic of Modena/Reggio Emilia (PDO)

This is certainly the easiest to identify by quality. The ingredients listed are grape must only; there is the stamp of its DOP/PDO status; along with its region's distinctive official bottling and labelling.

Aceto Balsamico Tradizionale di Modena (Traditional Balsamic of Modena)

> Minimum 4.5% acidity.

> Sold in a 100ml bulbous-shaped bottle that looks a bit like it has swallowed an onion.

> Two age distinctions: a white cap for twelve years; a gold cap for the *extra vecchio* that is gauged to be twenty-five years old or older.

Aceto Balsamico Tradizionale di Reggio Emilia (Traditional Balsamic of Reggio Emilia)

> Minimum 5% acidity.

> Sold in a 100ml upside-down-tulip-shaped bottle.

> Three age distinctions: a red label for twelve years; a silver label for eighteen years; a gold label for twenty-five years or more.

The older the *Tradizionale*, the sweeter, more intense, deeply coloured and dense it will be.

Balsamic Vinegar of Modena IGP

This is the balsamic you are most likely to buy or be served. The official stamp of IGP status tells you that it has been made to the minimum criteria of production and regionality. Unfortunately descriptions of the considerable variances in production are not included on the label of a IGP balsamic but there are clues to be found.

Ingredients list

- 'Cooked grape must' is better than 'concentrated grape must' and will result in a fuller-bodied balsamic.

- Look for the ratio of wine vinegar to grape must. If wine vinegar is the lead ingredient you are closer to buying a wine vinegar than a balsamic.

- Any colouring or sweetener in the ingredients means that this is a lower-quality vinegar with shortcuts made in its production.

Colour and flavour: balsamic should always be clear and bright, deep brown, with a sweet-and-sour flavour and intense aroma with a hint of woodiness. The appearance of balsamic will vary according to how it has been made. The more intense those attributes – without the addition of colours or sweeteners to achieve them – the better the balsamic will be.

Density: A syrupy balsamic is good for drizzling over ice cream, but to cook with you want something less dense. Hold a bottle up to the light and you can see how thick or not it is. Alternatively, and more scientifically... The minimum density for Balsamic Vinegar of Modena is 1.06 at 20°C. That means any Balsamic Vinegar of Modena with a higher rating is denser. As a comparison, the minimum density for *Tradizionale* is 1.24 and 1.2 for Modena and Reggio Emilia respectively. Denser balsamics are trying to get closer to being like a *Tradizionale* in this respect. There are good and not so good ways of achieving this (see page 71) – watch out for any kind of thickener or cornflour on the label.

Density might also be marked according to a leaf system that runs from a bronze-backed one-leaf grading at the less dense end, to four leaves on a black background for the most syrupy of balsamics. Note, though, that density gradings on labels are not officially monitored.

Age: when Balsamic Vinegar of Modena IGP says it is aged – *invecchiato* – that means it has been kept for a minimum of three years before selling. The label may not tell you much more than that, however.

'Condiment' balsamics

If a bottle is not marked as DOP/PDO or IGP/PGI then it is not an officially accredited balsamic. It has not met – or not had to meet – those criteria of authentic production. This is a broad and uncontrolled category but, as above, the density, age, colour and flavour will help you navigate a way through it.

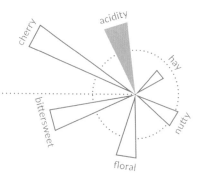

This a beautiful bowl of contrasts: there's the velvety smooth squash roasted in balsamic vinegar for depth of flavour and to bring sweetness to its caramelised edges; salty feta cheese; raisins soaked in cherry vinegar to give the vinegar a lovely sweetness for dressing the bitter radicchio leaves, alongside a hint of spicy cinnamon. Put it all together with the freshness of mint and parsley and you have a terrific lunch or supper that can be eaten as soon as it's made, or kept a day or so for the flavours to get to know each other. Serve with warmed flatbread.

Squash, Feta and Radicchio Salad

1 squash, approx. 1kg (try kabocha squash, butternut squash or pumpkin)
3 tablespoons olive oil
2 tablespoons balsamic vinegar
5 garlic cloves, unpeeled
60g raisins
3 tablespoons cherry vinegar
1 head radicchio (2 if small)
1½ tablespoons extra virgin olive oil
½ teaspoon ground cinnamon
200g feta
2–3 tablespoons chopped mint leaves, to taste
2–3 tablespoons chopped flat-leaf parsley, to taste
salt and freshly ground black pepper

VINEGAR VARIATION
You could use all balsamic or all cherry vinegar here; any other dark fruit vinegar or a fruit balsamic could be swapped for the cherry vinegar, as could a sherry vinegar.

serves 4–6

Preheat the oven to 220°C/200°C Fan/Gas Mark 7. Quarter the squash, scoop out the seeds, then peel and cut the flesh into chunks.

Mix the olive oil and balsamic vinegar together in a large bowl with a pinch of salt. Add the squash pieces and the whole, unpeeled garlic cloves and toss together. Spread it all out in a single layer on a baking tray and roast for 25–30 minutes until tender and the squash is caramelised at the edges. Remove from the oven and set aside.

While the squash is roasting, soak the raisins in the cherry vinegar for about 20 minutes. They won't be fully immersed so stir a few times.

Remove any damaged outer leaves from the radicchio. Halve it and cut out the white core, then shred the bright leaves into a large serving bowl. Drain the raisins and add to the radicchio. Left behind will be 1 tablespoon or so of cherry vinegar: whisk into that the extra virgin olive oil, cinnamon and a little seasoning. Toss the radicchio and raisins with this dressing.

Add the now cooled and caramelised squash pieces. Squeeze the sweet, tender, roasted garlic out of its shells and toss with the rest of the salad. Crumble in the feta cheese, then add the chopped mint and parsley. Toss again and serve when ready.

This very easy and absolutely delicious soup takes the principle of roasting roots with vinegar to bring out their sweetness, purée it up with roasted garlic and add balsamic for that all-important vinegar finishing touch. Excellent hot or cold.

Roasted Beetroot and Garlic Soup

1kg raw beetroots
1 whole garlic bulb
4 sprigs of rosemary
**120ml red fruit or
 apple vinegar**
120ml olive oil
approx. 500ml vegetable,
 chicken or beef stock
**3-4 teaspoons
 balsamic vinegar**
grated zest of 1 orange
salt and freshly ground
 black pepper

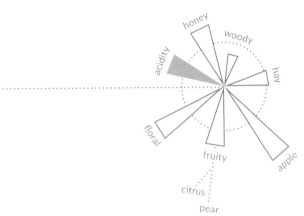

serves 4–6

Preheat the oven to 190°C/170°C Fan/Gas Mark 5.

Wash the beetroots, cut their tops and tails down to a few centimetres, then put the whole roots into a baking dish. Add the garlic bulb, broken up into individual unpeeled cloves. Then add the rosemary, fruit vinegar and 75ml of water. Toss to combine. Cover tightly with a lid or foil and roast for 1–1½ hours until the beetroots are tender.

Leave to cool before rubbing off the beetroots' skins and slipping the garlic cloves out of their shells. Cut the beetroots into chunks and purée with a stick blender or in a food processor along with the garlic, olive oil and a little salt.

Put the root purée into a saucepan and add enough stock to achieve your preferred consistency. Season to taste with the balsamic, pepper and salt. As you serve, finish each bowl with a smattering of orange zest.

VINEGAR VARIATION

A red wine vinegar is especially good for roasting beetroots so that would be my first-choice variation here instead of the fruit vinegar. Otherwise play around with fruit, cider, honey or infused vinegars that are all good for drawing the sweetness from root vegetables. Try seasoning with sherry vinegar at the end, in place of the balsamic.

I absolutely love an onion roasted 'in its overcoat', as Dylan Thomas put it. With the skins kept on as a protective outer layer, the insides become sweetly intense balsamic-baked onion flesh. Just the best thing with sausages.

Whole Roasted Onions

8 medium onions, unpeeled
8 sprigs of thyme
2 tablespoons olive oil
3 tablespoons
   balsamic vinegar
100ml vermouth or cider
knob of butter (roughly 10g)
salt and freshly ground
   black pepper

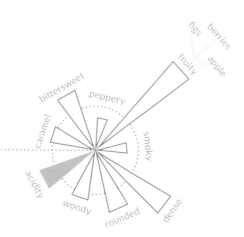

serves 4

Preheat the oven to 180°C/160°C Fan/Gas Mark 4. Pull off any very loose bits from each onion but be sure to leave as much skin on as possible. Cut just enough from the base of each one to give it a flat edge so the onion can stand straight. Cut about 1cm or so off the top and score a cross into the now-revealed onion flesh.

Sit the onions in a baking dish that will take them fairly snugly. Stuff the thyme sprigs into the crosses in the onions, then drizzle over the oil followed by the balsamic vinegar. Season with salt and pepper. Pour the vermouth or cider into the dish, but not over the onions – it is just there to stop them sticking. Cover with a tight lid or foil and put into the oven for 45 minutes.

After 45 minutes, take the lid off, baste the onions with the juices that have been released into the baking dish, and dot the butter over them. Return to the oven – uncovered this time – for another 45 minutes, so they are gorgeously browned and each onion is deliciously soft inside its coat.

VINEGAR VARIATION
You need a full-on vinegar to contend with the onion, and ideally with an edge of sweetness, so try a Pedro Ximénez sherry, another fruit balsamic, or an intense red wine vinegar. Malt vinegar would be good too, but add a teaspoon of sugar to the vinegar before drizzling over.

I much prefer a cooked oyster to a raw one, and especially these, where the oyster is cooked with a lush tarragon butter and then finished with balsamic to cut through with its sweetness and acidity. A very fine starter or canapé.

The recipe calls for oyster shucking, so you will need an oyster shucker tool to stand an outside chance of achieving this with as many fingers left as you started with. Hold an oyster firmly in a tea-towel in one hand, its flatter side facing up. Find the hinge between the shells – it is at the pointed base – and use your other hand to insert the shucker tip just there. Give it a forceful twist so that the hinge breaks and the shell starts to open. Now wiggle and slide the knife up and under the top shell to separate them and lift the top shell off. Use the knife to gently loosen the oyster in its shell.

Oysters with Tarragon Butter and Balsamic

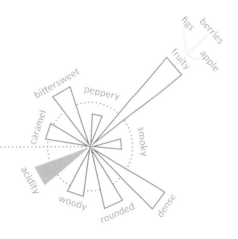

75g salted butter, at
   room temperature
3 tablespoons chopped
   tarragon
½ garlic clove
12 oysters
2 tablespoons
   balsamic vinegar

serves 4

Combine the butter, tarragon and garlic in a food processor to create a smooth tarragon butter. Set aside in the fridge until needed. To do this by hand, first crush the garlic into a bowl, then use the back of a spoon to smoothly mix it with the butter and tarragon.

Preheat the oven to 240°C/220°C Fan/Gas Mark 9. Crumple tin foil into a baking dish, making 12 indents to hold the oysters. Shuck the oysters (see introduction) and sit each open half-shell holding an oyster on the foil. Dot the tarragon butter over the top and then sprinkle over 1 tablespoon of the balsamic. Roast for 4 minutes and serve immediately, with the remaining balsamic sprinkled over to taste.

VINEGAR VARIATION

A fruit vinegar would be good, or malt vinegar. Chinese black vinegar would take it in a totally different – but delicious – direction.

Balsamic and apples are a super combination. The acidity of the vinegar brings out and emphasises the flavour of the apples, while their two sweetnesses mingle underneath. Here, the apple slices are doused in balsamic vinegar for a mouthful of fruity quick-pickled flavour to cut through the intensity of the game meat.

Ask the butcher for skin-on breast fillets but if you can only get hold of the whole bird, here's how to do it yourself: use a very sharp, small knife to cut along the breast bone then prise the breast flesh away. Trim as necessary. Use the rest of the carcass for a delicious stock.

Partridge with Red Cabbage and Quick-pickled Balsamic Apples

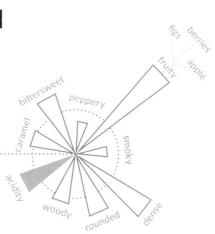

2 small eating apples
4 tablespoons
 balsamic vinegar
1 teaspoon juniper berries
2 garlic cloves, chopped
1 teaspoon thyme leaves
½ large red cabbage
2 tablespoons olive oil
8 partridge breasts, skin on
25g butter
salt and freshly ground
 black pepper

serves 4

Quarter the apples, cut out the core, then slice each piece into lengths about 1cm thick. Lay the apple slices in a single layer in a bowl and pour over the vinegar. Turn the apple slices over so that the vinegar coats all sides. Set aside, turning the slices every now and again.

In a pestle and mortar, crush the juniper berries, garlic cloves and thyme with some salt. Prepare the cabbage by cutting out and discarding the white core, chopping the leaves finely, then rinsing and draining them.

Heat the oil in a frying pan. Season the partridge breasts and lay them skin-side down in the hot oil. Leave for 2 minutes, then turn them over and give them another 2 minutes. Lift out onto a plate, set aside and cover to keep the meat warm.

Melt the butter in the same pan, then add the pestled juniper, garlic and thyme mix. Stir for a minute or two (make sure the garlic doesn't start to burn), then drop in the chopped cabbage. Season and cook for 3–5 minutes, stirring occasionally, until the leaves are wilted but retain their bite and colour.

VINEGAR VARIATION
Try a bittersweet fruit vinegar or another fruit balsamic that is a good flavour match for the game, so ideally a dark fruit such as cherry, plum or any of the berries.

Serve straight away by dividing the red cabbage between four plates, with two partridge breasts sitting on top of each pile, and arrange the balsamic apple slices alongside. Pour over any vinegar left in the apple bowl and finish with a good grinding of pepper over everything.

Beef brisket is cut from the lower part of the animal's breast and is perfect for pot roasting or braising. Done any other way it has a tendency to toughness, which probably explains why it is one of the less popular joints at the butcher's. That's a shame as it is also one of the least expensive joints, and when cooked long and slow like this – with vinegar to act as both a tenderiser and flavour enhancer – the meat has no option but to yield into tender succulence. This recipe works just as well with a venison joint. Serve with dumplings, or a mash of potatoes or any other root veg. Lots of horseradish sauce, too (or cranberry sauce if you switch the beef brisket for a venison joint).

I use a combination of deeply fruited vinegar and balsamic. This is not the time or place to blow the budget on your best balsamic, but do check that, whatever you use, the acidity isn't below 5% or the vinegar isn't going to be tenderising enough.

Pot-roasted Brisket with Balsamic and Honey

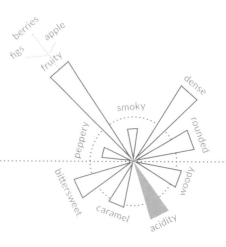

approx. 1.8kg beef brisket,
    rolled and tied
1 teaspoon juniper berries
6 sprigs of thyme
100ml balsamic vinegar
100ml red fruit vinegar, such
    as cherry, blackcurrant
    or plum
200ml red wine
juice of 1 orange
1 teaspoon black peppercorns
25g unsalted butter
2 tablespoons olive oil, plus
    extra if needed
3 medium onions, peeled
    and cut into eighths
5 carrots, roughly chopped
4 garlic cloves, crushed
2 tablespoons honey
salt and freshly ground
    black pepper

serves 6–8

Sit the brisket in a deep dish. Lightly crush the juniper berries and mix them with the thyme, vinegars, red wine, orange juice and peppercorns. Pour the whole lot over the brisket, cover and set aside for up to 8 hours if you can – in the fridge if longer than 8 hours, or if your kitchen is warm, but be sure to return the meat to room temperature before cooking. Turn the meat over from time to time to give it all a fair go.

When it is time to cook, lift the brisket out and pat it dry. Keep the marinade. Season the brisket all over with salt and pepper. Choose a large ovenproof earthenware pot or roasting tin that can take the brisket and also be used on the hob.

Preheat the oven to 160°C/140°C Fan/Gas Mark 3. Heat the butter and olive oil in the pot or tin on the hob. Sear the brisket on all sides: you want it to be nice and browned on the outside with a good caramel colour. Lift the beef out and set it aside. Add more oil to the pot if needed, and cook the onions and carrots, stirring frequently, so they soften and the onions start to take on some colour. Just as the onions seem nearly ready, add the garlic and season it all with salt and pepper. While the veg are cooking, whisk the honey into the reserved marinade.

Return the brisket to the pot and sit it on the bed of onions and carrots. Pour over the honeyed marinade and bring to a simmer. Cover with the pot's lid or a tight piece of foil and pot-roast it in the oven for 4 hours, turning it over halfway through.

To serve, lift out the brisket and set it aside to rest for 10 minutes. Take a look at the broth in the pot and make a decision. You will be spooning it over the meat, so is it too liquid for your liking? If yes, then bubble it on the hob for a few minutes to reduce it. Is it not liquid enough? Add a little wine, water or stock. It may, of course, be just right.

Slice the brisket thickly and serve, making sure each person gets a good spoonful of broth and vegetables.

VINEGAR VARIATION

Switch the balsamic for a sherry vinegar, and the fruit vinegar for a red wine or honey vinegar.

Slowly braising pig's cheeks into melting tenderness – with the helping hand of a vinegar marinade – is the best way to make the most of this delicious, meaty and inexpensive cut of meat. Serve with mash or rice to soak up the sauce, and wilted greens.

Braised Pig's Cheeks with Cherry Vinegar and Liquorice

2 pig's cheeks (around
      170g each)
4 tablespoons cherry vinegar
5 tablespoons olive oil
3 tablespoons plain flour
1 large red onion, sliced into
      half-moons
2 garlic cloves, crushed
1 stick of celery, finely diced
1 tablespoon honey
250ml red wine
250ml chicken stock
1 stick of liquorice root, broken
      into two pieces
2 bay leaves
a sprig of thyme
50ml single cream
salt and freshly ground
      black pepper

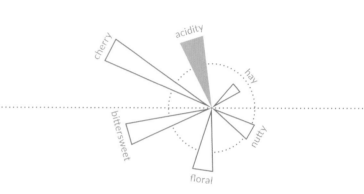

serves 2

Put the pig's cheeks, 2 tablespoons of cherry vinegar and 2 tablespoons of olive oil into a bowl, cover and leave to marinate for a few hours or overnight – in the fridge if more than a couple of hours. Lift the cheeks out of the liquid and pat them dry on kitchen towel. Keep the marinade.

Preheat the oven to 140°C/120°C Fan/Gas Mark 1. Place the flour in a shallow bowl and season with salt and pepper.

Heat 2 tablespoons of olive oil in a casserole dish. Roll the pig's cheeks in the seasoned flour, then sear them in the oil until browned all over. Use a slotted spoon to transfer them to a plate and set aside.

Add the remaining tablespoon of oil to the casserole dish, then add the onion, garlic, celery and a good sprinkling of salt. Cook over a gentle heat until the vegetables have softened up, stirring every now and then and scraping off any bits that are stuck to the bottom of the pan. Return the pig's cheeks to the dish and stir in the honey.

Stir in the red wine, stock, pieces of liquorice root, bay leaves, thyme, the remaining marinade and a few grindings of black pepper. Bring to a high simmer then put the lid on and transfer to the oven for 2½ hours.

Use a slotted spoon to transfer the pig's cheeks into a serving dish along with as much of the onion and celery as you can fish out. Cover to keep the cheeks warm while you finish the sauce.

Strain the cooking liquid into a saucepan over a medium heat and bring to the boil for around 10 minutes to reduce. Remove from the heat and let it all calm down before stirring in the remaining 2 tablespoons of cherry vinegar and the cream. Check the seasoning, then pour the sauce over the cheeks and serve.

VINEGAR VARIATION

Cherry vinegar matches perfectly with both the pork and the liquorice, while also cutting through the dish's tendency towards richness. It can be easily swapped for red wine vinegar or a good malt vinegar in the marinade, but when it comes to making the sauce at the end another fruit vinegar such as plum would work well, or go for sherry vinegar.

Marinating pork chops in vinegar, garlic and herbs is a hassle-free way to ensure they will be gorgeously tender and flavoursome. Then after cooking they are finished with a quick deglaze of the meat pan with vinegar and cider for a burst of freshness (the opened cider will be great to drink alongside, too).

The green beans and spring onions with sesame on page 184 are very good with these chops.

Garlic and Herb Pork Chops

1 garlic clove, chopped
1 tablespoon chopped tarragon
1 tablespoon chopped
  rosemary
3 tablespoons quince vinegar
2 pork chops
20g butter
50ml cider
**1 tablespoon red fruit vinegar,
  such as plum, black cherry
  or cherry**
salt

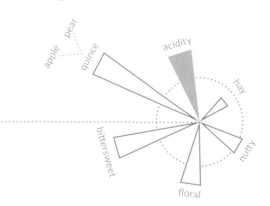

serves 2

Crush the garlic in a pestle and mortar with a good pinch of salt until it becomes a paste. Stir in the tarragon, rosemary and quince vinegar, then smear over both sides of the chops, cover and set aside for 2 hours. You can increase or reduce this time to suit your own plans – put the chops in the fridge if more than 2 hours, or if your kitchen is warm, but be sure to return them to room temperature before cooking.

Put the butter into a large frying pan over a medium–high heat. Once melted, lift the chops out of the marinade and lay them in the pan. Cook for 4 minutes each side – you want them to be nicely browned.

Lift the pork chops out of the pan and transfer to warmed plates. Pour the cider and fruit vinegar into the same pan and stir over a high heat for about 1 minute to bubble and reduce. Pour over the chops and serve.

VINEGAR VARIATION

The quince vinegar in the marinade could be swapped for apple vinegar, pear vinegar, a herb-infused vinegar, honey vinegar, rice vinegar (of at least 5% acidity) or white wine vinegar. I think a deeply fruity vinegar is exceptionally good here for the finish it gives, but you could also go for red wine vinegar in place of the fruit vinegar.

Plump grapes roasted with balsamic vinegar become deeply flavoured, with a perfect blend of sweetness and acidity. A terrific addition to a cheeseboard or served with pâté. I think black grapes work best here, but red or green are good too, and a combination can be best of all. Seedless grapes essential.

Balsamic Roasted Grapes

4 tablespoons
balsamic vinegar
400g seedless grapes of your choice, on the vine
¼ teaspoon sea salt flakes
2 teaspoons light brown soft sugar

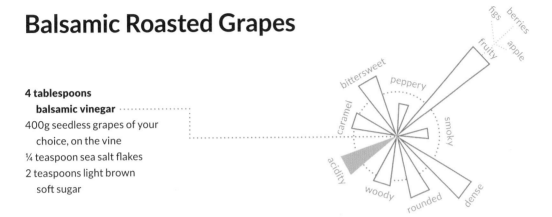

serves 4–6

Preheat the oven to 200°C/180°C Fan/Gas Mark 6.

Pour the balsamic over the grapes in a mixing bowl, then sprinkle over the salt and sugar. Toss gently so as not to pull the grapes off the vine.

Transfer to a baking tray, pouring over all the vinegar mixture left behind in the bowl. Roast for 15 minutes, turning the grapes halfway through. They are done when shrivelled and starting to burst.

Carefully transfer to a plate, pour over any juices from the tray, and allow to cool before serving.

VINEGAR VARIATION

Try a sweet Pedro Ximénez sherry vinegar or another fruit balsamic vinegar.

Think of the best baked apples you've ever had. All that lovely, slightly spicy, dried fruit packed inside an apple that is roasted so that its flesh is almost bursting out of its seams. Then add another flavour dimension that takes that baked apple up a notch or dozen. The extra dimension is balsamic vinegar. Its mellow acidity brings out the best in the sweet fruit. These are gorgeous with ice cream, cream or yoghurt.

Baked Apples with Balsamic

20g walnut halves
80g raisins
½ teaspoon ground cinnamon
grated zest of 1 lemon
**6 tablespoons
  balsamic vinegar**
6 medium apples
small knob of butter

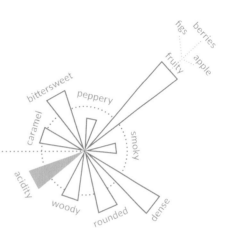

serves 6

Crush the walnuts in your hands, then combine them in a bowl with the raisins, cinnamon, lemon zest and balsamic. Set aside for 30 minutes, or as long as it takes to prepare the apples.

Preheat the oven to 180°C/160°C Fan/Gas Mark 4. Use an apple corer to take the core out of the middle of the whole apples. Keep the apples whole and cut a line around the equator of each to pierce the skin. Grease a shallow baking dish with most of the butter and sit the apples in it.

Drain the dried fruit mix, being sure to retain all the liquid that comes away. Fill each apple cavity with the dried fruit mix and dot a little butter over the top of each filled apple. Bake for 30 minutes, until the apples are tender.

Allow the apples to cool a little, then lift them onto a serving plate (or into individual bowls).

VINEGAR VARIATION
Try another of the fruit balsamics or sherry vinegar.

Add any juices that have seeped into the baking dish to the reserved vinegar marinade and pour all of that into a small saucepan. Simmer over a medium heat to reduce to a syrup consistency, then drizzle over the apples before serving.

This sweet balsamic-reduction sauce that is rippled into the ice cream towards the end of its churning is incredibly useful to know about. You could also use it as a sauce for drizzling over ice creams and sorbets (from vanilla or rum and raisin, to fruits such as strawberry, fig or cherry that will marry well with the balsamic). It is also very good as a sauce over roasted fruits, pancakes, brownies and other chocolate desserts.

Note that if you have a dense balsamic to start with, you don't need to make a reduction, just use as-is. Tip the bottle – if it coats the sides then use without reducing.

Balsamic-ripple Ice Cream

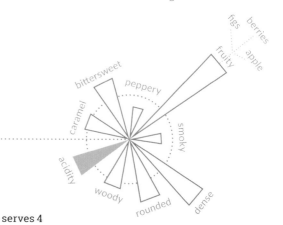

FOR THE BALSAMIC SAUCE
75ml balsamic vinegar
25g caster sugar
or 50ml dense balsamic vinegar

serves 4

FOR THE VANILLA ICE CREAM
4 egg yolks
100g caster sugar
300ml whole milk
150ml double cream
1 vanilla pod

To make the balsamic reduction: put the balsamic and sugar into a small saucepan over a medium heat and stir until the sugar has dissolved. Bring to the boil then let it bubble for 3–5 minutes until the vinegar has reduced to the consistency of a syrup. Set aside to cool before using. It will keep in the fridge for a few days.

For the ice cream, beat together the egg yolks and sugar in a large mixing bowl until thoroughly mixed and becoming lighter in texture.

Pour the milk and cream into a saucepan. Use a knife to split the vanilla pod down its length, then scrape out the seeds and add those to the milk and cream. Put the pod in too and heat until almost – but (crucially) not quite – boiling. Whisk the hot milk mixture into the sugared eggs, little by very little to avoid scrambling the eggs.

Pour it all back into the saucepan and stir over a low heat to make a custard that is thick enough to coat the back of a wooden spoon. Then take it off the heat and pour the whole lot – pod and all – into a bowl or large jug. Cover and chill for at least 6 hours.

Once the ice cream mixture is chilled, remove the vanilla pod then churn the mixture according to the instructions of your ice cream machine. Add the balsamic sauce (or your dense

VINEGAR VARIATION
Try one of the other fruit balsamics.

balsamic) when nearly fully churned to achieve a rippled effect. Freeze until ready to serve.

To churn by hand, remove the vanilla pod, then pour the ice cream mixture into a deep baking dish or mixing bowl and freeze for 45 minutes. Give it a vigorous mix with a spatula or whisk and return to the freezer. Repeat at 30-minute intervals until frozen. Add the balsamic sauce (or your dense balsamic) at the last hand-mix.

SHERRY, WINE AND CIDER VINEGARS

This soup combines a light texture with a beautifully deep flavour that is helped along by cooking the apples with sherry vinegar. The sprinkling of sumac to finish gives it an extra flavour lift.

Apple and Chestnut Soup

20g butter
1 tablespoon olive oil
1 leek, trimmed and sliced
2 garlic cloves, crushed
1 celery stick, chopped into
    3cm pieces
½ teaspoon coriander
    seeds, crushed
300g cooked and peeled
    chestnuts, roughly chopped
250g sharp, crisp eating apples,
    such as Cox
2 tablespoons sherry vinegar
2 tablespoons double cream
1 teaspoon sumac
salt and freshly ground
    black pepper

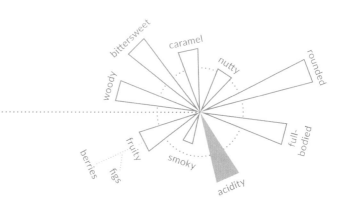

serves 6

Heat the butter and oil in a large saucepan. When the butter has melted, add the chopped leek, garlic and celery. Cook over a low heat until the vegetables have softened but not coloured.

Add the coriander seeds and chestnuts to the pan and stir round. Peel, core and roughly chop the apples, adding them to the pan as you go. Stir in the sherry vinegar and use it to deglaze any bits that have stuck to the bottom of the pan. Season, then pour in 1¼ litres of water and simmer for 20 minutes with a lid half-on.

Allow the soup to cool slightly, then blend until smooth. Check the seasoning and if the soup seems thick, add more water. Reheat if necessary and serve with a drizzle of double cream and a sprinkling of sumac.

VINEGAR VARIATION
Try another of the rich Spanish vinegars – so Condado de Huelva or Montilla-Moriles. Otherwise, go for a 50/50 combination of malt vinegar and a deep red wine vinegar.

The classic onion soup is French, of course, but I cannot in good faith call this version French as it makes use of Spanish sherry vinegar. It's well worth the name switch, though, for the depth the sherry vinegar gives, and best of all if it is a sweet Pedro Ximénez vinegar. I like to use a mix of red and white onions for the extra sweetness from the red onions. This is tasty, warming and comforting. A real treat.

Rich Onion Soup

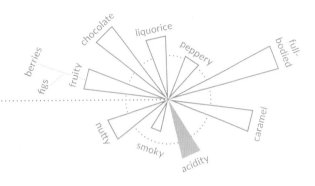

80g unsalted butter
1 tablespoon olive oil
750g white onions, thinly sliced into half-moons
250g red onions, thinly sliced into half-moons
2 garlic cloves, crushed
2 sprigs of thyme
1½ tablespoons plain flour
4 tablespoons Pedro Ximénez sherry vinegar
1 litre beef stock (the best you can get hold of)
200ml red wine
12–18 slices of baguette, approx. 1.5cm thick
100g strong cheese (think Comté, Gruyère or Cheddar), grated
salt and freshly ground black pepper

VINEGAR VARIATION

A balsamic or any sherry vinegar other than PX would work well, as would a 50/50 mix of a good malt vinegar and a deep red wine vinegar (in which case I might be tempted to add a teaspoon of sugar). For anything other than PX sherry vinegar, reduce the amount of vinegar to 3 tablespoons.

serves 4–6

Heat the butter and oil in a large pan over a low heat, add the onions and stir round. Give them a good pinch of salt and cover the pan with a lid. Cook the onions for around an hour (possibly more), stirring occasionally to make sure they don't burn, until they become thoroughly soft and are caramelising to an appealing light brown. Remove the lid for the last 10 minutes or so of cooking to encourage them to caramelise.

When they are nearly ready, stir the garlic into the onions along with the thyme. Allow to cook for a few minutes to allow the garlic to soften, then stir in the flour, followed by the vinegar, stirring for a couple of minutes and deglazing any delicious sticky bits from the base of the pan.

Warm the stock and red wine together in a separate pan, then add to the onions. Bring to the boil, turn the heat down, then let the soup simmer gently for 45 minutes or until you achieve the consistency you want. Check the seasoning. Don't worry if it tastes a bit heavy on the vinegar as the cheese topping will balance that.

While the soup is cooking, toast the baguette slices. Preheat the oven to 220°C/200°C Fan/Gas Mark 7.

When the soup is ready, ladle it into ovenproof bowls and sit the toasted baguette slices on top. Sprinkle the cheese over and bake for 3–5 minutes until the cheese melts. Allow to cool slightly before eating.

The trick to getting gazpacho absolutely right lies in three things. Firstly, you need ripe tomatoes, packed with flavour – insipid tomatoes will make for insipid gazpacho, and there is no point in that. Secondly, remember it is an Andalucían dish so the sherry vinegar needs to be good and the amount well-balanced – I accept that what this means will differ from person to person, so I like to serve it with the sherry vinegar bottle on the table so that people (meaning me) can help themselves. Thirdly, the gazpacho has to be served super-cold.

I like my gazpacho quite thick, so that is how this comes; thin it with water if you prefer. Note that there is no need to skin the tomatoes as they will be blended and strained before serving.

Gazpacho

1kg very ripe tomatoes,
   roughly chopped
1 cucumber, peeled and chopped
1 green pepper, deseeded
   and chopped
80g slightly stale white or brown
   bread, torn into pieces
3 garlic cloves, chopped
**3 tablespoons sherry vinegar,
   plus extra to taste**
125ml extra virgin olive oil
salt and freshly ground
   black pepper

TO GARNISH (OPTIONAL)
chopped hard-boiled egg
chopped spring onion
chopped cucumber
chopped mint
croutons
sherry vinegar

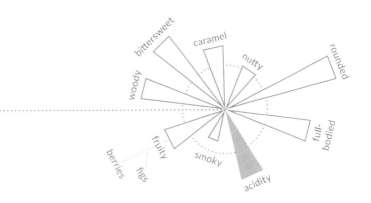

serves 4–6

Place the tomatoes in a large bowl with the cucumber, green pepper, bread pieces, garlic, sherry vinegar and half of the oil. Give it a good pinch of salt, mix to combine, cover and chill for 2 hours.

Transfer to a blender and blend it all together, adding the rest of the olive oil. Season and strain into a bowl through a fine sieve, pushing at it with a spoon to get as much through as you can. Taste it for seasoning – remember that chilling dulls the seasoning slightly – and take a look at the resulting soup. If it is too thick for your liking, thin it down with some water.

Chill until needed, then serve in small bowls or cups with a drizzle of sherry vinegar on top and with your choice of garnishes arranged on the table for each person to help themselves to.

VINEGAR VARIATION
One of the other intense Andalucían non-sherry – Condado de Huelva or Montilla-Morales – wine vinegars would be good here. Or I'd be tempted to try finishing it with a good balsamic, tomato balsamic, maple vinegar or cucumber vinegar.

Red cabbage leaves are wrapped around an intensely flavoursome mix of mushrooms, lentils, fruit and herbs, with sherry vinegar to give depth. Bundles of deliciousness to serve with herbed yoghurt.

Stuffed Red Cabbage Leaves

bittersweet · caramel · nutty · rounded · woody · full-bodied · fruity · smoky · berries · figs · acidity

1 head of red cabbage
15g dried mushrooms
120g dried Puy lentils
30g butter
1 tablespoon olive oil, plus
a little extra
3 shallots, chopped
3 garlic cloves, chopped
300g mixed wild mushrooms,
roughly chopped
1 tablespoon chopped
tarragon leaves
1 tablespoon chopped
sage leaves
1 pear
3 tablespoons sherry vinegar
2 tablespoons chopped
coriander leaves
2 tablespoons chopped dill
250g plain Greek yoghurt
**1 tablespoon balsamic
vinegar, to drizzle**
2 tablespoons roughly chopped
flat-leaf parsley
salt and freshly ground
black pepper

VINEGAR VARIATION

A a rich fruit vinegar would be good instead of the sherry vinegar, and instead of the classic balsamic to finish you could go for a fruit balsamic.

serves 4

Preheat the oven to 180°C/160°C Fan/Gas Mark 4. Bring plenty of water to boil in a pan that is large enough to fit the whole red cabbage. Trim the base off the bottom of the cabbage and – carefully – lower the cabbage into the boiling water. Cook for approx. 15 minutes until you start to see the outer leaves begin to unfurl. Carefully lift the cabbage out of the water, set aside for a few minutes until cool enough to handle, then gently peel away whole leaves. If you get to a point where they will no longer come away easily, return the cabbage head to the pan for a few more minutes. Aim to get eight whole leaves and a few nearly-whole. Set your peeled leaves aside.

Pour 75ml of boiling water over the dried mushrooms and set aside. Simmer the lentils in water for 20 minutes until tender with a bit of bite. Drain and set aside.

Heat the butter and oil in a large frying pan and gently cook the shallots until softened. Add the garlic and wild mushrooms to the pan, stir round and season well. Lift the dried mushrooms out of their water (but don't throw the water away), chop them and add to the mushrooms in the pan, along with the tarragon and sage.

While it is all cooking, peel, quarter and core the pear. Chop into 1cm squares and add to the mushrooms. Pour over the reserved liquid from the dried mushrooms, give a good stir and leave to cook for 5 minutes. Then take off the heat and stir in the lentils, sherry vinegar and chopped coriander. Season to taste.

Get your eight whole cabbage leaves ready for stuffing. Use the others to line the base of a baking dish – they'll be useful for catching any filling that falls out. Now spoon the mushroom mix into the whole leaves, and roll/wrap the furls of the cabbage round to seal them as tightly as possible. Sit them in the baking dish on top of the broken leaves with the sealed side downwards. Drizzle over 100ml of water, sprinkle over a little salt and bake in the oven for 35–40 minutes. They should be cooked through and just gently crisping on top.

While they are cooking, stir the chopped dill into the yoghurt and season. Before serving, drizzle the balsamic vinegar over the stuffed bundles and scatter over the chopped parsley. Serve with the herbed yoghurt on the side.

Many is the spring-time *feria* in Andalucía at which my husband and I have tucked into this as a breather in the midst of that festival of food, fino and fun. It is essentially a rich tomato sauce cooked with chunks of chorizo, with clams (*almejas*) added at the end. There's sherry in there too, of course , as well as sherry vinegar for the depth, balance and deeply Andalucían flavour it gives.

Clam and Chorizo Stew

5 tablespoons olive oil

2 medium onions, chopped

3 garlic cloves, crushed
   or chopped

250g cooking chorizo, cut into
   1.5cm chunks

2 bay leaves

400g can of chopped tomatoes

2 tablespoons sherry vinegar

50ml fino or manzanilla sherry

500g clams

2 tablespoons
   chopped tarragon

sweet 'condiment' sherry
   vinegar (optional), to drizzle

salt and freshly ground
   black pepper

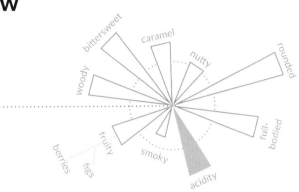

serves 4

Heat the oil in a large shallow pan that has a lid. Cook the onions in the oil over a medium heat until softened. Add the garlic and chorizo and stir; as it heats you will start to see the chorizo release deeply coloured and flavoured juices. Allow to cook for 5 minutes. Then add the bay leaves, tomatoes, vinegar and sherry. Stir well, season, bring to the boil, then turn the heat down so it is gently simmering. Partially cover with the lid and allow to simmer on a low heat for 20 minutes, stirring occasionally. You could prepare the dish to this point ahead of time and keep it in the fridge for a day, making it a very quick cook-and-serve in its final stages.

Prepare the clams by washing them thoroughly in cold water and discarding any that are broken or open. Drain the clams only when you're ready to cook them.

Bring the tomato and chorizo sauce to the boil, tip in the drained clams, put the lid on the pan and leave it alone for 6 minutes. Then check to see if the clams are starting to open, put the lid back on and give it all another 2 minutes, or as needed until the clams have opened up.

To serve, sprinkle over the tarragon and a drizzle of sweet sherry vinegar, if using. Discard any unopened clams, and then enjoy how these rustic yet elegant flavours come together.

VINEGAR VARIATION

Condado de Huelva or Montilla-Moriles wine vinegars would be good for the all-important Andalucían feel.

The strong flavours of rabbit and radicchio are tempered here with the acidic punch of the vinegar and the sweetness of the plums. Serve with farro, mashed potatoes or red rice, each stirred through with olive oil, seasoning and parsley.

Rabbit with Plums and Radicchio

2 tablespoons olive oil
25g butter
1 large rabbit, jointed into
    8 pieces
180g pancetta, cubed
1 onion, chopped
2 celery sticks, chopped
1 tablespoon sherry vinegar
3 garlic cloves, crushed
1 tablespoon honey
2 bay leaves
200ml white wine
6 plums, halved and stoned
1 large radicchio (or
    2 small ones), leaves
    roughly chopped
handful of basil leaves
salt and freshly ground
    black pepper

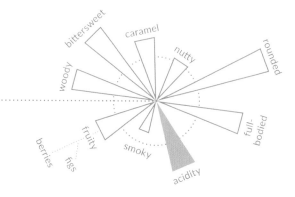

serves 4

Heat the oil and butter in a large casserole dish or pan. Once sizzling, add four of the rabbit pieces to sear them. As they achieve a good deep colour, remove them to a plate with a slotted spoon and repeat with the rest of the rabbit.

Tip the pancetta cubes into the pan and stir for a minute until the fat starts to run. Add the chopped onion and celery, then the vinegar, which will give enough liquid to let you rub at the base of the pan to deglaze it. Add the garlic and cook for a few minutes until all the veg is softened and taking on colour.

Return the rabbit pieces to the pan, stir in the honey, tuck in the bay leaves and mix well. Season, pour in the wine and 150ml of water. The rabbit shouldn't be submerged – the liquid should just gently lap at it. Bring to a high simmer, cover, then reduce the heat and simmer gently for 1 hour, stirring halfway through.

Lift the rabbit pieces onto a serving dish and set aside, covered, to rest. Turn up the heat and bubble the contents of the pan for 8–10 minutes to reduce the liquid. Turn the heat down, stir in the plum halves and cook for 5 minutes, uncovered. Stir in the radicchio and cook for a further 5 minutes. Take off the heat and pour the sauce all over and around the rabbit. Roughly tear over the basil and serve.

VINEGAR VARIATION
Switch the sherry vinegar for a deeply fruity red wine vinegar, or even a good malt vinegar.

The Pedro Ximénez sherry comes via its vinegar and is all the better for that. Its sweet sharpness cuts through the berries and chocolate to bring all those elements together deliciously.

Berries in Chocolate and Pedro Ximénez Sauce

400g blackberries
200g raspberries
2 tablespoons caster sugar
4 tablespoons Pedro Ximénez sherry vinegar ·······
150g dark chocolate
100ml double cream
vanilla ice cream
salt

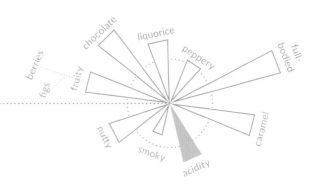

serves 4–6

Sit the blackberries and raspberries in a shallow bowl. Add the caster sugar and vinegar. Stir round, cover with cling film, and set aside for a couple of hours at room temperature.

Strain the berries into a bowl; be sure to keep the juice. Break the chocolate into a bowl that is sitting over a pan of simmering water. Once the chocolate has melted, whisk in the cream and the juice from the berries along with a pinch of salt until you have a smooth, thick sauce.

Divide the berries between bowls. Add a scoop or two of ice cream to each bowl, then drizzle over the chocolate and Pedro Ximénez sauce, and eat straight away.

····**VINEGAR VARIATION**
A balsamic vinegar would be great here, as would a really lovely red wine vinegar or maple vinegar if you added another tablespoon of sugar to compensate for their relatively lower sweetness.

Sherry Vinegars

I am sometimes asked what my 'desert island' vinegar would be. If I could have just one vinegar to use for ever more ... which one? It's a question I take barely a second to answer: sherry vinegar. It has – for me and I think many others – the perfect balance of acidity and body that I love in a good red wine vinegar, with a nod towards balsamic with its sweetness and depth. Hence its place here as a bridge between balsamic vinegars and wine vinegars. I often use it as an alternative to both. Versatile, delicious, fascinating.

My introduction to sherry vinegar came thanks to falling in love with a man who a good few years earlier had fallen in love with Andalucía (via a football trip at the age of twenty-one, a local girl and friendships made that have proven to be life-long). He has shared with me his love for the culture, language, food and drink of his 'second family' in the glorious corner of Cádiz, where the town of Rota sits on the coast. There I had my first sherry that did not involve Christmas-time Bristol Cream connotations. The very dry fino sherry (or, more typically in Rota, its close cousin manzanilla) was a shock at first, but the tastebuds soon realise its dryness is exactly the thing to refresh in the searing Andalucían heat.

It was at the end of that very first trip to Cádiz when I first encountered Jerez vinegar, too. I bought a bottle at the airport, I think, not really knowing what it was or what I'd do with it. For longer than I would now care to admit, that bottle sat unopened on the kitchen shelf. When I eventually opened it, the vinegar was as much a revelation as Andalucía itself.

Sherry vinegar – *Vinagre de Jerez* – is wonderfully rich and mellow, ranging from gold to mahogany in colour. Being born from sherry wine, which has a higher alcohol level than other wines, the sherry vinegars marry relatively high acidity with relatively high residual alcohol. Some have a sweetness that can threaten to dominate but is straight away tempered by other complex characteristics. Depending on the type and age of a sherry vinegar, your senses of smell and taste could be embracing almost sixty distinct aromatic elements. Complex indeed, and very much part of what makes sherry vinegar stand out, even if our sensorial interpretation of all those compounds is that a vinegar sits at a point on a nutty/woody spectrum.

Vinegar-making has become such an important business to the legendary sherry-making *bodegas* of the region that its production is now similarly controlled and protected. To understand the wine is to understand the vinegar, and vice versa.

HISTORY OF SHERRY VINEGAR IN ANDALUCÍA AND BEYOND

Making wine has been fundamental to this region for millennia. We know for certain that by the time the Romans invaded in c.200 BC, wine production was already established and much to the Roman taste. They expanded production and exported this wine from the region they called 'Ceret' to areas right across the Roman empire. It survived the conquest by the Moors in the eighth century AD, and when the land was reclaimed from the Moors some 500 years later, it became known as Xérès, and later, Jerez. Through and beyond the Middle Ages, the sherries of the region were hugely popular as exports to England and France, whose visiting merchants found them just as appealing as the Romans had.

By then sherry was well on its way to being big business for Andalucía, and you feel it all around when you are there. The culture is steeped in it. I've walked past many a bar on a stifling hot day to see an Andalucían man outside on his horse, sipping his fino as if it's the most normal thing in the world. From the drive out of Jerez airport and onwards, *bodegas* or vineyards seem to line the roads everywhere. All of them must abide by the rules of DO (*Denominación de Origen*) status, which classify and protect the quality and production of certain Spanish foods and wines, and which apply across the production of Jerez sherries and sherry vinegars.

Denominación de Origen (DO)

Spanish classification of protected status with specific and controlled requirements of where and how the product is made.

First, in 1933 (and first in all of Spain) was the DO awarded to *Jerez-Xérès-Sherry* – the three names reflecting the wine's historic and ongoing popularity in Spain, France and England. Then came the DO for *Manzanilla-Sanlúcar de Barrameda*, the lighter, coastal wines from the neighbouring area to the west of Jerez. Only in 1994 did *Vinagre de Jerez* get its own DO status and protection. It subsequently also garnered the EU protection and status of DOP (*Denominazione di Origine Protetta*), which guarantees production, place of origin and ensuing quality (see page 64).

That should in no way suggest that sherry vinegar is a new thing. Sherry vinegar will have been (accidentally) produced in the region for as long as it has been producing wine; it is just that for a very long time those vinegars were not considered something to shout about. They were the product of sherry wine becoming somehow unfit for use during the course of its complicated production process. Sherry that had gone wrong, if you like. For many centuries (even millennia), these spoiled sherry wines were being quietly aged and matured into sherry vinegars for non-commercial use. To any extent they were traded, it would only have been locally. Andalucíans were more than happy to use the vinegar themselves, given how well suited it is for cooking and serving with the local cuisine. What they had not yet realised was that the wider world would love it too.

Change came in the mid-1900s and is accredited to an enterprising Andalucían called Antonio Páez Sánchez, who decided to fully embrace vinegar as a commercial product. He saw that the Andalucíans were sitting on something truly wonderful with, in both the culinary and business sense, huge potential in the rest of Spain and internationally. The starting point for Antonio was the family stock of sherry vinegar, which his father had tended from some old sherry wines since the early part of the century. In 1945, twenty-two-year-old Antonio, with a keen eye for a good thing, decided the vinegar was so fabulous that he was going to make a business from it, and spent the next few years spreading the word far and wide about the glory of this local product. Not for nothing did Antonio come to be affectionately known as the 'Vinegar King'. For his ninetieth birthday, Antonio's family baked him a cake in the shape of a large vinegar bottle.

In the fifty years between Antonio having that 'eureka' moment and sherry vinegar being given its own DO status, Andalucíans began to understand that their vinegar was something very special indeed, with the potential to become a premium product. That last sentence is possibly more true for those producing or selling it, than for the locals for whom sherry vinegar is an everyday ingredient. There is still quite a high degree of nonchalance about it from them: they love it, they use it, but I've found my excitement about it tends to be met with a disarming insouciance. Yet these days most, if not all, of the main *bodegas* in the Jerez region will produce vinegars alongside their sherries – and be thankful for the business they bring. The DO sherry and sherry vinegar producers are so intertwined now that they share a regulating council.

PRODUCTION

To be truly worthy of the very real value and prestige that the name *Vinagre de Jerez* brings, the vinegar is produced from sherry wine to traditional methods of production and ageing that are tightly controlled.

Only wines made from Palomino, Pedro Ximénez and Moscatel grapes can be used to make *Vinagre de Jerez*. The area where the grapes may be grown – and the base wines made – is also restricted. The rural vineyards of the production area extend beyond Jerez itself to embrace eight municipalities of Cádiz – from v to the coastal regions of El Puerto de Santa Maria, Sanlúcar de Barrameda, Chiclana, Chipiona, Puerto Real, (my) Rota, then to Trebujena more inland – plus Lebrija in the province of Seville. If you ever get the chance to put memories to those names they will be of mountains, white towns and villages, and a coast to lose yourself in.

The *terroir* in these areas is hugely important in determining the characteristics and quality of the end result, just as in all wine production. Here there is soil that retains moisture well; a balmy climate of barely 5°C lows in winter and 35°C highs in summer that can be tempered by cooling winds; around 300 days of sunshine

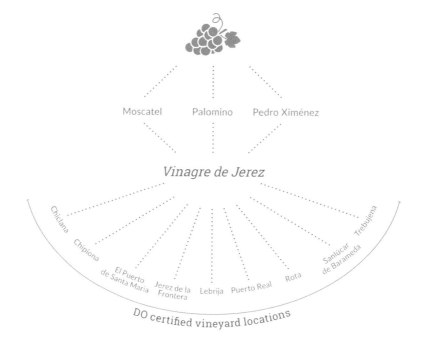

Vinagre de Jerez production regulations

Moscatel   Palomino   Pedro Ximénez

Vinagre de Jerez

Chiclana   Chipiona   El Puerto de Santa Maria   Jerez de la Frontera   Lebrija   Puerto Real   Rota   Sanlúcar de Barrameda   Trebujena

DO certified vineyard locations

a year; and rain – when it comes – only really in November, December and March. It is the combination of moisture-retaining soil and vines that bask in long hours of sunlight that make it one of the best wine-producing (vinegar-producing) regions in the world.

It is a still more restricted area where the base wines are aged into *Vinagre de Jerez*: that is only in Jerez de la Frontera, Sanlúcar de Barrameda and El Puerto de Santa Maria, known as the 'sherry triangle'. The dynamics of the cellars they use for ageing the vinegars play a vital role, just as the *terroir* does. Their gabled roofs and high ceilings envelop lots of air, lessening the impact inside of temperature changes outside. Thick walls provide insulation, while high windows allow air to circulate from the night breezes known as Poniente, but are high enough so that the barrels aren't in direct light.

Typically, and most traditionally, the sherry wine becomes acetified into sherry vinegar with bacteria on the surface of the wine in wooden barrels which are only about two-thirds full. The air in the gap in the barrel makes direct contact with the bacteria and stimulates the process of turning the alcohol to vinegar.

The best, most traditionally made sherry vinegars use a rolling system of acetifying and ageing the vinegar to achieve blends that combine the depth of a more mature vinegar with the relatively spiky freshness of the younger ones just poking through underneath. The blending of the batches makes for excellent *Vinagre de Jerez*.

It is a process that shares much with *Tradizionale* balsamic. In Jerez it is called *criaderas y solera*. *Solera* refers to the barrels at ground level, which contain the oldest vinegars in the system. As fully-aged vinegar is removed from the *solera* barrels or *botas*, they are replenished from the barrels that form the next tier (*criadera*) up. And so it continues with ever-younger vinegar, up through the levels of the *criadera* to barrels whose contents are just starting out on their journey to becoming *Vinagre de Jerez*. The barrels are typically made of American oak as an acknowledgement of the early days of wood and wine being traded between the two countries, as well as the fact that oak is really well-suited to embracing the wine/vinegar. Not that it has to be American oak barrels; chestnut can be used well too.

The number of barrels used in the system, and therefore the time the vinegar takes to move its way through, depends on each *bodega*. The minimum ageing time is six months. Bottles labelled as *Reserva* contain vinegar that has aged for an average of at least two years, and *Gran Reserva* is vinegar that has aged for at least ten years on average. What the lengthy blended ageing in the wooden barrels does is really develop the pungency, intensity and richness of aroma, 'woody' flavour and general character of the vinegar – all those factors increase the longer the sherry vinegar is aged. Crucially, it is the same system used to age sherry wines (although obviously, in the case of wine, without the bacteria that turn the wine into vinegar).

There is an alternative – faster, cheaper – way to turn the wine into vinegar. Stainless steel vats are used to hold the wine, the bacteria is submerged in it and air is pumped through the vessels to move the acidity process along. That can take just twenty-four to thirty-six hours, but even then the sherry vinegar regulations insist that it is aged in a wooden barrel for at least the minimum six months to give the vinegar its distinctive characteristics. Sherry vinegars aged in this way (without being mixed with vinegars of previous years) may be labelled as *añada* if aged for at least two years.

Although static ageing in the same barrel for the whole time is allowed, vinegars aged by the *solera* system will undoubtedly have a more complicated, rounder, deeper and many-layered profile, as you would expect when it is achieved through a blending of the different ages. It stands to reason that it will be more interesting than a statically-aged, unblended vinegar, which has been kept in the same barrel all the way through.

THE VINEGARS

The result of all this is vinegars that share lots of characteristics between the different types. They are all intense of colour, flavour and aroma. Their acidity and residual alcohol are relatively high, making them very versatile to use. There are exciting differences, too. In part those are due to the distinctions of static ageing, *añada* or *criaderas y solera*. In larger part, the choice of grape will determine the profile of the sherry vinegar. The three allowed grape varieties of Palomino, Pedro Ximénez and Moscatel can produce vinegars of quite different styles.

Palomino is the most commonly used grape for sherry vinegar. If the grape variety isn't named on a bottle of sherry vinegar, then it is Palomino. The vinegars it produces come with notes of wine, wood and hay; with deep flavour, colour and aroma. Its minimum acidity is 7% (8% for the *Gran Reserva*), and maximum residual alcohol is 3%. Compare that to a 'straight' wine vinegar, which will be around 6% acidity and 1–1.5% alcohol.

Often the Palomino is blended with one or both of the other grape varieties for the sweetness they can bring to Palomino's relatively dry and tart elements.

Sherry vinegar characteristics

Palomino
minimum acidity 7%;
maximum residual
alcohol 3%

Moscatel
less acidic (6%);
maximum residual
alcohol 4%

Pedro Ximénez
good acidity of 6%;
residual alcohol
up to 3%

Moscatel sherry vinegar is more sweetly acidic, floral, yet somehow light at the same time. These vinegars are less acidic (6%) and the residual alcohol is allowed to be slightly higher at 4%.

Then there are the **Pedro Ximénez** (PX) grapes. They give sherry vinegar a plummy richness that those who love the sweet wine these grapes make will know to expect. In the case of the vinegar that sweetness is cleverly tempered with acidity. PX sherry vinegars are often described as having a 'raisin' quality that is a direct result of the grapes being left to dry in the sun after harvesting. That reduces the water content and intensifies both sweetness and flavour. Again, slightly less acidic than a standard sherry vinegar at 6%, but certainly a high enough acidity to do most of the cooking 'jobs' needed of vinegar. It is this mix of acidity with sweetness and depth of flavour that makes a PX sherry vinegar, or a PX blend, such a treat.

THE FUTURE FOR SHERRY VINEGAR

There has been a surge of interest in sherry vinegar in recent years – possibly as the reliability of the quality of balsamic vinegar has become more of a concern. International chefs are using it more, and that is developing a wider general awareness. Most of the sherry vinegar produced is still sold in Spain, then France; America is third, but it is interesting to note that sherry vinegar is moving up the US imported vinegar sales chart to nudge at France's wine vinegars in the number two spot (balsamic is ahead of them all). Germany, Italy and the UK are other key markets for sherry vinegar and I anticipate they will all continue to grow.

The trick for the sherry vinegar producers will be to manage the supply to meet growing demand. Their advantage over the balsamic industry is that the interest in sherry vinegar has been much more gradual than Modena experienced in the 1970s and 1980s. There has been time for more *bodegas* to produce quality sherry vinegar and therefore increase total production year-on-year. This will undoubtedly stand the producers in good stead to manage output and quality.

IN THE KITCHEN
Sherry Vinegar

When it comes to choosing a sherry vinegar, first look for the *Vinagre de Jerez* DO mark; look for an indication that it has had *solera* ageing; then consider the impact of the ageing (younger vinegars are fresher and sharper; older vinegars are deeper and richer); and the grape varieties used or blended.

To cook with, its high acidity makes sherry vinegar an excellent choice for meat marinades, ceviches and for sauces and dressings. Think about using a sunflower oil as its partner for salad dressings – the lightness and relative sweetness of the oil will allow the character of the vinegar to come through more clearly than olive oils with bitter, peppery notes.

The marriage of depth of flavour, acidity and sweetness make it a go-to choice for adding at an early stage of a dish. It balances and brightens other elements. Think about making it the base for all manner of meat- and tomato-based dishes; and for stews or soups whether they are meat, fish, bean or vegetable led.

Then for the more grape-specific vinegars: Moscatel is a little sweeter and lighter, great for fish and seafood, and another super choice for salad dressings; Pedro Ximénez vinegar can be used in more robust dishes that can take its weight. Think about using it to deglaze a meat pan. A light finishing spritz can offer a perfectly balanced lift of seasoning of acidity, depth and sweetness. Macerate strawberries in it, pour over roasted fruits, or reduce with sugar over a low heat to make a reduction for sauce or glaze.

Wine Vinegars

Wherever there is a wine-making culture around the world, there has been, is and will forever be wine vinegar too – from European classics to the 'New World' wines, to ice wines in Canada, and any in between.

The details of the origins of wine vinegars are hazy. There is evidence from mentions in manuscripts and residues in urns that leave us in little doubt that ancient cultures enjoyed wine vinegar, but how that was first discovered is lost in time. It is a mystery that adds to the mystique of it all. A safe assumption, however, is that wine vinegars began as a mistake, or at least as a by-product of wine-making.

Once grapes have been fermented into wine, they are then only one fermentation away from becoming vinegar. If the wine is badly stored or otherwise exposed to air and its naturally occurring bacteria, that can be all it takes to kick-start the bacterial fermentation that turns the alcohol into acidic vinegar. We all know this from having left wine open at home, which then becomes vinegary. Modern wine-makers know how to make sure that does not happen to their wines, and modern vinegar-makers know how to carefully control and craft that acetic fermentation, but it is not at all hard to see that in the past it just naturally happened as a consequence of wine-making. Any sadness at the idea of wine spoiling is, I hope, swiftly mollified by knowing gorgeous wine vinegar can be the result.

ORLÉANS

The best-known story of how vinegar-accident became vinegar-industry is that of Orléans. In Western vinegar-making the word 'Orléans' comes up again and again, and you still see it on some bottles of vinegar. In vinegar terms, these days it seldom means a French city seventy miles or so south-west of Paris. What it means is a process of making wine vinegar (and other vinegars too, sometimes) and is a by-word for slow, artisan, traditional vinegar-making that is indeed rooted in that city's port on the Loire, going back 600 years and more.

Imagine, if you will, Orléans in the fourteenth century. It's a bustling port, ideally positioned on the Loire river to receive produce destined for the capital. The Loire, being France's longest river, weaves its way through much glorious wine-producing country, meaning that wines formed a significant wealth of the cargo flowing into Orléans.

Now imagine the journey those wine barrels had en route: the conditions – the air – they may have been subjected to. Some of the wines were spoiled on the journey to Orléans, and for the traders there was little point in taking that wine any further, knowing that it would be impossible to sell in Paris, and being taxed on it to boot. So the 'off' wine was offloaded in Orléans and as a consequence a whole industry sprang up there, turning the wine into vinegar. Orléans was the right place at the right time to became the epicentre of France's wine vinegar production.

Orléans method

a by-word for slow, artisanal, traditional vinegar-making, rooted in the fourteenth century style of making vinegar in Orléans.

Its success – domination, really – was born out of a burgeoning public interest in what had until then only really been considered by the French as an accident of wine-making, or something that was made at home or in monasteries, but not made and sold at a commercial level. The wine vinegar-makers of Orléans changed all that. The *vinaigriers* there became a corporation – rather like a guild – under official statute. There was even an initiation ceremony that included an oath taken never to reveal how the vinegar was made.

It is an oath that the early Orléans vinegar-makers would have had little trouble keeping. For while all kinds of alchemists would go on to be employed to come up with the best ways of making the best vinegars from these less-than-best wines, initially at least the science didn't really move on from the absolute simplicity of what had been happening with wine all over the world: it was left to interact with the air and natural bacteria, and to become vinegar. The vinegar-makers knew something magical, miraculous – and ultimately hugely marketable – was going on, but not the facts behind it. It is a situation best summed up by an old French expression used when something inexplicable happens: *c'ést le secret du vinaigrier.* Such a secret, most of the vinegar-makers didn't even know it.

As the corporation became more established and demand for vinegar grew, the Orléans method of slow fermentation of wine into vinegar became a much more understood practice: wines in oak casks were fermented with natural bacteria into vinegar; the vinegar would then be siphoned off, but about a fifth was left behind in the barrel so that when new wine was added, there were the right bacteria already there to begin the acetic fermentation again. It was – is – a continuous process, that is still famed and used today.

By the sixteenth century there were hundreds of vinegar-makers in Orléans doing this. Royal decree set out that Orléans-style vinegar could only be made in Orléans and its immediate area; it was no longer a way of using off-wine on its way to Paris. Just as we appreciate today that the best wine vinegars start with high-quality wines, so it was that wines were being transported to Orléans specifically for vinegar-making, then being taken all over France and sold to what had become a market so significant it was worth putting a tax on it.

Louis Pasteur was hugely important in discovering and clearly setting out just what was happening to make Orléans-style vinegar in the 1860s. But by then others were working to come up with vinegar-making methods that would be quicker, more reliable, more consistently high-yielding than Orléans in order to fill the demand that had been stoked. You can find more detail on the science of vinegar-making and the more high-tech innovations that have been introduced since on page 22. What matters here, in thinking about modern wine vinegar production across the world, is just how much the Orléans story still resonates and in varying degrees applies to any and all wine-producing countries and their wine vinegars.

WINE VINEGAR TODAY

Some modern wine vinegars are made by wine-makers as a sideline to their primary wine business. And some producers focus purely on making and selling really good wine vinegar. There are makers who use great wines as the basis for vinegar, others who don't. Many make their wine vinegars as fast as possible, using the latest technology in huge tanks. Then there are those who take it slow, Orléans-style, in oak barrels. All of these play an important role in the worldwide market for wine vinegars – and it truly is worldwide.

I am going to pick out here particularly interesting wine regions and grapes that are producing distinctive wine vinegars. But a word first on 'generic' red or white wine vinegars. Those inverted commas are not intended to denote any snobbery or sneer. I have bottles of big-brand, non-specific wine vinegars in my cupboard and I bet you do too, for use as baseline, hard-working wine vinegars. Nothing wrong with that. But. But, but, but. The point is that they are just the tip of the gloriously versatile wine vinegars you might come across, which make a feature of the wine region or the wine grapes at their heart. Those factors will determine the acidity, density and flavour profile of the vinegar and therefore what you can use it for in the kitchen.

In all wine vinegar-making, the end result in the bottle in your kitchen is going to be determined by three things: the type and quality of the base wine; the microorganisms used to turn the alcohol to vinegar; and the process used for that acetic fermentation. I am not sure I could tell you which element is most important. What matters is how they work together – and this is the balance being alchemised by producers working across the world's wine vinegar regions and grapes, in order to achieve the vinegar they want.

That balance for many modern wine-vinegar-makers increasingly lies in choosing to create sweeter vinegars labelled as bitter-sweet, or *agrodolce* or *aigre-doux*. They are different names for the same thing and it can be achieved in various ways. Some producers use sweet wine as the base to be turned into vinegar, which as you will see accounts for many interesting wine vinegars. Some use late-harvest grapes that will be a bit sweeter for being dried, or 'raisined', in the sun. Others – increasingly many – add grape must to the wine vinegar.

Grape must, from cooked-down grape juice, seeds and skins, was used by the ancient Romans as a sweetener known as *saba*, and serves the same purpose for the wine vinegars. Wine vinegars with added grape must will list it on the bottle as an ingredient. Sometimes they are described as 'condiment' vinegars and can be absolutely lovely – especially excellent as salad dressings – but the thing to watch out for is if the addition of the grape must has reduced the vinegar's acidity. Anything below 5% and you should be wary of using that wine vinegar for anything other than a sauce or dressing. Dishes such as marinades, ceviches or pickling need the higher acidity these must-sweetened wine vinegars sometimes do not have.

Ageing of wine vinegars is another thing to consider. One producer told me with impressive candour that the merit and impact of ageing in wine vinegars is sometimes questionable. It is one of those things that we as consumers like the idea of, and savvy makers can play into that. Ageing sounds artisan and interesting, as if it is bound to produce a better vinegar. And indeed it can help a wine vinegar develop its colour, flavour and become more rounded – it is just not necessarily as straightforward as to assume that ageing means good, non-ageing means less good.

WINE VINEGARS BY REGION/WINE TYPE

For many wine-vinegar-making regions, it is a balance of the grapes together with the area's natural characteristics – its *terroir* – and the methods of production that combine to create something exciting in the bottle. For these wine vinegars, the environment it has been produced in matters as much as, or maybe more than, simply the profile of the grapes used.

A decent rule of thumb is that if a wine vinegar shares some or all of the characteristics of a good wine, the likelihood is you are on to a good thing. For that reason I am always drawn to wine vinegars from regions with a good wine pedigree, and especially those with protected status of production such as the EU PDO (Protected Designation of Origin) or PGI (Protected Geographical Indication), see page 64. Even if the protected status doesn't extend to the vinegar – and mainly it doesn't – the integrity is often still very much there in the vinegar.

France

France has not forgotten how much it loves making wine vinegar. There are lots of French wine vinegars about, some of the best being made in France's wine-making AOP (*Appellation d'Origine Protégée*, see page 135) or Vins de Pays regions.

Think in broad terms first. Of regions such as Corbières, which is famous for red wine, so I know its red wine vinegars are worth a look too. Similarly with Anjou in the Loire Valley, for still more red wine vinegars, made with Gamay or Cabernet Franc grapes. There is the mountainous region of Jura, over in the east between Burgundy and Switzerland, which is turning out some gorgeous vinegars that share the breadth and quality of the Arbois AOP wines, with vinegars ranging from crisp white Chardonnay to light, fresh Poulsard reds. (It is maybe not so much a tribute as a coincidence that Arbois, Jura's capital, was home to Louis Pasteur as he was growing up, but given his huge importance to our modern understanding of just what vinegar is, it is fitting nonetheless.)

Then focus in – to wine vinegars based on local, specific wine specialities. This is where things can get really exciting. As in Anjou, again, where there is a terrific vinegar made from the region's rather special Coteaux du Layon sweet white wine. Its vinegar is a fabulous rich golden colour, with the sweetness of the wine deliciously tempered by fruity acidity – a favourite for anything where a light balance of sweet and sour is appreciated.

Or there is Pineau des Charentes, another interesting AOP wine being turned into vinegar. The area where this sweet aperitif wine is made has almost exactly the same geography as the Cognac region, making it nothing of a surprise at all for this to be made with local Charentes region grapes plus a healthy measure of young Cognac in there for its fermentation. When young it is pale yellow, sweet and floral, then it ages up to get a bit more character and colour. The Cognac gives the Pineau des Charentes vinegars extra body, even in the lighter styles.

Vinegars made from Banyuls AOP take on much of the character of this gorgeous dessert wine. Banyuls is right on the southern edge of France, with Catalunya just over the border. Here the wines are predominantly made by small growers with immense pride in their local speciality wine that is starting to gain the more widespread recognition it deserves. As it does, I hope the Banyuls vinegars gain a similar head of steam. These are vinegars full of lush fruity body and to be used accordingly.

Spain

Vinegar culture is interwoven with the Spanish way of life, with its food: olive oil and vinegar, hand in hand.

The truth of this is in the fact that Spain has three of the five vinegars in Europe with PDO classification (the other two are the *Tradizionale* balsamics of Italy). Note well: these are not vinegars that are just born of PDO wine – these are vinegars that have the classification, status and protection in their own right. All three Spanish PDO vinegars are found in Andalucía, at the very core of Spain's olive oil production. It's another Andalucían vinegar triangle, with Jerez at its most southerly point, Condado de Huelva further up the coast to the west and then Montilla-Moriles heading east inland. Jerez has the rights on world-famous sherries and sherry vinegars; for the other two it is wine and wine vinegars that are rather less well-known and – currently – less widely sold than they deserve to be.

Does Spain's dominance of the vinegar PDOs mean it has the dominant European vinegars? Certainly not in terms of profile. Balsamic is the worldwide star. Yet the Italians have posed a number of objections to the EU about Montilla-Moriles wine vinegars being given PDO recognition. All were dismissed out of hand, but it makes me wonder whether there is some underlying nervousness about balsamic being able to keep its place when these Spanish wine vinegars are coming through on the inside and their production is resurging. If the Andalucían local vinegar-making industry can continue to be reinvigorated to a significant scale of high-quality production, they may – *may* – pose a serious challenge to balsamic in the future.

Montilla-Moriles

Montilla and Moriles are the two towns of the Córdoba province that are at the centre of, and give their names to, the Montilla-Moriles wine-producing region. It may be only a couple of hours' drive from Jerez, but it is drier, with greater daytime extremes of heat and cold. The

impact on the grapes, the wines and therefore the vinegars, is that they are that bit rougher than their sherry cousins. In Montilla-Moriles it is the Pedro Ximénez grape that is dominant (not sherry's Palomino), giving an emphasis on the sweet. These vinegars have good acidity (6%), with residual alcohol up to 3%.

The Montilla-Moriles wines share with sherry (and Condado de Huelva) the way they become vinegars: either by being aged using the traditional *criaderas y solera* system described on page 115, where the vinegar moves through wooden *botas* or barrels as it matures; or in the *añada* style, by staying in one barrel the whole time and for at least three years (for *añada* sherry vinegar it is two years). For the 'dynamic' traditional way there are different categories depending on the ageing period – from *Crianza*, meaning at least six months; to *Reserva* being at least two years; and *Gran Reserva* for vinegar aged in wood for at least ten years. As it ages the colour and flavour of the vinegar intensify. What starts as a fresh young amber will become mahogany and then nearly jet black with deep roasted fruit notes. Think about how you use it in the kitchen developing accordingly: from dressings at the light end, through drizzling over langoustines, to the *Gran Reserva* being saved for use as a finishing touch (to a soup, perhaps).

The Pedro Ximénez grape varieties of these vinegars come with all the sweetness you would expect of grapes that raisined under the intense sun, but then with the wonderful acidic contrast. So they're good with ice creams or over roasted fruits. Still sweet but even more diversely useful for being rather lighter, are the Moscatel vinegar versions.

Condado de Huelva

The wine-making region of Huelva province stretches from the coastal Sierra de Aracena to the edge of the Doñana National Park, with its vast and wild marshlands. That gives a relatively mild, relatively wet climate with air so rich in oxygen that this part of the world is sometimes called the 'lungs of Europe'. With all that in its favour, the local Zalema grapes produce deeply flavoured alcohol-heavy wines and vinegars, which, as in Montilla-Moriles, have always been overshadowed by what is happening in Jerez.

Vinagre Condado de Huelva is a perfectly lovely, versatile wine vinegar, pale gold in colour, with a hint of apple that is gifted by the Zalema grapes. But with the addition of the word *viejo* – meaning 'with ageing' – is the *Vinagre Viejo Condado de Huelva*, which is much richer and, arguably, better than its unaged counterpart. These vinegars are literally enriched with Condado de Huelva liqueur wine during the vinegar's ageing process, and the resulting vinegar has much more body – and alcohol.

The residual alcohol allowed in the *Vinagre Viejo Condado de Huelva* is up to 3% (as in sherry vinegar). Compare that to the 0.5% allowed for unaged *Vinagre Condado de Huelva*. So these are full, deep wine vinegars packed with dried-fruit flavours that marry with the higher acidity of 7–8%.

The ageing and labelling of *Vinagre Viejo Condado de Huelva* follows the same system as Montilla-Moriles, whether in the dynamic sequence of *criaderas y solera* barrels or the *añada* way of staying in the same barrel the whole time. The difference is that the *Vinagre Viejo Condado de Huelva* does not have the *Gran Reserva* classification for prolonged ageing.

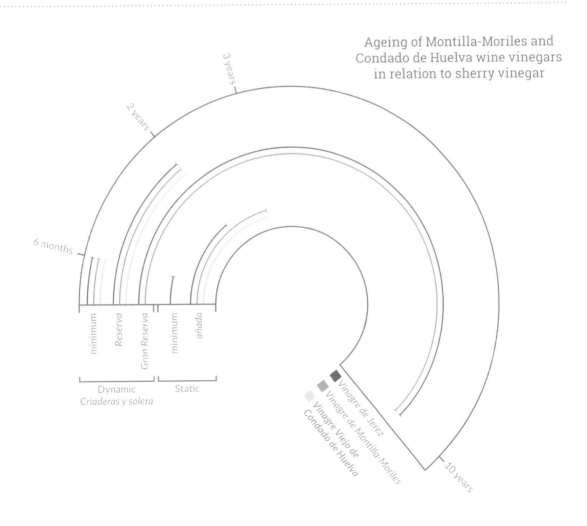

Ageing of Montilla-Moriles and Condado de Huelva wine vinegars in relation to sherry vinegar

Greece

The Greek peninsula of the Peloponnese is riven through any text on ancient Greek culture. That includes wine culture, and, by almost automatic extension, wine vinegars too. The romance of that legacy may be partly why I am so drawn to the modern wine vinegars – the *oxos* – of the Peloponnese and across Greece. I feel I can taste the legends of the land in the vinegar, and am imbuing my cooking with that mythology. Let me think it, at least.

Nemea on the north-east of the Peloponnese is well known for its red wines. What is particularly distinctive is just how varied the land and the climate is. The contrasting wines that are the result of its microclimate make for wonderful blends of Nemean red wine vinegars, made with the region's signature Agiorgitiko grape.

When it comes to Greek white wine vinegars they are usually made with the Rhoditis grape. When I tell you that this is the grape traditionally used to make retsina you may worry about the balance of the vinegar. Don't. Modern retsinas are far more refined than the foggy memories of Greek holiday nights of your youth might lead you to think, especially those of the grapes grown in the Patras region where the high altitude creates more rounded dimensions to the wines. As ever, that translates to the wine vinegars too. Look for Patras-region, Rhoditis-grape white wine vinegar and you will have something bright and fruity.

The Greek island of Crete is also turning out some excellent wine vinegars from its extensive wine-producing region. Of special interest are red wine vinegars of its local grape specialities, Kotsifali and Liatiko.

Italy

Thoughts of Italian vinegars tend to be dominated by balsamic. But it was not ever thus. Until relatively recently – forty years or so ago – balsamic was very much a local product, made and enjoyed locally. You couldn't get it in the rest of Italy, but the rest of Italy didn't mind so much as it was enjoying its own local wine vinegars.

That Italian wine vinegar market took a backseat as balsamic leapt to the fore, but it is interesting and exciting to see the resurgence of Italian single-variety wine vinegars produced from the grapes and wines that Italy is legendary for. Chianti and Barolo (and other fabulous Piedmont wines) are amongst those again being produced as wine vinegars. Sometimes the winery is making them; sometimes they sell the wine to a vinegar producer. Either way, they're something to look out for.

USA

So here's an interesting thing. Wine is now one of California's proudest achievements. It is acclaimed around the world, and more and more wineries are being set up there. Depending on the year and how you gauge it, the USA consistently comes in the top three, four or five wine-producing nations across the world. But wine vinegar – not so much. Which is as interesting to take note of as if they produced lots of it. The two fundamental reasons why there is so little US-made wine vinegar are that cider vinegar is much more the thing in America; and the wine industry is very young, having had to start from pretty much scratch after Prohibition. Let's not blame them for focusing on the wine first and foremost, ahead of the vinegar.

I wonder if it will come, though. It certainly should, judging by the wine vinegar being made by the few producers or wineries who are choosing to focus on it. The scale and scope of California's wine-producing regions make it impossible to ponder here in any detail on what its wine vinegars might be like if there were more of them. All we can say with certainty is that given wine vinegars are a distillation of the character of a region's wines, so Californian wines will – in their own time – have much to add to international wine vinegars.

Australia

Victoria may the second smallest state in Australia, but it punches well above its weight in terms of the nation's wine. It has more regions and individual wineries than any other Australian state. Its eminence as wine country goes back to the mid-1800s, as predicted in this essay from 1860 that I came across on Victoria's agriculture: 'As Victoria is likely to become a wine-producing colony, and as a large quantity of this wine may become sour, especially during the first few years, I will proceed to show you how easily it may be turned to the best advantage by being completely acetified or converted into vinegar...'

The unnamed author was right on all counts. Victoria by the 1880s was producing more wine than any other state. The youth of the industry would have led to accidental spoilage of wines in the making and storing of them. And certainly there is little more efficient to do with such wine than turn it into delicious vinegar.

Australia's wine industry would go on to hit a rough patch and then resurge from the 1970s onwards. And duly wine vinegars are coming through again now (with some especially delicious ones coming out of Victoria).

Wine vinegars by grape

The *terroir* and methods of production matter for all wine vinegars, but much wine vinegar is defined not by where it is made, but by its grape first and foremost. Using these vinegars is as simple as translating what we know about food and grapes from our wine drinking.

There are as many wine vinegars as wine styles or grapes. The following are just a few, but the logic when using them never differs: think about the wine that might go well with a particular food, then cook the dish with the wine vinegar as close in style to that wine as possible.

Sauvignon Blanc

A crisp white wine vinegar with fruity notes coming through. A great choice for marinades, ceviches and salad dressings.

White Burgundy

Made from Chardonnay grapes grown in the region of Burgundy. This is one of my favourite white wines, so unsurprisingly it is also one of my favourite white wine vinegars. It is elegant, rounded, with a vibrancy to its acidity. I'd use it for fish.

Riesling

Often found as a vinegar in the wine-producing regions of Austria and Germany. Australia, too. Fruity and floral with excellent acidity and medium body, it is a good alternative to cider vinegar in dishes.

Pedro Ximénez

The grape of so many Spanish wine vinegars, especially in the south of the country. Sweet from being dried out in the sun, they create intense sweet-yet-sharp vinegars. The Spanish wine vinegar producers do not have the monopoly on using Pedro Ximénez grapes to make vinegar, though. PX grapes from other countries will share the depth and sweetness (but won't have the same restrictions on how the grapes are processed and bottle labelling). Try over soft fruits, with cheese, or with shellfish such as oysters.

Zinfandel

These can be really super red wine vinegars, especially if *agrodolce*. The crisp acidity carries with it jammy fruits. Use for dressing tomatoes, drizzled over figs and cheese and in pork dishes.

Rioja

Another of the deep, full, heavy red wine vinegars.

Chianti

The red wine vinegar of choice for richness and depth. Imagine what you'd like to drink a nice Chianti with – for me that's a big bowl of pasta ragù – then use a Chianti vinegar to cook it with.

Champagne

Light, delicate, pale and good with fish. Almost like a nice glass of bubbly! These vinegars are a blend of the grape varieties used to make champagnes – usually Pinot Noir, Pinot Gris, Pinot Meunier and Chardonnay. There are no requirements for the champagne vinegar to be made in the Champagne region or in the champagne style. A champagne vinegar could mean it is simply a blend of the champagne grapes, or it could mean that actual champagne has been fermented into vinegar. If it is the latter then the vinegar will be slightly fizzy, but the main thing to note on champagne vinegars is that they are like white wine vinegars, with similar acidity, but lighter in body and flavour.

Merlot

Usually somewhere in between the Chianti and Cabernet Sauvignon red wine vinegars in terms of its body and intensity. Often sold as a sweetened version.

Pinot Noir

These vinegars can be fruity, spicy and yet somehow delicate, too. That makes them one of the most versatile red wine vinegars. Especially good with meat, game and red fruits.

Moscatel (in Spain)/Muscatel (in France or Italy)

An aromatic, bitter-sweet vinegar with fruity, floral and citrusy notes, which make this a versatile choice for salad dressings, especially as it carries other flavours so well.

Chardonnay

A fruity, crisp, floral and light vinegar. An excellent choice for fish dishes and salads, or any dish with mango or apples.

Cabernet Sauvignon

These grapes make for a plummy red wine vinegar that is usually of medium intensity, making it a versatile choice for marinades, sauces and deglazing pans. Excellent in mignonette sauce for oysters.

DESSERT WINES

There are lovely and distinctive sweet wines to be found all around the world, and many of them are being made into even lovelier vinegars. They tend to carry an underlying sweetness which is very appealing to modern cooks, as well as having 'proper' vinegar acidity. Pedro Ximénez sherry is a sweet wine and famously used in wonderful sherry vinegars; and I have already mentioned Banyuls. Those are two of the best known, but there are others too that are well worth knowing about. Wherever you encounter a regional sweet wine that has been acetified into vinegar you are likely to have something interesting.

Ice Wine

Ice wine just sounds exciting, I always think. And it is, both in the making and drinking. It is produced from vineyards that have the perfect ice-wine producing contrast of hot summers that give the grapes abundant life, and literally freezing cold winters. Grapes that have frozen on the vine are pressed to extract as much of the sweet juice as possible, but little of the iced-solid water. The resulting wine is sweetly divine and – as with so many of the wine vinegars – sweetness in the base wine translates to really interesting vinegar. The ice wines and ice wine vinegars are for obvious reasons only produced where the climate allows: look out for producers in Canada, USA, Germany and Austria.

Trockenbeerenauslese (TBA)

A wine style that is found in Germany and Austria, quite often as a vinegar. It is a very long word for a medium- to full-body dessert wine. The grapes – of varying varieties – are picked late in the harvest, which makes them sweeter. It is a similar idea to the raisining of PX grapes in Spain. The resulting vinegar is another that works well for its edge of natural sweetness.

Tokaj 'Aszu'

This time it is neither the weather nor the harvesting that causes the shrivelling up and intense sweetening of the grapes – it is mould. A very helpful 'noble rot' mould, thanks to which Aszu sweet wine is made in Hungary's Tokaj region. Its vinegar is sweet and crisp.

VERMOUTH

Vermouth vinegars are as diverse as the vermouths that are out there all over the world, and with as many layers of complexity as each vermouth will have from its own blend of ingredients. These are not vinegars where the flavours should be cooked away – use them as a finisher for fish, salad or poultry dishes, or for marinades. In Catalunya I encountered a glorious local way of eating cockles (*berberechos*) with vermouth vinegar (see page 159).

MAKE YOUR OWN

The final word on wine vinegars goes to making your own. For those of us who drink wine or live in a wine-drinking culture, this can be both easy and pleasurable to do. I half believe that.

For me – and this is a very personal thing – I don't particularly enjoy making my own wine vinegar. It's for the same reasons that if I want proper patisserie I go to a patissier. There is skill, craft, knowledge and experience at play in the end result. In the case of vinegar there is science, too, to contend with. I would rather buy a wonderful vinegar crafted by someone who knows exactly what they are doing.

But if you do want to have a go, making a basic wine vinegar is simplicity itself when done in the style that would be recognisable to country-house kitchens across France (and elsewhere) of really any period you might care to mention.

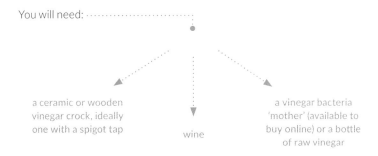

You will need:

a ceramic or wooden vinegar crock, ideally one with a spigot tap

wine

a vinegar bacteria 'mother' (available to buy online) or a bottle of raw vinegar

The wine goes into the crock with the mother (or raw vinegar), ensuring it is only about two-thirds full, and you leave it alone for vinegar to happen. Taste it after two months to see if it is to your required acidity. This is the bit that bothers me most about making my own vinegar – without specialist equipment you cannot tell how fully acetified the vinegar is. You will not know its acidity. But then, this is for your own consumption, not for sale, so maybe all that matters is that you like it.

Try to get the vinegar out with as little disturbance to the mother as possible. Using a 'wine thief' implement to suck some up is a good idea. Then just top up the crock with leftover wine as and when you have some. Note that mixing red, white or rosé wines would be a mistake, but otherwise you can freestyle it between wine varieties of the same colour.

IN THE KITCHEN
Wine Vinegar

The wealth of variety of wine vinegars means there is a similar wealth of things they can be used for. Think of wine vinegar and food partnerships as you do wine and food partnerships. Robust red wine vinegars will be best with heartier dishes, while lighter white wine vinegars lend themselves more to fish. But on the other hand, I'd often go for a red wine vinegar with seafood... Try wine vinegars for marinades, pickling, pan deglazes, over roasted meats, vegetables or fruits, a finishing spritz or drinking vinegar shrubs. So many choices for these are such deliciously versatile vinegars.

Cider Vinegars

There is a common theme to so many vinegars that – at least to start with – in all likelihood came about as a happy accident of drinks-making going 'wrong', or going too far. Cider vinegars are another example. They are simply one fermentation on from apples being fermented into cider, and have become a staple around the world.

I say staple – do I mean ubiquitous? It definitely seems so in some regions. Japan and America especially are very big on consuming apple cider vinegar (apple cider vinegar, ACV and cider vinegar are names that can be used interchangeably). Much of that popularity is to do with cider vinegar's proclaimed health benefits, which are certainly interesting but which I feel sometimes overshadow our understanding of cider vinegar's culinary pleasures, rather than being appreciated as a complement to them.

None of which is to throw a damp towel onto the magical powers of cider vinegar that deserve their own detail (and will get it, see page 138). It's just that it reminds me a little of the story food historians in the UK tell: of how before the food writing of Elizabeth David, the nation's olive oil was more likely to be found in the medicine cabinet (good for unblocking ears) than in the kitchen. Many decades on from that, we seem to be in a place where people are thinking of cider vinegar as something to take as a tonic rather than to cook with, and at the very least that seems a shame. Cider vinegar, with its mild flavour and good acidity, is one of the most useful of all vinegars for a cook.

CIDER APPLES AND CIDER VINEGAR-MAKING

I love that the literal roots of this elixir are with the orchards of gnarled old cider apple trees. The *terroir* of those trees is all-important to the production of cider vinegar. Across the world, wherever there have been rural farming communities with the soil and climate that are generous to those orchards flourishing, chances are there will have been the production of cider and therefore cider vinegar. From Britain to northern Spain, from the east coast of America to the French countryside of Normandy and Brittany, for centuries farmers have been producing the best cider vinegars which retain the distinctive character and essence of those regions' orchards. Cider vinegars might range in colour from pale straw to rich gold, each absolutely tasting and smelling of the apples from which they are made – surely a base level requirement for any ACV, but not something to be taken for granted.

Terroir aside, other key factors in making cider vinegar are the apples themselves, and then the process. The level of sugar and acidity varies among apple varieties, season and maturity, all of which affect the cider and cider vinegar. Less ripe fruits have more acidity; over-ripe fruits have a sweeter but sometimes also flatter flavour. Many cider and cider vinegar producers would grow and therefore use a blend of cider apples to achieve just the balance they are after. A real mix of bitter-sweets, bitter-sharps and sweet apples that were typically ready for harvesting later than other crops, so

ACV

Apple cider vinegar, also known simply as cider vinegar.

farmers could get the main harvest done before turning their attention to the cider and cider vinegar that would be produced through November and December when little else happened on the farm.

One of the simplest, oldest ways of extracting raw juice from the apples for its alcoholic fermentation was to pile ripe apples into a hollowed-out tree or into a trough and just beat at them with sticks to release the juice. Left somewhere warm and damp, the naturally-occurring yeasts would organically ferment the apple into alcohol. To make vinegar, that now-cider would be left again to move to its next stage of fermenting into vinegar.

While there is a definite appeal to such a natural, hands-off way of doing it, for a farmer intending to use or sell the vinegar in any meaningful quantities, it came with various problems: of the alcoholic fermentation not being quite complete; of the process taking a long time; and producing a low yield of cider and vinegar. Farmers were understandably keen to embrace more sophisticated production processes as they came along, both in terms of making cider and then of turning that to vinegar. Speed and cost became the driving forces over time, with flavour the loser in that equation.

Modern craft cider producers are now re-embracing some of the old ways of making. There are some small-scale producers around who still have and are using again those old-style presses. In regions where cider vinegar has that kind of cider heritage it is not too hard even to find small-batch cider vinegar producers using traditional Orléans-style surface-fermenting, with its commercial disadvantages of a slow, low yield of vinegar, but a flavour upside.

AGEING OF CIDER VINEGAR

Ageing of cider vinegar after it is made can be of huge flavour benefit. Ideally it is done in wooden casks, just as wood is used for ageing balsamic or sherry vinegars. Or whiskies and wines come to that. The wood allows it to breathe in a way that stainless steel tanks (which are sometimes used) cannot. Those tanks which have rather less character about them and so allow rather less character to develop in the cider vinegar are better than no ageing at all, though. Or the very minimal one or two months that the mass-producers choose to 'afford'. From their purely commercial point of view it is easy to see that ageing vinegar costs money in terms of production costs and just the basic factor of not having it out there on sale as fast as possible. Yet storing cider vinegar for a year or so knocks off its harsher flavour edges, to develop a rounder profile. The aroma develops. The colour changes. With the wood casks that allow some air through, additional reactions take place that develop deeper, fruity notes to the vinegar.

PASTEURISING AND FILTERING ... AND THE 'MOTHER'

A couple of other things matter when making cider vinegar. Actually, they matter when making any kind of vinegar, but especially cider because of its health-boosting momentum.

If a vinegar is to be pasteurised, this happens after the ageing (if there is any). Like any pasteurisation, the idea is to subject the vinegar to fast heat and wipe out any harmful pathogens. Many think – and I agree – that while there are definite upsides to pasteurisation, it can also kill off some of the bacteria that are not only acceptable from a health and safety perspective but also part of the product's character, even of its benefits. It is the same argument as for raw – unpasteurised – milk, for example. A vinegar that has been made with care and knowledge about using the 'right' bacteria – so any vinegar that is safe to be sold commercially – does not really need to be pasteurised. Look out for raw vinegar.

Then there is filtering. Unfiltered vinegars are those that have the vinegar bacteria 'mother' floating around in the bottle (see pages 138). For many producers the message seems to be that having the mother in the bottle is the thing that makes the vinegar 'good'. The jury is out on that one. More interesting to me than whether or not the apple cider vinegar has the mother in it, is the risk of filtration removing some of the precious colour and flavour profiles of the vinegar. So, look out for unfiltered cider vinegars, too.

MODERN CIDER VINEGAR

In the end, what really matters – to me, at least – is that the cider vinegar has been made well, with depth and balance that will be good to cook with. Such ACVs can be found all around the world. Still of special interest are the regions I mentioned earlier, with a long-standing, proud and fascinating cider-making – and cider vinegar-making – heritage: Britain, France, America and Spain. Also of note are Canada, Austria and Germany. Each has wonderful stories of its cider vinegar past, and is producing excellent cider vinegars now. Some are taking their cider vinegars to another level and blending their traditional cider vinegars with other fruit extractions or infusions.

First, though, a small note of caution. Where cider vinegars are being produced by small cider farms, they are generally made using some traditional processes of fermentation with their own or local apples. Especially in the areas given special protected status for their ciders. It is worth remembering, however, that even in those areas there is no established legal protection putting a stamp on how ACVs are made. It isn't like the sherry vinegars of Jerez, where the wine and the vinegar are both protected. It is possible for a cider producer to be selling a cider vinegar that is maybe not made from their cider or apples, maybe not made in the same region, maybe not made by any traditional processes, but maybe giving the impression of being some or all of those things.

Of course, if you are lucky enough to be there at the farm with the producer you can ask. Otherwise, check the label for clues when buying.

Britain

'Where there's muck, there's brass' is an old Yorkshire saying, and the southern England equivalent in the seventeenth century could well have been, 'Where there's apples, there's cider'. Meaning cider vinegar too, of course. There were apples aplenty in the cider orchards across the farms of Devon, Somerset, Shropshire and even across the Welsh borders to the shires of Monmouth, Brecon and Radnor. Where the climate was mild (relatively) and moist (definitely), with rich meadow grass, cider orchards were abundant, growing apples with such wonderfully evocative yet mysterious names as Gennet Moyle, Coccagee or the Tom Putt. In the seventeenth century, as cider became the national drink, cider apple orchards were a hugely profitable adjunct to other farm activities. Crops could be grown in the wide spaces between the cider apple trees and, as previously mentioned, cider-making could happen when other aspects of farming were quieter. There are accounts of farms feeding the pomace remains of the cider apple pressings to their pigs for what I imagine must have been especially tasty bacon.

This was the highpoint of cider – and therefore cider vinegar – production. Its fall came as cider fell out of favour to beer. A nation in thrall to either hops or French wine imports meant the nation's cider apple orchards began to fall away through the Victorian era. It was a situation that worsened as you scroll on to post-World War II when, with mass food production coming through, swathes of British apple orchards were decimated to make way for other crops. The cider that was being made in the UK on any significant scale was being made with imported apple juice, and lacking those interesting local characteristics of apples from the regional orchards.

I haven't forgotten my thrust here is really about cider vinegar, not about cider. The point is that it is largely the same story. Without good, local craft cider – in the real sense – there is no good, local craft cider vinegar either. Or at least, not any that could be purchased by the public. Small-hold farmers would certainly have carried on producing cider vinegar for their own use, but it is only with the recent craft cider renaissance in those same counties that the wider market has access again to authentic cider vinegar.

Traditional presses have been bought or restored; orchards cultivated of heirloom cider apple varieties with wonderfully bizarre names; and there are now ciders across Herefordshire, Worcestershire, Gloucestershire and Wales with protected PGI status. Lessons have been re-learnt as to how to produce not just regional ciders, but good regional cider vinegars, too. These are the vinegars with it all: *terroir*, heritage, blending of apple varieties and a traditional and skilful process that is not rushed. As cider routes are opening up across parts of the British countryside, if you stumble across one be sure to ask the cider producers if they are doing a vinegar too.

France

The northern regions of France – especially Normandy and Brittany – with their cooler, calmer climate relative to the south and their lush landscapes, are prime apple-growing country. The *terroir* here is less suited to grapes, and so it is in these regions that cider dominates over wine in both production and consumption. Which means, naturally, this is cider vinegar territory, too. And just as in other rural cider-producing parts of the world, it is only relatively recently that the cider vinegar produced (maybe initially by accident) is available for more than use by just the family or for purely local trade.

In the last thirty or so years, these regions have reclaimed their status and pride in their apple produce, which had for centuries been one of the agricultural mainstays. Charlemagne is credited with the spread of cultivated cider apple trees in the region in the eighth and ninth centuries AD (interestingly, doing so after encountering *sidre* in Spain's Asturias region). By the fifteenth century, cider was embedded into the region's life thanks to enhanced production techniques, seedlings being grafted that were particularly suited to yielding fruit in that soil, and then in the sixteenth century the decision by Charles IX to restrict vineyards. Yet come the twentieth century and two World Wars, the story of cider production in northern France is a familiar one to that of Britain. The agricultural focus shifts away from fruit, and to any extent it rests there it is all about mass productivity. Traditional cider production techniques and regional characteristics disappeared, but happily now there are cider producers once again putting their regions' long-won time and skill and quality produce into their vinegars too.

The cider vinegars of this region share the characteristics of its cider. They are well balanced from being made with a base blend of bitter-sweet and bitter apples. The methods of production being used are the traditional, artisanal ones which give the cider and the vinegar their subtle, complex, rounded flavour. Even more fundamentally, the apples are imbued with the essence of what makes the regions' other produce so fabulous, and that cannot fail to make its way into the vinegar. Think about it – the land that makes the grass, that makes the milk, that makes the cheese so wonderful is the same land that gives life to the apples. The produce is all part of the same system.

A drive, cycle or stroll through modern Normandy reveals its green hills, valleys that run between quiet villages, sixteenth-century châteaux and the odd glimpse of the ocean. This is real country-life France, as unspoilt as can reasonably be expected. Dairy farms abound, producing the region's iconic cheeses; there are cattle grazing on naturally nutrient-rich green, green grass; and all around are hectare after hectare of cider apple orchards. Producing cider, of course, but not just cider – other apple products of Calvados apple brandy and Pommeau (apple brandy with cider apple must) are hugely important here too. But for vinegar purposes it is the cider that excites most.

In particular, there's a twenty-five-mile (almost a marathon's worth) circular route through the Pays d'Auge area where cider is the way of life. The farms on the cider route have AOP (*Appellation d'Origine Protégée*) protected status for their cider. The route is handily marked with signs that feature a big red apple, and many of them are open to visitors for tours or tastings. And purchasings too, of course. Many of these cider route farms also produce and sell cider vinegar, and very lovely it is.

While many of the cider apple trees that grow here are not terribly big because the soil doesn't allow for that, even that aspect of the *terroir* is still to the advantage of the cider (vinegar). Small apples mean the flavour is intensified, and the aroma too. In smaller apples there is a higher ratio of skin to apple flesh, and the skin – especially in red cider apples – is where the most tannins are. The tannins are where the polyphenols are, and so they are where the really good-for-you bits of the apple can be found. Extracting more from apple skin in proportion to flesh means extracting a higher proportion of tannins too.

Over the south-west border of Normandy lies Brittany, where exciting cider and cider vinegar things are also happening; not quite as much as in Normandy, but still exciting. The local cider here makes use of blends of mainly bitter-sweet cider apples. Inland from the wild moors and jagged cliffs of its western coast, is the 'department' of Finistère where – just as in the Pays d'Auge – farmers have worked hard to breathe life into their eminent cider apple heritage. Here is Fouesnant, famous for its orchards and Breton cider; and Cornouaille (Cornwall's cousin), with another French AOP status/protected cider.

Brittany's cider vinegars again share many of the qualities of the region and its cider. What there aren't – yet – are nearly as many as over in Normandy, or as many who are so set up to welcome visitors and sell their cider vinegars. But keep your eye out.

Appellation d'Origine Protégée (AOP)

French classification of protected status with specific and controlled requirements of where and how the product is made. Formerly AOC (*Appellation d'Origine Contrôlée*).

USA

America's love affair with apple cider vinegar is both old and new. A significant part of its modern incarnation is in taking it as a health tonic. And in truth, that was a big part of its old popularity too. From the mid-seventeenth century onwards there are reports of apple cider vinegar being used as a medicine, as well as for cooking and pickling.

It would be a mistake, though, to imagine there has been a continuous line. The twentieth century saw a huge drop-off in cider and cider vinegar production and use – but for totally different reasons than when the same thing happened in Europe. It was the Prohibition of the 1920s and early 1930s that decimated the US cider industry. Heartbreakingly, many cider apple orchards were burned down by Prohibitionists. With 'hard cider' (i.e. alcoholic) prohibited, there was also a cap put on how much 'sweet cider' (i.e. non-alcoholic) could be produced per orchard. Farms had little choice but to turn away from cider to make money from other crops. Depletion of cider – hard or soft – fairly obviously meant the same for cider vinegar.

This was devastating, of course, especially given how quickly cider and cider vinegar had taken a hold in the rural farming communities of New England. Colonists arriving from England had found only native crabapples, so they introduced dessert and cider apples, which flourished in the soil that took much more readily to the apple trees than to the grains needed for beer-making or the vines for wine. Cider was soon hugely popular – as was cider vinegar – and it spread west across the States.

Farms began to produce more cider and cider vinegar than they needed in order to use it in exchange for places at local schools and the services of doctors. In 1817, pomologist William Coxe Jr (what a great name for an apple-lover) wrote in his *A View of Cultivation of Fruit Trees, and the Management of Orchards and Cider*, that while vinegar was admittedly expensive for poor rural cider farmers to produce, the endeavour

was well worthwhile as the cider vinegar could be sold for three times the price of cider.

By the early 1900s, German and Eastern European immigrants to the USA wanted beer over cider, and the ground of the Midwest could grow barley well. That might have put a dint in cider production, but as I have already sighed over, it was Prohibition that did the real damage to America's cider (and cider vinegar) production.

Fortunately – as in Europe – this story has a happy ending. Or at least a happy now. The craft beer trend that has spread across the USA in the last few decades is now turning to craft cider, and looking for inspiration to the ciders of the UK. Where orchards have been replanted, many US cider (and cider vinegar) producers are going for varieties such as Dabinett and Kingston Black, which are more commonly associated with Britain's cider's heritage.

There's a large variety of cider styles being made right across the States now, from Washington State in the west, back to those same eastern states of New England (Maine, Vermont, New Hampshire, Massachusetts, Connecticut and Rhode Island), and leaning into New York State. All are dense again – relatively – with interesting cider producers, many of whom are making cider vinegars of a quality that laughs at the mega-brands on every supermarket shelf and in a heck of a lot of American homes.

Just like their European counterparts, these producers are considering what types of cider apples are best suited to their land and to the blend they want to achieve; they are reinvigorating old-style, nearly-forgotten production techniques; and they are producing cider and cider vinegar that are distinctive with local character and apple-ness. This is cider vinegar to take as a tonic, if you will, but that is also glorious to cook with.

Spain

In the north of Spain, in the Asturias and Basque regions, there is a cider-making heritage that has driven local economies there since the eighteenth century. This is lush, green land – the absolute opposite to Andalucía in the dry south where it is all about sherry and sherry vinegar. Here in the north, cider rules. The *sidra* in Asturias (the cider that so excited Charlemagne that he got cider apples going in modern-day France) has won itself PDO (Protected Designation of Origin) EU status (see page 64). In Basque it is *segardoa*. Cider-related products abound in both, and while cider vinegar has not at the moment received its fair share of modern focus or production, it yet might.

IN THE KITCHEN
Cider Vinegar

Cider vinegar is typically sweeter and less acidic than a generic white wine vinegar (but more acidic than a rice vinegar). That gives it a glorious combination of mildness and acidic usefulness.

Cider vinegar is very versatile. Use it in dressings, sauces, pickling, marinades and for meringues where its mild flavour won't get in the way. It's also the go-to choice for making drinking-vinegar shrubs from fruits and other fresh produce.

APPLE CIDER VINEGAR – THE HEALTH TONIC

I said I would give apple cider vinegar its moment as a tonic under my vinegar lens, and here it is.

So many of the wondrous health benefits that vinegar has had its name put to tend to centre upon apple cider vinegar. For centuries, where there has been cider vinegar in the kitchen, there has been cider vinegar taken as a tonic.

If you are one of the many people who want to say how wonderful ACV has made you feel, then absolutely 'hurrah' to that. When so many different cultures have for centuries believed that taking cider vinegar is good for you, then I am prepared to believe there is more than a grain of truth in it, even if the science isn't *quite* there. It's just I don't think it is the cure-all elixir it is sometimes cracked up to be. And so, with scepticism duly declared, I am going to set that aside to focus upon the positive.

Apples are high in pectin, and some varieties of cider apple have even higher levels than dessert or cooking apples. Similarly with cider apples and antioxidant polyphenols. Both pectin and polyphenols are known to have health benefits from heart disease to possibly strokes and cancer too – and both pectin and polyphenols make it through the vinegar-making process into ACV. So that is good.

'Raw', 'unfiltered' and 'with the mother' are the modern buzzwords of ACV for health. 'Raw' means unpasteurised; unfiltered is obvious; 'with the mother' means it has the filmy substance that has done this marvellous thing of creating vinegar still floating in the bottle. They are terms that could be applied to any vinegar made that way – they are not of themselves distinctive or particular to ACV. It is only because ACV is the most usual choice for a health vinegar, and those are the aspects that producers are focusing upon, that they are often tied together.

I happen to steer away from pasteurised, filtered vinegars because those processes can remove some of the vinegar's compounds of aroma and flavour. Given that, I have no problem believing that pasteurising and filtering can also remove some of the beneficial compounds of natural vinegar. For more on pasteurisation of cider vinegar I refer you back just a few pages to the section on the production processes (see page 132). Because here I want to focus on the 'mother of vinegar'.

It is a curious switch-around of vinegar fashion that it used to be that vinegars were pasteurised and filtered to get rid of the pesky mother floating around, and which was considered a bit of a turn-off for consumers. Now the mother is a selling point – even if the seller may not quite understand why. I always smile to hear about shop assistants telling people with great excitement that the vinegar they are eyeing up 'contains the mother', but under questioning have no idea why that is a good thing.

To be fair, that is not really their fault. My smile is a wry one because I think too little is known to really make a firm case for the mother, despite the fact that many people do. Acetic bacteria are what make vinegar, the mother is where they thrive and that is why the mother is present in vinegar. The mother itself is primarily cellulose. And cellulose is best described as the main structure of plant cell walls, or what is used to make cardboard.

Mother of vinegar

Acetic bacteria are what make vinegar and the mother is where they thrive, which is why the mother is present in vinegar. The mother itself is primarily cellulose, which is best described as the main structure of plant cell walls.

The concentration of bacteria in the mother may well have probiotic qualities that contribute to gut health. More research is needed to be sure. It is also true that cellulose is a great source of fibre, and so the mother may be good for bowel health. Again, more research is needed. Where research into the mother has got people excited is a US study that showed the mother has a higher presence of some phenolic compounds and iron than the vinegar it is in does. Note, though, that the study made a comparison between ACV and pomegranate vinegar, and it was the pomegranate vinegar that came out 'best'.

In short, what does all this mean? Until more research is done into the benefits of the vinegar mother, any answer to that is going to be subjective. What is known with much more certainty is that there are real health benefits to natural vinegar; and where there is a concentration of nutritious and healthy compounds found in its base ingredient – e.g. apples – then there are health benefits in those particular vinegars, too. For my money, what those words 'raw', 'unfiltered' and 'with the mother' can actually tell us is that this is a well-made vinegar that has not been overprocessed in a way that would remove some of its most positive health – or flavour – characteristics.

Any lack of scientific research into the health benefits of ACV is possibly made up for by the weight of anecdotal evidence. There is no shortage of people who believe in its powers, and that has been the case for centuries. As cider became the national drink in England in the mid-1600s, there was much emphasis on the medicinal powers of the cider and its ensuing vinegar. It was also a medicinal tonic for America's New Englanders of the seventeenth, eighteenth and nineteenth centuries; their recipes of blending it with herbs and spices are now being revived as the basis of several modern ACV tonics.

The most common way to take ACV as a tonic is to dilute a couple of tablespoons (or to taste) in water and honey, and take once or twice a day before meals. Some people put it into their morning smoothie.

Or you could just cook with it, of course.

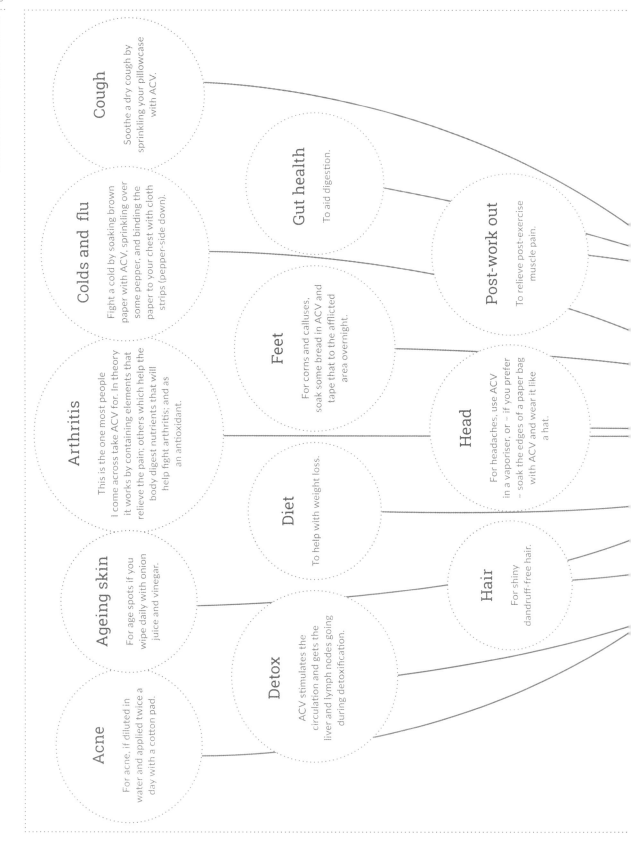

Cough
Soothe a dry cough by sprinkling your pillowcase with ACV.

Colds and flu
Fight a cold by soaking brown paper with ACV, sprinkling over some pepper, and binding the paper to your chest with cloth strips (pepper-side down).

Gut health
To aid digestion.

Post-work out
To relieve post-exercise muscle pain.

Arthritis
This is the one most people I come across take ACV for. In theory it works by containing elements that relieve the pain; others which help the body digest nutrients that will help fight arthritis; and as an antioxidant.

Feet
For corns and calluses, soak some bread in ACV and tape that to the afflicted area overnight.

Head
For headaches, use ACV in a vaporiser, or – if you prefer – soak the edges of a paper bag with ACV and wear it like a hat.

Ageing skin
For age spots if you wipe daily with onion juice and vinegar.

Diet
To help with weight loss.

Acne
For acne, if diluted in water and applied twice a day with a cotton pad.

Detox
ACV stimulates the circulation and gets the liver and lymph nodes going during detoxification.

Hair
For shiny dandruff-free hair.

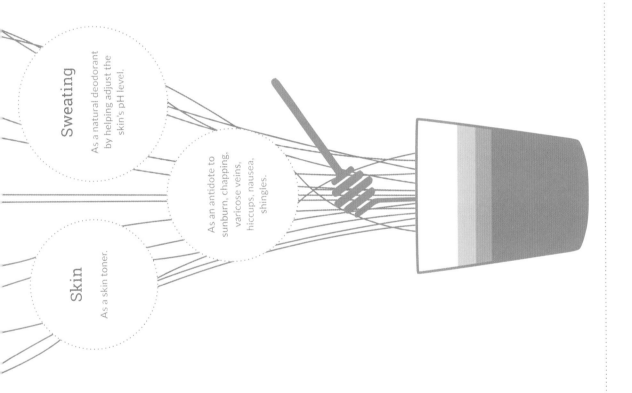

Sweating

As a natural deodorant by helping adjust the skin's pH level.

As an antidote to sunburn, chapping, varicose veins, hiccups, nausea, shingles.

Skin

As a skin toner.

Apple cider vinegar as health tonic

Here are just some of the afflictions that ACV has at various times been claimed to relieve, or the benefits it might bring. It is a list that straddles the plausible to the laughable to the worth-a-go. What I hope it shows is the extent to which people have put their faith in cider vinegar. That is for me is where some of its credibility lies. They are listed in no particular order, and to each our own judgement on the likely efficacy...

This is typical of what vinegar can do: something already pretty great (fried eggs) is given a touch of vinegar and it becomes the best ever version of itself. The vinegar is reduced – in the same pan, after the eggs have cooked – to take its harsher edges off, and is then poured over the egg. You don't taste vinegar, you taste an egg with its flavour potential amplified. This is not just for morning eggs, of course. It is a useful trick for any fried-egg cooking, and is also good over a bowl of roasted vegetables for lunch.

Fried Eggs for Breakfast

a small knob of butter
2 eggs
**3 tablespoons white
    wine vinegar**
a pinch of sumac (optional
    for extra heat)
salt and freshly ground
    black pepper

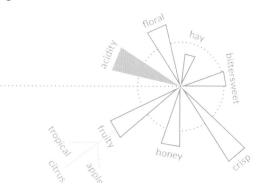

serves 1–2

Fry the eggs as usual: melt the butter in a small frying pan, break the eggs in, season, and lift them out of the pan when cooked to your liking.

Now pour the vinegar into the same pan and let it reduce by about half. It will take barely 10 seconds if the pan is hot. Pour the vinegar over the eggs and finish with a little sumac, if using.

VINEGAR VARIATION
Try red wine vinegar, cider vinegar, vermouth vinegar, honey vinegar or a vinegar infused with a flavour that will go especially well with eggs, such as tarragon.

This very quick, very versatile sauce is based on the classic Sicilian salmoriglio of pestled oregano, parsley, oil, garlic and lemon juice. Here, the acid element of lemon juice is swapped for cider vinegar, which gives a more rounded flavour, but you still get a citrusy hit from the lemon zest. It is great with lamb chops, steak, flash-fried langoustines or tuna steaks.

Wild Garlic and Oregano Salmoriglio

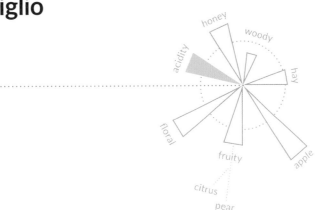

4 tablespoons finely
   chopped wild garlic leaves
   (if out of season use 2 garlic
   cloves instead)
6 tablespoons finely
   chopped oregano
3 tablespoons finely chopped
   flat-leaf parsley
grated zest of 2 lemons
½ teaspoon chilli flakes
150ml extra virgin olive oil
50ml cider vinegar
salt

serves 4–6

Combine the dry ingredients in a bowl with a pinch of salt, then simply stir in the olive oil and vinegar.

VINEGAR VARIATION
Try a white wine vinegar
or an infused vinegar
with flavours that go well
with whatever the sauce
is accompanying.

Pickling is a great way to ensure that even in the depths of winter we're still able to enjoy the crisp bite and flavour of good cucumbers. If you can get them, do use the shorter, slightly stubby ridge or 'kirby' cucumbers that will have rather more about them than the longer, thinner variety.

Cucumber Pickled with Hot Spices, Garlic and Bay

2 ridge cucumbers
(approx. 400g)
4 bay leaves
1 teaspoon coriander seeds
1 teaspoon black mustard seeds
1 teaspoon fennel seeds
½ teaspoon dried chilli flakes
4 garlic cloves, crushed with the
back of a knife
6 sprigs of dill
250ml cider vinegar
3 tablespoons fine salt

You will need: 2 sterilised glass
storage jars, each with a
capacity of 500ml

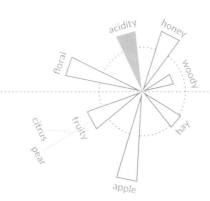

makes two 500ml jars

Cut the cucumbers into uneven chunks. Pack the jars evenly with half of the cucumber chunks. Then evenly divide the bay leaves, coriander seeds, black mustard seeds, fennel seeds, chilli flakes, garlic cloves and dill between the jars. Pack the rest of the cucumber pieces on top.

Heat the cider vinegar in a pan with 250ml of water and the salt until it is just boiling and the salt has dissolved. Pour evenly between the jars, making sure the cucumber chunks are immersed. If they aren't quite immersed then top up with a little more vinegar.

Seal and leave the jars in the fridge for at least 2 days before eating. They'll keep just fine for a couple of months. (Don't worry if the garlic turns blue over time in the fridge – that is just the garlic reacting with the acid of the vinegar and is absolutely fine to eat.)

SERVING SUGGESTIONS

Try to think beyond putting these on burgers, and consider how they can become the base for other dishes – see the recipe ideas below. However you use them, be sure to keep the pickling liquid, as it makes a terrific base for a salad dressing.

Salads

Slice into salads such as a courgette ribbon, feta and beetroot salad: use a vegetable peeler to create ribbons from a yellow courgette, dress with a light vinaigrette (try using some of the pickling liquid), add a handful of rocket, some crumbled feta, sliced beetroot, mint, basil and slices of pickled cucumber.

Soup

Pickled cold cucumber soup (based on Elizabeth David's recipe in *Mediterranean Food*): chop 200g pickled cucumbers and simmer with 1 litre of chicken stock for 30 minutes. Strain into another pan. Heat through with 1 tablespoon of sugar, gratings of nutmeg and 140ml of double cream. Season, chill to serve and garnish with fresh mint.

Deep fried

Deep-fried pickles: pat dry the pickled cucumbers. Prepare three separate bowls of seasoned plain flour, beaten egg and breadcrumbs. Dip each pickle in the flour first, then the egg, then the breadcrumbs. Heat about 5cm of deep-frying oil in a large saucepan to 180°C (test by dropping in a small piece of bread: it will sizzle and brown). Use a slotted spoon to carefully lower the pickles into the hot oil. Don't crowd the pan. Cook for 2 minutes until golden brown, then lift out with the slotted spoon and drain on kitchen paper. Repeat for the rest of the pickles, straining the oil as needed to remove any breadcrumbs. Serve straight away with mayonnaise. A 'classic' of the American South and compulsively good.

Pickleback

For a 'pickleback', chase a shot of bourbon with a shot of the pickle juice.

VINEGAR VARIATION

Try using white wine vinegar or honey vinegar.

Tiny pearl onions are lightly pickled for an elegant cocktail garnish with real bite. Their classic use is in the Gibson martini, where a little of the brine is added to the drink too. Both the onions and the brine can also be very useful in the kitchen, for adding to a casserole or the like.

Pickled Pearl Onions (and a Gibson Martini)

250g pearl onions (choose
the smallest ones)
200ml white wine vinegar
9 juniper berries
½ teaspoon coriander seeds
1 bay leaf
¼ teaspoon thyme leaves
¼ teaspoon whole
black peppercorns
2 tablespoons caster sugar
2 teaspoons fine salt
2 broad strips of orange zest
75ml dry vermouth

FOR THE GIBSON MARTINI
75ml gin
2 teaspoons dry vermouth
¾ teaspoon cocktail onion brine
cocktail onions

You will need: a sterilised
glass storage jar with a
capacity of 500ml

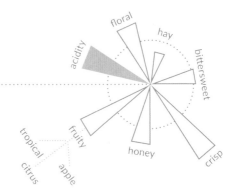

makes one 500ml jar

Peel the onions by immersing them in a bowl of boiling water for 1 minute. Drain, then trim off the tops and bottoms and the skins should slide off easily. Set the peeled onions aside.

Put all the ingredients except the onions and the vermouth into a pan. Heat gently until the sugar has dissolved, then add the onions to the pan for 1 minute. Take off the heat and allow to cool. Add the vermouth and transfer it all to the prepared jar. Seal and store in the fridge. The onions will be ready to use in a week and will keep for months in the fridge.

To make the Gibson martini, fill a cocktail tin (or tall glass or jug) with lots of ice. Pour over the gin, vermouth and the brine from the jar of cocktail onions. Stir over the ice for a minute, then strain into a chilled glass. Garnish with a cocktail onion dropped into the glass, or three on a cocktail stick.

VINEGAR VARIATION
I think a vermouth
vinegar could be very
exciting here.

As a child, a sure sign of the arrival of summer was my mum serving pretty much every night's 'tea' (our main evening meal in Lancashire) with a side of pickled beetroot. This was a treat she could keep all for herself, as to the rest of the family these crinkle-cut slices of fiery root held no charm whatsoever. Its charms have definitely grown on me as I have got older, however, and not just for nostalgia's sake. Now I too can appreciate how good a slice of pickled beetroot can be with summer salad, pork or game. Crinkle-cut is still optional.

Beetroot Pickled with Dill and Orange

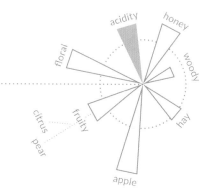

500g uncooked beetroots

75ml red wine vinegar

2 bay leaves

2 teaspoons coriander seeds

1 teaspoon black mustard seeds

2 sprigs of dill

4 broad strips of orange zest

2 teaspoons black or
  mixed peppercorns

300ml cider vinegar

3 teaspoons fine salt

100g caster sugar

You will need: 2 sterilised glass
  storage jars, each with a
  capacity of 500–750ml

makes two 500ml jars

Preheat the oven to 190°C/170°C Fan/Gas Mark 5.

Wash the beetroots and cut their tops down to about 5cm, leaving the roots in place. Put into a baking dish with the red wine vinegar and 50ml of water and toss round. Cover tightly, either with a lid or foil, and roast for 1–1½ hours until the beetroots are tender. Allow to cool before rubbing off the skins and cutting into slices about 3mm thick.

Divide half the beetroot slices evenly between your two jars. Then divide the bay leaves, coriander seeds, black mustard seeds, dill, orange zest and peppercorns between the jars. Sit the remaining beetroot slices on top.

Put the cider vinegar, salt, sugar and 300ml of water into a saucepan and heat just until the salt and sugar dissolve. Divide between the beetroot jars, seal, and keep for at least a week before using. They will keep for several months in the fridge.

VINEGAR VARIATION

The pickled beetroot my mum so loved was made with malt vinegar, so I suppose that has to be the most obvious variation. Or a white wine vinegar, vermouth vinegar or cider vinegar.

Making your own cheese – any kind of cheese – has to be one of the most pleasing, smug-inducing things to do. I mean that as a good thing. You have made cheese appear from where there was no cheese. What could be better?

Ricotta means 'twice-cooked' in Italian and refers to how it is made using the whey that is a by-product of cheese-making. Make yours by mixing warmed milk with the acidity of vinegar to create curds of creamy ricotta. Raw (unpasteurised) milk is great in this recipe if you can get it, but don't worry if you can't – it will still be lovely.

Ricotta

1 litre full-fat milk
25ml white wine vinegar
salt

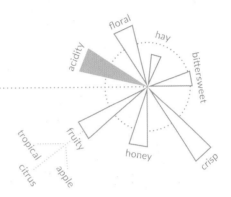

Makes approx. 250g

Heat the milk in a saucepan with a good pinch of salt. Just as it is starting to get close to boiling (look for steam and small bubbles; it should be approx. 85°C on a thermometer but no more), take the pan off the heat and stir in the vinegar for a minute or so. You will start to see curds come together and your ricotta is already on its way. Cover with a clean cloth and set aside for 3 hours. If you are worried curds are not forming, add a little more vinegar, but go steady as you do not want your ricotta to taste vinegary.

Line a colander with a dampened piece of muslin. Spoon the milky curds of your would-be ricotta into it and allow to drain for an hour. The longer you leave it to drain, the firmer your ricotta will be.

Spoon the ricotta into a bowl, taste to see if it needs more salt. It can be used straight away or kept in the fridge for 4 days.

VINEGAR VARIATION

Try a cider vinegar, or even an infused herb or flower vinegar for an extra undertone of flavour.

Soda bread is the easiest bread to make and one of the best to eat – it has such a rich, nutty, rustic flavour and appearance. Its ease is due to its reliance for its rise on the chemical reaction of acid with the alkaline bicarbonate of soda. There is no yeast, barely any kneading and no rising time. The acid ingredient is traditionally buttermilk, but that can be replaced by mixing cider vinegar into whole milk. This is certainly as good a substitute for hard-to-get-hold-of true buttermilk as the 'cultured' buttermilk available at supermarkets.

Soda Bread

400ml whole milk
2 tablespoons cider vinegar
300g plain wholemeal flour,
    plus extra for dusting
200g white bread flour
1 teaspoon salt
1 teaspoon bicarbonate of soda
1 tablespoon maple syrup,
    or honey
drizzle of mild olive oil or
    sunflower oil
freshly ground black pepper

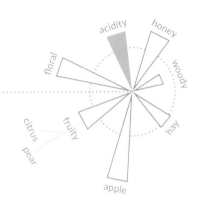

makes 1 loaf

Preheat the oven to 200°C/180°C Fan/Gas Mark 6. Stir the milk and vinegar together in a bowl and set aside for 5 minutes.

In a large bowl, mix together the flours, salt and bicarbonate of soda, plus a good grinding of pepper. Stir the maple syrup or honey into the milk/vinegar mix, then pour this, in stages, into the dry ingredients. Work quite quickly, initially with a fork, and then with your hands, to bring it into a soft, slightly sticky dough in the bowl. You may not need all the liquid – sometimes I only use 300–350ml or so.

Finish it by kneading quickly and briefly on a floured surface so that it is smooth. Shape into a round loaf and transfer to a baking sheet lightly greased with the oil. Use a sharp knife to mark three slashes into the loaf and sprinkle wholemeal flour over the top. Set aside for 30 minutes if you have the time, but this isn't essential.

Bake in the oven for 40–50 minutes, until the top is crusted and when you knock on the base it sounds hollow. Transfer to a wire rack to cool before slicing. This is best eaten on the day of baking: toasted and buttered, or – my favourite – smothered in ricotta (see page 151) and piled up with pickled beetroot (see page 150).

VINEGAR VARIATION
Try red wine vinegar,
white wine vinegar or
honey vinegar.

This recipe is based on a classic Greek octopus salad. Tender, meaty octopus is nestled upon salad leaves to serve as part of a mezze feast, or with the saffron-roasted potatoes (see page 246) and mayonnaise (see page 45).

When it comes to octopus, 'tender' isn't necessarily a given, but the multiple steps – and the vinegar – help no end. The initial blanching in hot water tenderises the meat, then poaching the octopus in the vinegar's acidity breaks down the toughness of the meat and the job is completed by marinating the cooked octopus in more vinegar before serving. If all of that sounds like a bit of a faff – it isn't. Just a bit of in-and-out of hot water, poaching and a marinade.

Octopus in Red Wine Vinegar

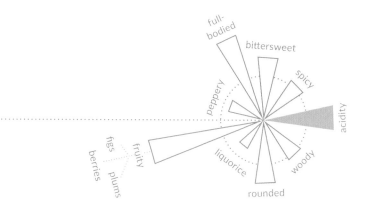

1kg octopus (cleaned by
   the fishmonger so it is
   ready for cooking)
100ml vermouth
150ml white wine vinegar
juice of ½ orange
2 bay leaves
100ml olive oil
100ml red wine vinegar
½ teaspoon dried oregano
1 garlic clove, crushed
3 handfuls of salad leaves
   of your choice
salt and freshly ground
   black pepper

serves 3–4

Blanch the octopus to tenderise it: bring a large pan of water to the boil, lower the octopus into it for 1 minute, then lift out and refresh in cold water. Repeat three times with fresh water each time. You will see the tentacles curl up with each immersion in the hot water, then relax in the cold. Clean the pan thoroughly if you want to use it for the rest of the recipe, as there may be scum on the sides.

Put the vermouth, white wine vinegar, orange juice and bay leaves into a large pan. Bring to a simmer, then add the octopus. Cover and gently cook for 45 minutes–1 hour. It is ready when tender to the prick of a fork.

VINEGAR VARIATION

The white wine vinegar used for poaching can be any kind of basic vinegar. But for the marinade, go for an interesting, bright – but not too heavy – red wine vinegar.

...continued on page 158

Remove the octopus from the poaching liquid, retaining 50ml of the liquid and discarding the rest. If you would like to give your octopus a bit of 'charred' colour, then quickly put it under the grill, or return it to the now-empty pan it cooked in, for 30 seconds each side. Afterwards, charred or not, cut the tentacles off and put into a bowl.

Mix together the olive oil, red wine vinegar, oregano, garlic and the reserved 50ml of poaching liquid. Season and pour this over the octopus tentacles – they should be just about submerged – cover and chill for 6 hours or overnight, turning occasionally.

When you are ready to serve, remove the octopus from the fridge and allow to come to room temperature. Arrange the salad leaves on a serving plate, then lift the octopus pieces out of the marinade and arrange on top of the leaves. Drizzle over 3 tablespoons or so of the marinade and serve.

I first heard of 'Sunday cockles' while visiting Judit Badia, who makes vinegar in Catalunya. She was telling me about their vermouth vinegar being used for the local dish of cockles (*berberechos*) and crisps, with vermouth drizzled over both, which is eaten on a Sunday. Hence the name. They usually use tinned cockles, but I am going for fresh ones, cooked in olive oil, garlic and vermouth vinegar to open them up. I am keeping the crisps.

Sunday cockles make for an excellent lunch or tapas. Or for a heartier meal, ditch the crisps and cook some pancetta with the garlic before adding the cockles, then stir it all through linguine for cockle pasta. This dish reminds me of a Cretan mezze speciality called *boubouristoi* – snails cooked in salt, then finished in oil, garlic and red wine vinegar. It is endlessly fascinating how, over the centuries, different cultures have come up with similar yet different ways of cooking with their local produce, including their local vinegars.

Sunday Cockles

1kg fresh cockles in their
   shells (use clams if you
   can't get cockles)
3 tablespoons olive oil
1 garlic clove, crushed with
   the back of a knife
2 sprigs of rosemary
125ml vermouth vinegar
large bag of ready-salted crisps
salt and freshly ground
   black pepper

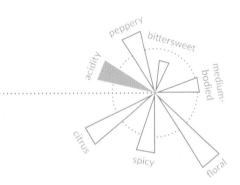

serves 4

Wash the cockles and discard any with a broken shell.

Heat the oil in a large saucepan that has a lid, and add the garlic. Stir round for 30 seconds or so, then add the cockles, rosemary and 100ml of the vinegar. Put the lid on the pan and leave over a medium heat for about 3 minutes.

Check to see if the cockles are opening. Once they are open, transfer the whole lot – juices and all – to a serving dish. Discard any stubborn cockles that haven't opened. Season, then serve with the crisps alongside or in a separate dish, and with the rest of the vinegar drizzled over it all.

VINEGAR VARIATION

A bittersweet white wine
vinegar is a good option.

Salmon fillets are 'cooked' in the acidity of champagne vinegar, along with raisins for sweetness and the kinds of herbs and spices you'd associate with pickling. The end result doesn't taste like pickled salmon, though. This is a surprisingly delicate way of preserving the fish's own flavour – even more so than smoking salmon, I think. It may take three days for the vinegar to do its work, but the cook's labour is mere minutes. Serve on slices of buttered soda bread (see page 155) with minted cucumber ribbons (see page 237) piled on top.

Pickled Salmon

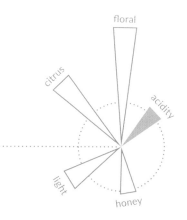

250ml champagne vinegar
60g soft brown sugar
1½ teaspoons yellow
    mustard seeds
2 bay leaves
1 star anise
40g raisins
1 teaspoon juniper berries,
    lightly crushed
1½ teaspoons coriander seeds,
    lightly crushed
2 very fresh salmon fillets
    (approx. 150g each)

serves 2–3

Put all the ingredients except the salmon into a saucepan with 150ml of water. Heat until the sugar has dissolved, then set aside until cool. Lay the salmon fillets into a dish in one layer and pour the spiced liquid over them. Add more cold water if needed to make sure the fillets are just immersed. Cover and leave in the fridge for 3 days.

After 3 days, lift the fillets out of the marinade, rinse and pat them dry. Flake or slice the flesh for use straight away, or keep tightly wrapped in the fridge for 3–4 days.

VINEGAR VARIATION
Swap the champagne vinegar for any other white wine vinegar, vermouth vinegar, cider vinegar, or a herb or flower vinegar such as tarragon or nasturtium.

This is a great way to lightly and quickly cook fish fillets such as salmon or trout. You make a simple 'court-bouillon' of water, vinegar and aromatics, then cook the fish in that. I much prefer it to fish stock, largely because I so rarely have any of that around. This can be made with store-cupboard ingredients in a smidge over half an hour.

Kindzmari is a Georgian sauce, taking its name from *kindz*, meaning coriander, and *mari*, meaning vinegar. There's sumac and garlic in it too, but essentially it is coriander and white wine vinegar. A punchy sauce for any fish (and very good with steak or pork chops, too).

Poached Fish Fillets with Kindzmari Sauce

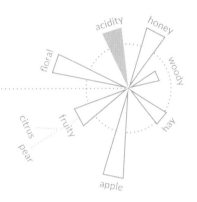

225ml cider vinegar

stalks from a bunch of
flat-leaf parsley

2 teaspoons peppercorns

1 teaspoon coriander seeds,
lightly crushed

1 star anise

1 leek, trimmed and cut into
rounds about 1cm thick

1 bay leaf or sprig of rosemary

4 fish fillets, such as salmon
or trout

salt

FOR THE KINDZMARI SAUCE

50g coriander, leaves and stalks
roughly chopped

1 garlic clove, roughly chopped

**3 tablespoons white wine
vinegar, preferably quite
a sweet one**

¼ teaspoon sumac

VINEGAR VARIATION

Try white wine vinegar
instead of the cider
vinegar in the court-
bouillon. And vice-versa
for the sauce.

serves 4

Pour 1 litre of water into a large saucepan or frying pan that has a lid. Add the vinegar and bring to the boil. Turn down to a simmer and add the parsley, peppercorns, coriander seeds, star anise, leek, bay leaf or rosemary and a good pinch of salt. Cover and leave to gently simmer for 30 minutes.

Strain the liquid, discarding the solids, and you have the court-bouillon in which to poach your fish. You can make the court-bouillon ahead of time, if desired, and store overnight in the fridge.

For the kindzmari sauce, use a blender to blitz the coriander and garlic along with the vinegar, sumac and a hefty pinch of salt, and set aside. (It will also be fine to keep overnight in the fridge.)

To cook the fish: bring the court-bouillon to a simmer, then slide in the fish fillets. Cook for 5–8 minutes – longer if thicker – until the flesh of the fish becomes opaque. Carefully lift the fillets out of the water and onto plates, and serve with the kindzmari sauce alongside.

Boquerones are fresh anchovies, which in this recipe are marinated/pickled in vinegar to 'cook' them. The flesh becomes white – so these are very different from brown anchovy fillets in brine or oil – and they are kept in oil with garlic and herbs. If you are familiar with Spanish tapas, I am sure you will be just as familiar with these.

Boquerones en Vinaigre

500g fresh anchovies, as
    fresh as possible, cleaned
    and butterflied
1 tablespoon salt
250ml white wine vinegar
4 garlic cloves, crushed
a small handful of flat-leaf
    parsley, finely chopped
500ml extra virgin olive oil

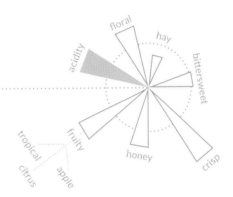

serves 8 as tapas

It is certainly easiest to ask your fishmonger to clean and butterfly the anchovies for you. If that isn't possible, then scrape each anchovy with a table knife under cold water to remove the scales; cut the head off at an angle, then cut down the middle to open the anchovy up and remove its insides and spine. Rinse well in cold water. Now you can get started with the recipe proper.

Lay the anchovies opened out in a baking dish, cover and freeze for 3 hours to kill off any parasites. Remove from the freezer, sprinkle over the salt and pour over the vinegar. Make sure the anchovies are submerged. If they aren't, add more vinegar. Cover and chill for 6–12 hours.

VINEGAR VARIATION

A light red wine vinegar can work very well here. The fish ends up a slight blushing pink, and that is rather lovely in its own way. Vermouth vinegar or a light sherry vinegar is also excellent in this.

Lift the now creamy-white fillets out of the marinade and transfer to another baking dish, layering them up with the crushed garlic, chopped parsley and olive oil. At the end, make sure the fillets are submerged and add more oil if they aren't. Cover and keep in the fridge. They are best if you can wait a day before using, and will keep in the fridge for a week or so.

Onions done in the *agrodolce* style are a classic of Italian cooking. *Agrodolce* means sweet and sour (and is a description that is increasingly cropping up on wine vinegar bottles, especially those with added grape must to sweeten). The onions are prepared here with butterflied sardines, which finish cooking in the vinegar sousing along with the onion, bay and dill. You could souse from raw, but I prefer to part-fry the sardines first for a charred look, before finishing them in the acidity of the sousing. This is a such a pretty dish with the red onion, red wine vinegar, shiny sardines and lushly green herbs. Perfect for lunch on toast rubbed with olive oil; with some dressed leaves; or as part of a tapas feast.

To prepare *agrodolce* onions for use in other dishes, just skip the part with the sardines. They will keep for a week in the fridge.

Soused Fresh Sardines with *Agrodolce* Onions

1 tablespoon olive oil
4 small sardines butterflied
    and boned
a sprig of dill
2 bay leaves
½ red onion, finely sliced into
    half-moons
**100ml bittersweet red wine
    vinegar (see variation below)**
40g caster sugar
salt and freshly ground
    black pepper

serves 2

Heat the oil in a frying pan. When hot, sit the sardines in it skin-side down and cook for 2 minutes. You want to be able to see the upturned flesh start to colour at the edges as it cooks, but no more than that. Carefully lift the sardines out and sit them skin-side down in a shallow bowl that can fit them in one layer. Arrange the dill and bay leaves on top.

Put the onions into the same frying pan, season, and cook for 2 minutes until only just starting to soften. Spoon the onions over the sardines, then return the pan to the heat and pour in the vinegar and sugar. Stir round on a low heat just long enough for the sugar to dissolve. Pour this over the sardine and onion mix, then season with salt and pepper. You need to make sure the fish is just about submerged under the liquid. Cover and set aside for 4 hours, or overnight in the fridge.

To serve, use a slotted spoon to lift the sardines and onions out of the liquid and onto a plate.

VINEGAR VARIATION

I like to use a sweet red wine vinegar in this recipe to emphasise the *agrodolce*-ness, but the vinegar's acidity must be at least 5% or it will be too weak to do its job of 'cooking' the fish. If the red wine vinegar you choose isn't particularly sweet, add another teaspoon of sugar to the measurements above. Honey vinegar is also good here, or cider vinegar, maybe a herb-infused vinegar or vermouth vinegar.

This is a very special kind of pork joint, which I would be more than happy to serve for any grand occasion – maybe/especially Christmas or New Year. The crackling should be worthy of a celebration in itself.

The loin's rich fig and walnut stuffing – which adds to the sense of occasion of this dish – is helpfully cut through with the vinegar. It is packed inside the joint before you tie it up, but don't worry if any oozes out in the cooking; it will just nestle in amongst the bed of fennel and onions (tossed in vinegar to draw out maximum flavour) that the joint is pot-roasted on.

Pot-roasted Loin of Pork with Fig and Walnut Stuffing

3 tablespoons olive oil
½ leek, trimmed and
    finely chopped
180g fresh figs, finely chopped
1½ tablespoons finely
    chopped lemongrass
40g walnuts, finely chopped
½ teaspoon ground cinnamon
grated zest of 1 orange
125ml cider vinegar
20g dried breadcrumbs
    (not panko)
2kg boneless loin of pork (ask
    your butcher to cut the loin
    under its eye to create a flap
    for the stuffing)
1 large bulb of fennel,
    roughly chopped
2 onions, roughly chopped
3 garlic cloves, crushed
salt and freshly ground
    black pepper, plus extra
    sea salt flakes

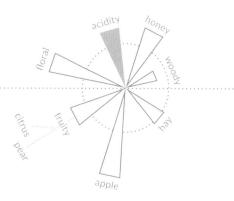

serves 6

Heat 1 tablespoon of the oil in a frying pan and cook the leeks until softened. Turn off the heat and stir in the figs, lemongrass, walnuts, cinnamon, orange zest, 75ml of the vinegar and the breadcrumbs. Season it well.

Open the loin out, skin-side down, and stuff the flap opening with the fig mix. Don't pack too much in – you want to be able to close it tight when you tie it.

Cut off at least six times the length of the joint in kitchen string. Pass the string under the joint at one end, bring round to the seam of the stuffing and tie a knot, leaving a short end of string (around 7–8cm) and a very long end. Pull the long end a couple of centimetres to the side of the knot, hold in place with your finger, pass the string under the joint then bring up to where your finger is and pass the long end under the string you are holding down to form a knot. Keep going along the length of the joint to tie it together. Once you get to the end, turn the joint over, run the string along the centre of the tied joint and tie with the short end you left at the beginning. You should — hopefully — have a tightly tied-up loin.

Preheat the oven to 170°C/150°C Fan/Gas Mark 3. Heat the remaining oil in a large casserole dish suitable for oven and hob. Sit the pork loin fat-side down in the oil and leave for a few minutes to brown. Turn over and sear the underside, then remove and set aside. Add the fennel, onion and garlic to the hot fat and allow to just start to soften but not colour. Pour over the remaining vinegar, season, stir round, then sit the joint on top, fat-side up. Cover with a lid and put into the oven for 2 hours.

After 2 hours, increase the oven heat to 220°C/200°C Fan/Gas Mark 7. Remove the lid and sprinkle salt flakes over the would-be crackling. Let it finish in the high heat for 30 minutes, then remove from the oven. Set aside to rest for 10 minutes then lift the joint out and carve. The fennel and onion mix on the bottom of the pan (there won't be much, but it is delicious) can be spooned into a bowl for serving.

If the joint is difficult to carve through with the crackling, you could cut the string, lift the crackling off and serve it on the side for people to help themselves to — then carve.

VINEGAR VARIATION

Try an apple, pear, quince, malt, honey or a herb-infused vinegar instead of the cider vinegar that goes into the stuffing. A white wine vinegar or herb-infused vinegar can be used to toss amongst the fennel and onions.

This recipe is dedicated to the ladies of the Lyon region of France and their heritage of mighty vinegar crocks, which no doubt inspired this classic dish of the area. Once you get over the fact that this is called 'chicken in vinegar', you are all set to enjoy a feast of a dish with bold, rustic flavours, yet – in the eating – none of them are directly identifiable as vinegar.

Poulet au Vinaigre

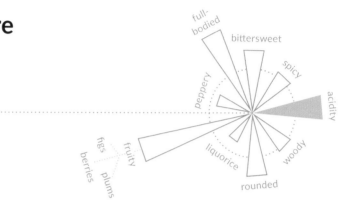

1.8kg chicken, jointed into
    8 pieces
50g butter
1 tablespoon olive oil
2 medium onions,
    roughly chopped
4 garlic cloves, crushed with
    the back of a knife
150ml French red wine vinegar
100ml dry vermouth
1 tablespoon tomato purée
1 tablespoon double cream or
    crème fraîche (optional)
2 tablespoons
    chopped tarragon
salt and freshly ground
    black pepper

serves 4–6

Preheat the oven to 180°C/160°C Fan/Gas Mark 4. Season the chicken, and choose a pan that will fit the chicken pieces in one layer, and is happy in the oven as well as on the hob.

Heat the butter and oil in the pan until good and hot, then put the chicken in to brown on all sides. Once the chicken is browned all over, lift it onto a plate with a slotted spoon and set aside.

Put the onions and garlic into the pan and cook until the onions have softened, but don't let them take on too much colour. While the onions are cooking, combine the vinegar, vermouth and tomato purée in a bowl.

Return the chicken pieces to the pan, nestling them into and on top of the onions and garlic. Pour the vinegar mix over it all and bubble for a minute to take the edge off the vinegar. Cover with a lid or some tightly-fitted tin foil and transfer to the oven for 40 minutes.

VINEGAR VARIATION
It really does need to be a red wine vinegar here, but you could use one that isn't French, at a pinch, or a good malt vinegar, too.

Remove the chicken pieces to a serving dish, cover and set aside. Sit the pan of cooking juices over a high heat on the hob and bubble rapidly to reduce to a sauce. It should take about 5 minutes to get a good consistency. Once reduced, stir in the cream or crème fraîche. Pour the sauce all over the chicken, sprinkle over the tarragon and serve.

Whether you call this cinder toffee or honeycomb, there can be no disagreement on what an exciting thing it is to make. The bicarbonate of soda reacts with the vinegar's acidity to make the sugar bubble up into an almost volcanic eruption. Then, as it settles down, you are left with the most beautiful amber honeycomb with such lovely toffee depth to it. It is a regular feature of my Bonfire Night celebrations, sometimes dunked into melted dark chocolate, sometimes just as it is. I like to use the small shards that break off to fold or churn into vanilla ice cream.

You'll need to work quickly once this gets going, so make sure that everything, including the prepared cake tin and glass of water, is close to hand. Use the largest stock-pot-style pan you have.

Cinder Toffee

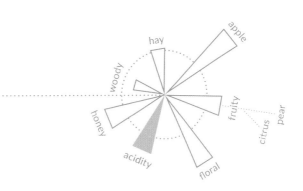

300g caster sugar

200g golden syrup

2 tablespoons cider vinegar

2 heaped teaspoons
   bicarbonate of soda

makes approx. 400g

Grease and line a 20cm round or square cake tin with baking parchment. Put the sugar, syrup, vinegar and 150ml of water into a large pan. Stir over a low heat to dissolve the sugar.

Once the sugar has dissolved, turn the heat up to high and stop stirring. The mixture will boil and bubble. It'll start to turn a lovely amber colour and to smell of toffee. Let it bubble for 8 minutes or so before testing if it's gone far enough on the toffee scale. What you are after is what is known as 'hard crack', and it is tested by using a sugar thermometer and waiting for it to reach 150°C; or by dropping a little of the mixture into the glass of cold water – if it goes brittle straight away, that is 'hard crack' and means your cinder toffee is ready.

As soon as you reach that point – do not leave it any longer or it will go too far and burn – take the pan off the heat straight away and stir in the bicarbonate of soda as quickly as you can. Now is the point to stand back and watch in awe as the toffee becomes bubbling lava. It will rise and rise, and just as it reaches the zenith of its eruption and threatens to bubble over, give the toffee a stir and it will subside.

VINEGAR VARIATION

Try using honey vinegar, palm vinegar or white wine vinegar.

Pour the toffee into the prepared cake tin and leave to cool. You will already be able to see its glorious bubbles. When it is totally cold, lift it out of the tin and break it up with a toffee hammer or rolling pin.

These meringues are every bit as indulgent and delicious as they sound. The little bit of vinegar in the meringue mix makes them nice and crisp on the outside, but chewy on the inside. Just how I like my meringues.

Salted Caramel Chocolate Meringues

350g caster sugar
75g unsalted butter, diced
125ml single cream
1 teaspoon sea salt flakes
50g dark chocolate
4 egg whites, at room temperature
1½ teaspoons white wine vinegar

makes 8–10 meringues, depending on size

To make the salted caramel sauce, put 150g of the sugar and 50ml of water into a small saucepan over a high heat. Heat so that it bubbles rapidly; watch carefully, and as soon as it turns a rich amber colour, take it off the heat and whisk in the diced butter and cream. Return to a low heat to gently simmer for a minute. Whisk in the salt and cook for another minute, then pour into a jug or bowl and set aside to cool.

Break the chocolate into small pieces and place in a bowl set over a pan of simmering water. Allow the chocolate to melt, then set the bowl aside to cool.

For the meringues, line two baking trays with baking parchment and preheat the oven to 100°C/80°C Fan/Gas Mark ¼.

VINEGAR VARIATION
The idea here is that the vinegar does a technical job, rather than give flavour. So you are choosing a vinegar for its acidity. A cider vinegar would work well, as would a palm vinegar.

Put the egg whites into a scrupulously clean mixing bowl and whisk to stiff peaks. Add the remaining 200g of sugar in two stages, whisking after each addition. Finally, whisk in the vinegar. It should become a billowy, firm, satin-sheened meringue. Use tablespoons to scoop 8–10 blobs of meringue onto the baking trays, around 10cm in diameter.

...continued on page 176

Drizzle a little salted caramel sauce over each meringue and use a cocktail stick to swirl it in. Repeat with the rest of the meringues, then do the same with the melted chocolate. There should be enough caramel sauce left for serving at the end.

Put the trays into the oven and check after 1 hour. Once you are able to easily lift the meringues off the paper, turn off the oven but leave the meringues inside with the oven door shut, to cool completely.

Serve with ice cream (the yolks you are left with could be used to make your own), or with whipped cream over the top and/or more of the salted caramel sauce. Store any unused meringues in an airtight container for up to 2 days.

This drinking vinegar is made by macerating rhubarb pieces in white wine vinegar and sugar to draw out the flavours; saffron and rose petals give it an additional, slightly Eastern feel. The result is a mellow shrub of sweet floral rhubarb, with a bit of an edge to it.

Serve with sparkling water, ginger ale or in a gin and tonic or a whisky-based cocktail. Like all shrubs, it is also good over desserts such as ice cream or sorbet. And I often add a couple of tablespoons of the undiluted shrub to a tagine for a one-stop burst of flavour, sweetness and acidity.

Rhubarb, Rose and Saffron Shrub

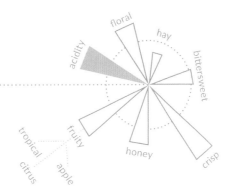

120ml white wine vinegar

160g caster sugar

¼ teaspoon saffron threads, crumbled between your fingers

500g rhubarb, unpeeled and cut into slices about 5mm thick

1 tablespoon edible dried rose petals

a pinch of salt

You will need: a sterilised bottle with a capacity of 250ml

makes approx. 250ml

Heat the vinegar and sugar in a small pan, just enough for the sugar to dissolve. Add the saffron threads, take off the heat and leave for 20 minutes to infuse.

Put the diced rhubarb, dried rose petals and salt into a bowl. Pour over the infused vinegar mix and stir round. Cover and leave in the fridge for 5 days, giving it the occasional stir. Don't worry if the fruit is not initially submerged by the liquid; that will change as the rhubarb starts to macerate.

Strain the liquid into a bowl or jug, discarding the solids left behind. The resulting shrub liquid should be a beautiful, quite-vibrant orange colour. Transfer to the bottle and store in the fridge for 3–5 days before using, to give the flavours time to mellow.

VINEGAR VARIATION

Use a cider vinegar instead of the white wine vinegar.

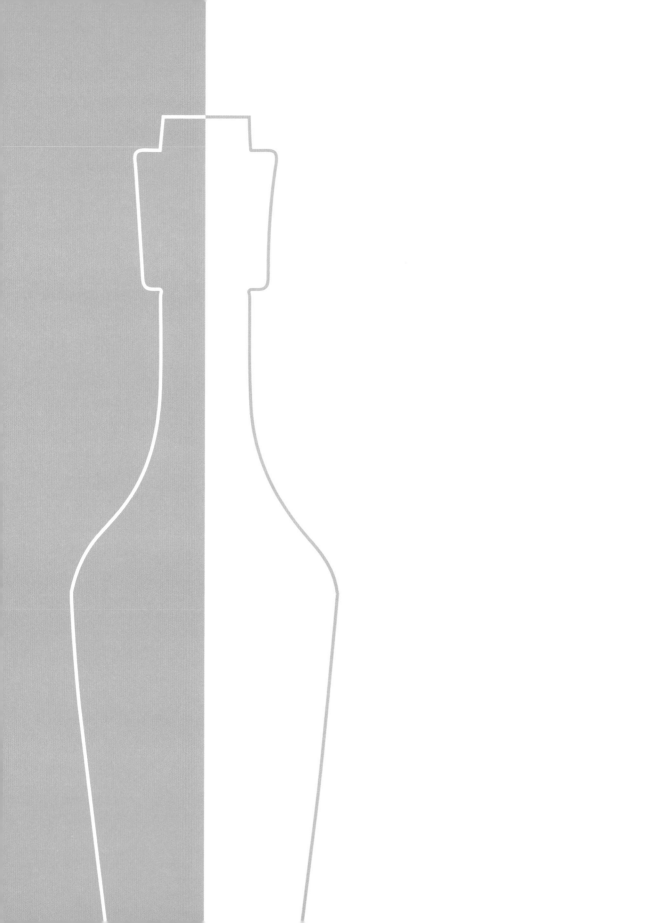

GRAIN VINEGARS

Plum shrub with notes of bay needs the ripest, tastiest fruit for maximum impact. Using rice vinegar sends it in a direction that fits well with the sake you might serve it with, but I find it better to combine it with the cider vinegar rather than using all rice vinegar, partly because rice vinegar typically has lower acidity, and also to balance the flavour.

Plum and Bay Japanese Shrub (for a Sake Tonic)

600g ripe, juicy purple plums
140g caster sugar
75ml Japanese brown rice vinegar
75ml cider vinegar
3 bay leaves

TO SERVE
50ml sake
150–200ml tonic water
or sparkling water

You will need: a sterilised bottle with a capacity of 350ml

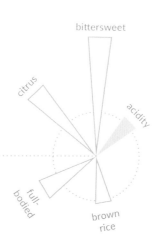

Makes approx. 350ml

Quarter the plums into a bowl, discarding the stones. Stir in the sugar, cover and set aside for 2 days for the fruit to macerate. It's best kept somewhere cool, but not as cold as the fridge. Give it a stir occasionally.

One day into this fruit maceration, mix together the vinegars in a non-corrosive jug or bowl (glass is ideal). Add the bay leaves, cover and set aside in the fridge.

After the fruit has had its 2 days of maceration it will have released lots of juices into the bowl. Strain the plums through a fine sieve into a bowl, then pour the vinegar mix into the sieve too and let it all strain through to give a clear mixture of plum syrup and infused vinegar that is your shrub. Stir well, pour into the bottle, and store for at least 5 days before using so that the flavours have time to develop and the vinegar mellows.

To create a sake tonic, put 1 tablespoon of the plum and bay shrub into a glass with the sake. Add ice and top up with tonic water to taste. Stir and serve. Alternatively, for a soft drink, dilute to taste with sparkling water and serve.

VINEGAR VARIATION
Anything other than a Japanese (or Chinese) grain vinegar takes this drink in a different – albeit delicious – direction. Go for all cider vinegar or white wine vinegar instead. A mild coconut vinegar could also be fun.

I think the key to this salad is its balance of elements: the mix of colours from the different leaves, the sharpness of the chicory, the mellow sharpness of the rice vinegar, the honey sweetness and then a caraway kick. It's great served with meat or fish.

Chicory and Caraway Salad

approx. 500g chicory, a mixture
    of green and red leaves
3 tablespoons rapeseed oil
**1½ tablespoons Japanese
    brown rice vinegar**
1 teaspoon honey
1 teaspoon caraway seeds
salt

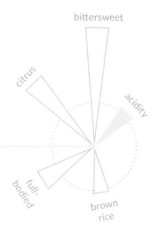

serves 4

Trim the base of each chicory head and discard any damaged outer leaves. Peel away the leaves into a mixing bowl, keeping them whole.

In a separate bowl or jug, whisk together the oil, vinegar and honey with a good pinch of salt. Toss the dressing through the leaves.

Toast the caraway seeds for around 30 seconds in a dry frying pan. Add to the dressed leaves and toss again, then serve.

VINEGAR VARIATION
Honey vinegar, coconut
vinegar or a rich fruit
berry vinegar.

Every time I make this salad I take a moment to reflect on its beauty. Pretty as a picture, with all its pinks and greens. The radishes are quick-pickled Japanese-style in *amasu*, a mix of rice vinegar, sugar and water that is heated until the sugar dissolves. The *amasu* gives a light pickling to the radishes, but these are not the kind of pickles that keep for ages; they need just an hour in the pickling liquid before the samphire and parsley are added and then it is served. Don't add samphire and parsley too soon before serving, however, or they'll lose some of their vibrancy. I sometimes use sea purslane instead of samphire; both are pretty salty, which is why there is no need for any additional salt in the recipe. The samphire here is raw – if you prefer, steam it lightly for 2 minutes and refresh in cold water before following the recipe.

If you fancy, the *amasu* rice vinegar pickling liquid can be retained and mixed with sparkling water for a delicious, prettily-pink drink.

Quick-pickled Radish, Samphire and Parsley *Amasu* Salad

180g breakfast radishes
**100ml Japanese brown
rice vinegar**
2 tablespoons caster sugar
2 broad strips of orange zest
2 sprigs of dill
a handful of samphire
(approx. 90g)
3 tablespoons chopped
flat-leaf parsley

bittersweet

citrus

acidity

full-bodied

brown
rice

serves 3–4

Top and tail the radishes, slice them thinly and put into a bowl.

Put the vinegar into a pan with the sugar and 50ml of water. Bring to the boil, then reduce the heat and simmer only until the sugar has dissolved.

Pour the hot liquid over the radishes. They should be just covered, but if they're not add more vinegar and water in a 2:1 ratio. Add the orange zest and dill to the bowl. Stir, then cover and leave for an hour at room temperature to cool and for the flavours to meld together.

VINEGAR VARIATION
A light white wine vinegar such as champagne vinegar could be used here.

Remove the orange strips and the dill. Strain away the liquid (or keep it – see introduction), then toss the radishes with the samphire and chopped parsley in a large bowl and serve.

Japanese rice vinegar gives these green beans a lift and just a hint of something Asian in flavour. A very useful accompaniment to lots of dishes, but also really good to nibble on as a snack.

Green Beans and Spring Onions with Sesame

300g green beans, trimmed
2 tablespoons sesame oil
1 bunch of spring onions, white
    parts only, finely chopped
2 teaspoons sesame seeds
1 tablespoon Japanese
    brown rice vinegar
salt

serves 4

Bring a large pan of water to the boil. Add the beans and cook for 3 minutes until just tender. Drain and refresh in cold water.

Heat the sesame oil in a wok. Throw in the green beans and spring onions. Stir for a minute, then add the sesame seeds, rice vinegar and salt to taste, and serve.

VINEGAR VARIATION
Take away the rice vinegar and I fear you take away this dish's identity. But you could give it a different identity by using an interesting fruit vinegar – maybe mango or pineapple – or coconut vinegar. A light apple or pear vinegar would work well too, as would a cider vinegar.

This is a truly fabulous way to cook liver. Marinating it in vinegar then cooking it quickly ensures it will be tender, while the Chinese black vinegar creates a super sauce. Serve the dish with rice to soak up that sauce.

Chinese Black Vinegar and Chilli-marinated Calf's Liver

1 large garlic clove
¼ teaspoon chilli flakes
2 tablespoons chopped
   coriander
**3 tablespoons Chinese black
   rice vinegar**
250g calf's liver, sliced
knob of butter
1 tablespoon olive oil
50ml chicken stock, or water
1 tablespoon crème fraîche
salt and freshly ground
   black pepper

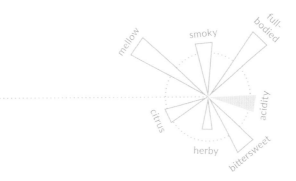

Serves 6 as a starter, or 2 as a main

Using a pestle and mortar, crush the garlic clove with a pinch of salt into a paste. Add the chilli flakes and coriander and pestle again, then mix in the Chinese black rice vinegar. Lay the calf's liver slices in a shallow dish in a single layer and rub over the marinade. Cover and set aside for an hour – in the fridge if your kitchen is warm.

Heat the butter and olive oil in a frying pan and, when hot, lift the liver slices out of the marinade and into the pan. Cook for 2 minutes, turn them over and cook for a further minute, then lift them out onto plates or a serving dish. Cover to keep warm and set aside.

Leave the pan on the heat and scoop into it the marinade that was left behind in the dish, along with the chicken stock, and whisk over a high heat for a minute or two to reduce the liquid. Whisk in the crème fraîche, then pour the sauce over the liver and serve with a grinding of pepper.

VINEGAR VARIATION

A balsamic or sherry vinegar would be good here, but I have to say not quite as good as the Chinese black.

*Manūl changac*hi is a Korean side dish of pickled whole garlic bulbs and is the basis for this recipe. It is an incredibly satisfying thing to make as the whole bulbs look so beautiful in the jar. This is a pickling of a few stages, but as is the way of pickling, even if the total time needed to make these is fairly lengthy (and it is), the actual time spent 'doing' is low – especially when you take into account the delight in serving these salty, crunchy pickled cloves.

Enjoy as a typical pickle as a side dish accompaniment, or consider cooking them by popping the pickled cloves out of their skins and sautéing them with vegetable greens or blending them into soups. Have a taste, and other options of how to use them will come to mind, I am sure.

Pickled Whole Garlic

10 whole garlic bulbs (avoid
    using old, flaky-skinned garlic
    if you can)
100g coarse salt
**1 litre Japanese brown rice
    vinegar, plus an extra 200ml**
600ml soy sauce
75ml honey
1 dried chilli, bay leaves or
    coriander seeds (optional)

You will need: a 2-litre capacity
    jar with a tight seal, sterilised

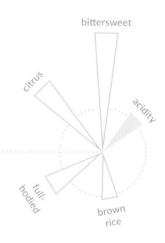

makes one 2-litre jar

Cut the top off each garlic bulb to reveal the tips of the cut cloves. Carefully peel away two layers of the skin, being sure that at least one layer is left on. Put the bulbs into the jar.

Stir the salt into 1 litre of water until it dissolves, then pour that over the garlic. It should cover the bulbs but, if not, add more water with the same proportion of salt. Seal and set aside somewhere cool and dark for a week.

Drain the bulbs of the salted water, return them to the jar and cover with 1 litre of brown rice vinegar. Seal and set aside for 2 weeks somewhere cool and dark.

Drain the bulbs and return them to the jar. Heat the soy sauce and remaining 200ml of rice vinegar in a pan with the honey and 200ml of water. Bring to a high simmer, pour over the bulbs to immerse, then allow the liquid to cool to room temperature before sealing. You could also add a dried chilli, bay leaves or coriander seeds for this final stage of pickling, if you like.

VINEGAR VARIATION

Change the vinegar and I think you change the style of the recipe so much that it is worth taking it in a whole different direction. Following the salting stage, for the first pickling cover the bulbs with a mix of 600ml red wine vinegar, 250ml red wine and 150ml water. Add some sprigs of fresh herbs, seal, set aside and in a month you will have a French-style version that will be delicious as a pickle (think about serving with terrines) or to cook with.

Set aside for at least a month (ideally 2 months) somewhere cool and dark before using. They will last for several months so long as they remain immersed in the brine and well sealed. Check on them after a week – as the bulbs take on the soy mix, you may find the liquid level falls below the top of the garlic. Just top up with more soy/rice vinegar in approximately the same proportions of three parts soy sauce to one part vinegar.

The black vinegar is used here as a finishing-touch garnish. This gives its flavours nowhere to hide and everywhere to shine, making it the ideal way to serve a well-made, rounded black vinegar. Try Chinese Zhenjiang or another of the Chinese black vinegars, or the Japanese black vinegar *kurosu*.

Pumpkin Soup with Enoki Mushrooms and Black Vinegar

1 tablespoon olive oil

2 onions, chopped

1 garlic clove, chopped

½ teaspoon ground coriander

¼ teaspoon ground cloves

1 star anise

approx. 800g pumpkin or other squash (weight after peeling and deseeding), chopped into approx. 2cm chunks

750ml vegetable stock

100ml sour cream

1 bundle of enoki mushrooms

2 tablespoons Chinese or Japanese black vinegar

salt and freshly ground black pepper

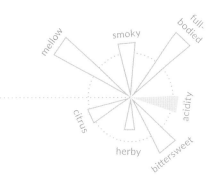

serves 6

Heat the olive oil in a saucepan over a medium heat and gently cook the onions until softened. Add the garlic, coriander, cloves and star anise. Stir round for a couple of minutes to release the flavours, then add the pumpkin pieces and stock.

Bring to the boil, then reduce the heat and gently simmer until the pumpkin is tender. It will take about 20 minutes. Remove the star anise and blend it all until super-smooth. Season and stir in the cream until you reach the consistency you want. Reheat in preparation for serving, then set aside to keep warm.

Cut the base off the enoki mushroom bundle and separate each one.

Divide the soup between serving bowls, with the raw mushrooms placed on top as a garnish, followed by a drizzle of black vinegar. Finish with a good grinding of pepper and serve.

VINEGAR VARIATION

Try balsamic, or a fruit balsamic such as fig or apple; maple vinegar would also work well here for its sweetness and woodiness.

The word 'sushi' refers to the vinegaring of the rice, rather than to the finished article with fish or what-have-you that accompanies it. I avoid buying ready-made sushi vinegar, partly because it tends to contain other preservative elements beyond the vinegar, sugar and salt, which are really all that are needed if you make it yourself. The other benefit of making your own is that you can develop the ratios of vinegar, sugar and salt to suit your taste. Just as sushi chefs will evolve their own ratio of rice to these ingredients, so can we.

Choose a mild Japanese rice vinegar. Colourless is the norm, but the traditional Edo *akasu* vinegar made from aged sake lees (see page 206) was the original choice for sushi, and that is a reddish-colour. So go for whatever style of Japanese rice vinegar you please, as long as it's a mild one of no more than 4.5% acidity.

Sushi

A guide to proportions when making rice:

Sushi rice	Water	Amount of cooked rice
200g	220ml	300g
400g	440ml	600g
1kg	1.1 litre	1.5kg

A guide to proportions when making rice vinegar dressing – remember, these can be tweaked up or down according to taste:

Cooked rice	Rice vinegar	Granulated sugar	Fine salt
300g	30ml	15g	7.5g (1½ teaspoons)
600g	60ml	30g	15g (1 tablespoon)
1.5kg	150ml	75g	37.5g (2.25 tablespoons)

VINEGAR VARIATION

Try a mild cider vinegar or white wine vinegar. Maybe even a spice-infused vinegar. Certainly the dashi-infused vinegar like the one described on page 41 could be very good.

Sit the rice in a large bowl, cover with cold water, stir well, then drain the water away through a fine sieve. Repeat three times with fresh water so that the final rinsing is clear as you drain it off the rice. After the last washing, leave the rice to fully drain in the sieve for an hour.

Put the rice and its proportionate amount of water (see guide above) into a saucepan and cover with a tight lid. Set over a medium heat to come to the boil. Listen for boiling sounds as – however tempting – it is important not to lift the lid and release the steam. Once you hear sounds of boiling, turn the heat down a little and let it cook for 5–8 minutes, depending on the amount of rice you are doing. Turn off the heat – still do not lift the lid – and let it finish cooking for 10 minutes in its own steam.

Make the vinegar dressing while the rice is cooking by stirring the required proportions of salt and sugar into the rice vinegar until they have dissolved.

While the rice is still hot, transfer it to your *hangiri* (see below) or other large shallow bowl. Moisten your *shamoji* (see below) or wooden spoon, and use it to cut through the rice and break it up. Pour the prepared vinegar dressing over the back of the spoon so that it covers the rice as evenly as possible. Continue to use the spoon to turn the rice over and coat the grains in the dressing. Try to fan the rice out as you do it. Avoid stirring – it is about turning the rice over.

Use the sushi rice on the day it is made. Form into shapes by dampening your hands in vinegar or water. If you are not using the rice immediately, cover the bowl with a damp cloth and leave somewhere cool and out of direct sunlight (not the fridge). It will keep happily at room temperature for up to 4 hours until you want to form it into the finished sushi, whether that's with sashimi, wasabi, seaweed, raw or lightly pickled vegetables, egg or whatever takes your sushi fancy.

Two aspects of technique for sushi

Making sushi uses less water in the cooking of the rice than you might for other rice dishes. Just 10% more water than the weight of the rice.

The idea is to make sure every grain of cooked rice has its fair share of the vinegar dressing, while also cooling the rice as quickly as possible to avoid it going mushy in its own steam. Traditionally, this would be done by using a large, shallow *hangiri* bowl to mix the rice in, and pouring over/mixing in the vinegar using a wide *shamoji* spoon which is like a paddle in shape. Both can be bought if you choose, or mimicked with any large shallow bowl and big wooden spoon.

I hope the recipes below will show just how versatile the light Japanese rice vinegars can be. Try to find a good one that has been made as well as you can discern from brown rice. Along with a few core Japanese pantry ingredients such as soy sauce, mirin (sweet rice wine), dried bonito flakes and kombu (sheets of dried seaweed), and you are all set.

Each one is very good as a dipping sauce for sushi, sashimi, fried fish or tempura. They can be reduced over heat if you are after a thicker style of sauce. I would also urge you to think about using these in your everyday cooking repertoire, not just when cooking a specifically Japanese dish or meal. They give a wonderful lilt and lift as a marinade or dressing for meat, fish, vegetables and salads.

For all the recipes, the methods of making and storing are the same (unless otherwise stated): just combine all the ingredients together well, then store in a sterilised jar or bottle in the fridge where they will be fine for a week or so.

Japanese Vinegar Sauces

SANBAISU

100ml Japanese brown rice vinegar
100ml light soy sauce
100ml mirin
2 garlic cloves, grated; or grated ginger (optional)

A traditional dipping sauce for tempura, or for pickling or marinating vegetables. It would have been made using small sake bowls to measure out equal quantities of the three liquid ingredients. Over time, the core ingredients have evolved a little: the mirin could be swapped for dashi stock, for example, in which case add a little sugar to taste.

makes 300ml

Combine all the ingredients together well.

NIHAISU

150ml Japanese brown rice vinegar
150ml light soy sauce

Use as a dipping sauce for sashimi, dumplings or fried fish. This contains two of the three ingredients of sanbaisu, again in equal quantities. The vinegar does a great job of lightening up the soy. This is a popular sauce in Korean cooking too, where it is called *cho ganjang* – the words for 'vinegar' and 'soy sauce' respectively.

makes 300ml

Combine all the ingredients together well.

TOSAZU

150ml sanbaisu (see page 192)
10g dried bonito flakes

The key ingredient here is the dried bonito flakes (*katsuobushi*), which gives this adaptation of sanbaisu a really fabulous umami depth. Use with fish dishes with enough strength not to be overwhelmed by it.

makes 150ml

Bring the sanbaisu to the boil in a saucepan, add the bonito flakes, then turn off the heat straight away. Leave to infuse for about 30 minutes, then strain out and discard the bonito flakes. Give them a squeeze as they will have absorbed some of the liquid.

GOMAZU

4 tablespoons white sesame
  seeds
**50ml Japanese brown rice
  vinegar or dashi vinegar
  (see page 41)**
25ml mirin
25ml light soy sauce

Roasted sesame seeds give this thick dipping sauce a wonderfully deep, rounded flavour. This is one to make as you need it, rather than to store. If you have any dashi stock on hand, you could use that instead of the water, but the amount used here is so small it isn't worth making a batch especially.

makes approx. 100ml

Lightly toast the sesame seeds in a dry frying pan, then grind in a pestle and mortar until smooth. Put the rest of the ingredients into a small saucepan with 25ml of water. Add the ground sesame seeds and simmer it all together for a few minutes to reduce and thicken.

PONSU

**75ml Japanese brown
  rice vinegar**
75ml mirin
20g kombu
10g dried bonito flakes
75ml light soy sauce
75ml citrus juice, such as yuzu,
  or half lemon/half lime

By now you will recognise the ingredients as being the fundamentals of many Japanese sauces – this time enhanced with a hit of citrus.

makes approx. 300ml

Heat the vinegar, mirin and kombu just until it boils and the kombu wilts, then add the bonito flakes and turn the heat off straight away. Leave to infuse for about 30 minutes, then strain out and discard the solids. Mix the soy sauce and citrus juice into the strained liquid.

This classic Japanese dish is rooted in the cooking styles of the Portuguese sailors and traders who arrived in southern Japan in the sixteenth century: the 'southern barbarians', which is what *nanban* refers to. Pieces of fish are deep-fried into surprising lightness, then marinated in a sweet *nanbansu* sauce, which has the familiar Japanese elements of rice vinegar, soy and mirin, with a little dried chilli in there too. The quick-pickle of some very finely chopped vegetables alongside makes this a lovely light dish for a starter, or as part of a sharing feast. Try with the sushi rice on page 190. I suggest using cod or salmon here, but other fish would work well, especially mackerel.

The dashi stock can, like all stocks, be achieved a few ways. There is dashi stock powder that you can buy from specialist Japanese ingredient stores; some supermarkets sell packets of prepared liquid dashi stock; or you can make your own: heat 150ml of water with a piece of kombu approx. 3cm square. As soon as it comes to the boil turn the heat off, take the kombu out and stir in 1 tablespoon of dried bonito flakes, leave for 3 minutes and strain the stock.

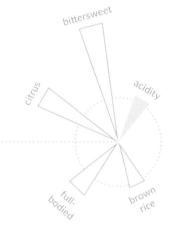

Nanbanzuke Fish

600g thick fillet of salmon
   or cod, skinned
1 litre vegetable oil
4 tablespoons plain flour
1 carrot, peeled and cut into fine
   matchsticks, approx. 6–7cm long
1 celery stick, cut into fine
   matchsticks, approx. 6–7cm long
2 spring onions, finely sliced
salt and freshly ground
   black pepper

FOR THE MARINADE
100ml dashi stock
**100ml Japanese brown
   rice vinegar**
50ml light soy sauce
50ml mirin
1 tablespoon granulated sugar
½ teaspoon dried chilli flakes

VINEGAR VARIATION
Cider vinegar would work
well here, too.

serves 4

Prepare the marinade by mixing together the dashi, vinegar, soy sauce, mirin and sugar in a bowl until the sugar has dissolved. Add the chilli, then pour into a tray that can take the fish and vegetables in one layer.

Chop the fish into 3 x 3cm cubes. Heat the oil to 180°C in a deep saucepan over a high heat (test with a thermometer, or by dropping in a small piece of bread: it will sizzle and brown but not burn).

Season the fish pieces, roll them in the flour, then carefully lower into the oil. You will need to do this in batches of four or so at a time so as to not crowd the pan. When each piece is crisped and nicely brown (2–3 minutes), lift out with a slotted spoon onto kitchen paper to absorb any excess oil, then transfer to the tray of marinade. Gently toss the fish pieces in the marinade. Add the carrot and celery, then cover and set aside for at least 2 hours or up to 24 hours. Baste the salmon occasionally with the marinade. If marinating for more than 2 hours, keep it in the fridge, but return to room temperature before serving.

To serve, lift the fried fish onto serving plates, arrange the carrot and celery matchsticks around, and drizzle over some of the marinade. Garnish with the spring onions and serve.

Chinese dipping sauces are a great addition to a cook's repertoire, served with dumplings, steamed vegetables, meat or fish. Here is a fairly classic version, using just Chinese black vinegar mixed with fresh ginger and a little sugar. Punchy and very versatile. I like it served alongside sea bass fillets wrapped around fine slivers of spring onion and steamed with a hint of tarragon. It is simple to cook, elegant to serve and delicious to eat. Serve it on a bed of rice with some steamed or stir-fried vegetables, or as a canapé or starter.

Steamed Sea Bass Rolls with Black Vinegar Dipping Sauce

4 skinless, boneless sea
   bass fillets
1 spring onion
5 sprigs of tarragon
salt and freshly ground
   black pepper

FOR THE DIPPING SAUCE
**4 tablespoons Chinese
   black vinegar**
1 tablespoon grated
   fresh ginger
½ teaspoon caster sugar

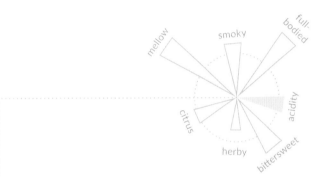

serves 2–4

Make the dipping sauce first, by mixing together the black vinegar and grated ginger in a bowl. Add half the sugar, then stir and taste. Add the rest of the sugar if you think it needs it – some Chinese black vinegars are sweeter than others. Then set the sauce aside while you get on with the fish.

Slice the sea bass fillets in half lengthways, to end up with eight long, thin strips of fish. Trim the spring onion, then cut through its length to end up with long, very thin strips of spring onion. Season the fish, lay a sliver of spring onion along the length of each fillet strip, and roll each one up to wrap up the spring onion. Hold each roll in place with a cocktail stick.

Bring the water in a steamer to the boil, throw in the tarragon, sit the sea bass rolls in the steaming basket, and cook over the water for 6–7 minutes. They are ready when the flesh turns opaque. Serve with the black vinegar dipping sauce.

VINEGAR VARIATION

This is one of those rare cases in which there isn't an alternative option really. Another intense grain vinegar such as Japanese *kurosu* would work, but otherwise ditch the dipping sauce and sprinkle the sea bass strips with rice vinegar or white wine vinegar before rolling.

Ribs marinated in Chinese black vinegar are a far cry from the tough, chewy spare ribs too often found in Chinese restaurants. The vinegar gives intensity to the marinade and the glaze, and it tenderises the meat gorgeously. A feast. And one to be shared with people who you don't mind having sticky fingers with.

Ask your butcher to prepare the racks by removing the thin film of membrane on one side. Or you can do it yourself by using a knife to lift up one edge and peeling it off. Note that these are racks of spare ribs from the loin of the pig, not from its shoulder.

Sticky Pork Ribs Marinated in Black Vinegar, Muscovado and Spices

juice of 1 orange (don't throw
    away the fruit's outer shells)
**4 tablespoons Chinese
    black vinegar**
6 tablespoons dark
    muscovado sugar
1 teaspoon English mustard
1 teaspoon ground fennel seeds
½ teaspoon ground cloves
2 racks of pork spare ribs, cut
    in half to create about 5 or
    6 ribs per portion
4 bay leaves
4 sprigs of rosemary
5 garlic cloves, unpeeled
salt

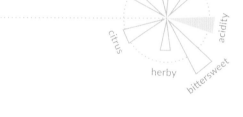

serves 4

To create the marinade, combine the orange juice, black vinegar, sugar, mustard, fennel seeds and cloves with a good pinch of salt and mix well.

Sit the rib racks in a roasting tin. You might need to use two, depending on the size of your racks and tins; if you do, just make sure everything is spread evenly across both tins and racks. Rub the marinade all over the racks and sit a bay leaf and a sprig of rosemary under each portion. Cut the reserved orange shells in half and put those into the tin too. Set aside for 5 hours – in the fridge if your kitchen is warm – turning the ribs in the marinade a few times.

When ready to cook, preheat the oven to 150°C/130°C Fan/ Gas Mark 2. Add the whole, unpeeled garlic cloves to the tin alongside the rib racks, rolling them in the marinade. Cover the tin and bake for 2½ hours, basting twice, until the meat on the racks is nicely tender. Dig out and discard the orange shells, garlic, bay and rosemary. Turn the oven up to 190°C/170°C Fan/ Gas Mark 5.

VINEGAR VARIATION

Chinese black vinegar really is best here, but a balsamic or rich sherry vinegar could work too.

Using a pastry brush, spread the marinade that is in the base of the tin all over the racks. Return to the oven, uncovered, for about 25 minutes so the ribs become sticky, turning the racks twice. When the racks are a glossy, sticky, rich brown colour, take them out and let them cool down before serving. You need to be able to hold them in order to rip them apart satisfyingly.

Baking figs with this combination of Chinese black vinegar, honey, thyme and cinnamon somehow manages to both enhance and cut through the fruit's richness of flavour and fragrance. Serve with a little dollop of crème fraîche (maybe with some orange flower water stirred through) or ice cream.

Honey and Chinese Black Vinegar Baked Figs

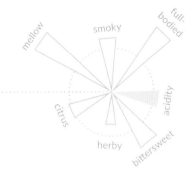

8 ripe figs
2 tablespoons Chinese black vinegar
2 tablespoons honey
2 tablespoons thyme leaves
½ teaspoon ground cinnamon

serves 4–8

Preheat the oven to 180°C/160°C Fan/Gas Mark 4.

Cut the tops off the figs and score a cross into the top of each one. Give them a squeeze to open them up, then sit them snugly, cut-side up, in a large piece of foil inside a baking dish.

Mix together the vinegar, honey, thyme and cinnamon in a bowl. Use a teaspoon to stuff the centre of each fig's cross with the soaked thyme mixture – this will open the fruit up even more. Use it all, pouring any that won't fit into the figs over the top of them.

Bundle together the foil loosely but securely to seal. Bake for 5 minutes, then open up the foil and bake for another 5 minutes. Check how they are doing – they might already be gorgeously tender, or may need another 5 minutes in the oven. It depends how ripe the figs were.

Serve one or two figs per person while they are still warm, with any juices in the base of the foil drizzled over the top.

VINEGAR VARIATION
Try using Japanese *kurosu* vinegar, sherry vinegar or red wine vinegar.

Japanese and Chinese Grain Vinegars

To the fascinated outsider that I can't help but be, there's much to understand in the twists and turns of Japan and China's distinct and numerous grain vinegar styles. There are so many different types between the two countries; and then within each country are local differences and regional specialities that you may only ever get the opportunity to experience by going there.

On emerging at the other side of this labyrinth, I feel the most fundamental things to know about the Asian grain vinegars are the main types; their heritage; the importance of the many regional differences; and how to get to grips with choosing and using the best modern vinegars available on the market. (See pages 18–19 for more on the history of these vinegars.)

TRADITIONAL PROCESS

There are core elements of the basic, traditional processes of Japanese and Chinese grain (primarily rice) vinegar-making which are shared across the two countries. What follows may seem quite technical but understanding it unlocks our appreciation of the different types and various modern incarnations of rice vinegar, in much the same way as understanding *Tradizionale* does for balsamic.

The most striking thing in grain vinegar is that it is about fermenting a solid, not a liquid. It's not like pressing grapes or apples, say, to extract their juice and then fermenting that. Typically – but not exclusively – in the traditional process the liquid element is added only *after* the grain has gone from starch to sugar, to alcohol, to vinegar. It is certainly true that rice wine sake can naturally ferment to vinegar as any other wine would, but that is not the traditional process.

The grain is first soaked and then steamed to activate its starch turning to sugar. This is then mixed with the all-important starter to get the alcoholic fermentation going. In Japan the starter is mould and called *koji*; in China it is *qu* (pronounced 'choo') and is both mould and yeast. This takes place in urns that are kept at an optimally warm temperature to allow the micro-organisms to do their thing.

The ensuing grain and *koji/qu* mash (known as *moromi*) is transferred to an empty urn or turned over in its own urn to help get air into it, which also plays a role in the chemical conversion. It takes five or so days for the sugar to become alcohol. It is now, if you like, a sort of very thick sake.

The next stage is to turn that alcohol into vinegar. This is done by adding a 'seed' of vinegar from a previous batch, and the aceto bacteria that will ensure acetic fermentation is completed.

Salt is then added so that as the vinegar stays in the urn to develop colour and flavour, it doesn't oxidise to carbon dioxide. Now the vinegar is washed three times in water in a process known as

Koji

the mould starter used in Japan for alcoholic fermentation.

Qu

the yeast and mould starter used in China for alcoholic fermentation.

'leaching'. It is the leached solution that is the actual vinegar, and each of the three washes will yield a different type or quality. This 'finished' vinegar is then aged to develop its flavour.

Now, get set to see how this process has, over the centuries, been adapted by various vinegar-makers across these cultures to create distinctive vinegars, and how modern makers continue to do it.

Japanese

Let me start by sharing something I have found incredibly useful to know when researching, shopping for or cooking with Japanese rice vinegar: the suffix '-*su*' or '-*zu*' at the end of a Japanese word is telling you it is vinegar or contains vinegar.

In the world of Japanese rice vinegar there is something of a clash between its modern rice vinegar production – with all the pressures of scale, consistency and commerciality – and the traditional processes and styles that have so much to commend them to modern consumers, and which some producers are endeavouring to retain or re-establish, or at least evoke elements of.

It is the same with wine vinegars, balsamic vinegars and cider vinegars, of course. And just as with those, the key to understanding modern rice vinegar production and its uses lies with understanding first where it has come from.

TRADITIONAL JAPANESE RICE VINEGARS AND THE WONDER OF *KUROSU* 'BLACK' VINEGAR

Japan learned brewing – and therefore vinegar-making – from China in around the fourth century AD. The Chinese methods of brewing rice first took hold in central Japan's Osaka, and from there spread widely throughout the country, so much so that there are records from the Nara period (AD 710–794) of vinegar being taxed in Japan as a variety of sake. (Making sake and making rice vinegar are based on the same basic brewing principles.)

Two main traditional types of rice vinegar produced

Komesu

Made from polished rice. That is white rice with its husk, bran and germ removed, which is then fermented into a milk, colourless or pale amber vinegar.

Kurosu

Made from unpolished rice (i.e. brown rice) which is fermented and then slowly, carefully aged into a vinegar sometimes known as 'black' or 'brown' vinegar, but in reality on a colour spectrum of light tan to deep mahogany, depending on its ageing.

I'll come back to *komesu* later as the forebear of most of our modern rice vinegars. For now I want to focus upon *kurosu/kurozu* (the *su* or the *zu* are used interchangeably). It literally translates as 'black vinegar', but I am going to avoid referring to it as such to avoid confusion with Chinese black vinegar. Let's all get our heads around the word *kurosu* and hope our tastebuds get the opportunity to follow.

Japan's most south-westerly island of Kyushu is where most of the *kurosu*-makers are now, and especially in Kiroshma City. Pay a visit there and you will see literally hundreds of thousands of huge crocks – known as *tsubos* – arranged in partially buried rows, knee-high or so out of the ground, in which this very special vinegar is fermenting and ageing.

The *kurosu* process begins just as for the basic traditional method (see page 202), but with water added much earlier, before the sugar becomes alcohol. Many producers will use the best, freshest, locally sourced spring water. It is a key ingredient and so its quality will tell. Some makers only transfer the liquid to the crocks once it is already alcohol; some do the entire process from start to finish in the *tsubo*. Either way, it is in the crocks that the vinegar magic happens in a way that is awe-inspiring for both its meticulous attention to detail, and its freedom in allowing the vinegar to take its own natural course.

The rows of crocks are set out from north to south, to give each crock its time in the sun as it goes from east to west. To protect the vinegar in the crocks from overheating in the summer sun, the grass is allowed to grow up and around each one as its own natural shade. Then in the winter the grass is cut back. Workers occasionally stir the contents of each crock with a bamboo stick; they talk of the 'sound of *kurosu*' that is emitted from the *tsubo* as the grains ferment.

It may become vinegar in just a few months, depending on the time of year. Some makers will then siphon the *kurosu* out, age it in tanks, filter it and pasteurise it for selling. For others, it can take several years in the *tsubo* for the vinegar to achieve the depth of colour, flavour and aroma its maker wants. It doesn't move from *tsubo* to *tsubo* – as balsamic would move from barrel to barrel – but it does evaporate in the air over time in the same way, and intensify in the same way. The oldest *kurosu* vinegars are the thickest in texture, the most intense of flavour and the deepest of colour.

In case you are planning to pay a visit to this part of Japan, I should maybe warn you about something beyond the beautiful, striking rows of urns in the sunlight: you will not be alone there. Quite the tourist culture has built up around *kurosu* of late. The industry has begun to reinvent itself with a new modern appeal – and why not. *Kurosu* is, you may remember, made from unpolished rice, so has the health associations of brown rice. Add to that its fermentation, and beliefs in the health-giving properties of naturally produced vinegars, and you have all the makings of a modern trend. The huge popularity and fashion in Japan for drinking vinegars has led to many people taking *kurosu* with fruit juice as a daily health tonic. Personally, I love it for its heritage and flavour.

The *kurosu*-makers are happy to embrace all those reasons and more for its resurgence. Tourists are bussed in, and many makers have shops and restaurants on site. Demand will, inevitably, make its mark on production as it always has, and there are now versions of *kurosu* being made by more modern methods of fermentation in other areas of Japan, too. Let price and authenticity be your guide, yes, but also taste.

Tsubos

traditional urns used for making and ageing vinegar in Japan.

IN THE KITCHEN
Kurosu

A young, milder *kurosu* will be the cook's choice for versatility where you want depth but nothing too overpowering. An older, more powerful *kurosu* would stand up as a meat marinade, for example,

or as a finishing touch, in the way you might use a deep balsamic. Try a shot in a glass of cold milk for a morning tonic.

MODERN JAPANESE RICE VINEGARS

I am aware that it may seem rather mean-spirited of me to exclude *kurosu* from a section on modern Japanese rice vinegar. Especially when I have just said it is making a resurgence. Yet I mean it as the best possible compliment. For all its wonder and history, *kurosu* is just a tiny proportion of modern Japanese rice-vinegar-making. *Kurosu* is made in a distinct, traditional way. Other – by which I mean most – modern Japanese vinegars are not.

Most Japanese rice vinegar is the pale, milder-flavoured type, with its roots in the traditional *komesu* style using polished white rice, although brown rice is often used now. The best characteristics of this Japanese rice vinegar are its lightness and freshness due to its relatively low acidity. The acidity level is often marked as a percentage on Japanese rice vinegar bottles by the character for *san*, meaning acid. It is typically about 4.5% acidity. Compare that to a wine vinegar, which would be around 6%. That may not sound like much of a difference, but it is sizeable when it comes to how rice vinegar can be enjoyed and used. Rice vinegar is simply milder than most other vinegars, which opens it up to being used in all kinds of dishes across the globe – those that need a little bit of acidity but not too much, and don't want to be knocked off balance with too large a hit of flavour. It is an incredibly useful and versatile ingredient, and one that is well worth embracing.

The majority is made in a way that is a far cry from the traditional process of *komesu*, although this is what modern producers are trying to emulate in their end result. The move towards industrial ways of making rice vinegar is in many ways an inevitable part of the modern supply chain and has its echoes around the world. In Japan's case it began with rice shortages in World War II; the Japanese simply had to find others ways to make their rice vinegar. Now, as we are seeing all over the world in connection with each country's heritage vinegar, it is exciting to see modern vinegar producers trying to bring back some authentic ways of making.

There's a wide spectrum of methods of vinegar production. At one end are the handful of huge producers making industrial rice vinegars, much of which is sold on to smaller companies to retail under their own label. That accounts for around two-thirds of the 500 or so 'vinegar-makers' in Japan. On the whole, these big companies are mass-producing their rice vinegars with the sole focus of getting a vinegar out quickly and cheaply. Quality and production are, inevitably, compromised in the result.

That vinegar could be labelled as *kokumotsusu*. *Kokumotsu* means 'grain', and *su* tells us it is vinegar. So this is grain vinegar made from any or a mix of grains (not just rice), distilled into spirit vinegar.

Or there is rice vinegar from the sake lees sediment that is left behind in sake-making. This is based on an old tradition of making *akasu* vinegar (see below), but the modern method cuts out the technique and ageing involved in that process. Where sake lees is used for mass production of rice vinegar, it is mixed with distilled grain alcohol and then converted to vinegar. (See page 26 for an explanation of the difference between distilled and fermented vinegars.)

You might see rice vinegar bottles list 'rice vinegar and water' as their ingredients, and rightly wonder: how can rice vinegar be an ingredient – surely it is the end result? Yes – but also no in an industrial process where rice is washed, soaked, steamed, mixed with a sake mash to give it high levels of alcohol, then processed quickly through an acetator to become vinegar. This way of doing it results in rice vinegar of very high acidity – too high for use. It is basically a vinegar concentrate. Its high concentration has real benefits for the maker, however, as it is cheaper for transporting and storing, but it has to be watered down for bottling, which is how rice vinegar can appear on a label as an ingredient.

When I include rice vinegar in a recipe, I am referring to the modern ones that appear towards the other end of the production spectrum I alluded to earlier. These vinegars begin with rice (polished white, or these days unpolished brown) and then undertake slow fermentation that takes time to become vinegar. Typically, these are the vinegars with words like 'brewed' or 'fermented' on the label. The ingredients will be listed as rice and water, and some of them may even tell you how many grams of rice were used per litre. The more the better. It will run from around 40g per litre, to 120g per litre or even 300g per litre at the top end. The highest-quality versions are sometimes labelled as *junmai-su*, meaning 'pure-rice' vinegar.

I hope very much that opportunities for buying really good Japanese rice vinegars outside of Japan will improve, as it can be hard at the moment. Even more than that, I hope that within Japan there is a movement back towards using more authentically made rice vinegars, rather than settling for the mass-produced ones that so dominate. The obstacle to that happening is that Japanese vinegar culture has changed so much. I have heard about how many Japanese children are growing up these days with a far greater sweet tooth than the sour one previous generations enjoyed. There is literally less of an appetite for the *sunomono* of lightly vinegared vegetable dishes (such as seaweed or cucumber) that would traditionally have been served to begin a meal or to complement main dishes. It will be a shame if that gets lost altogether.

IN THE KITCHEN
Modern Rice Vinegar

A good, modern *komesu*-style rice vinegar will be lightly sweet, full-bodied, mild, acidic without the sharpness of the overly industrialised ones, with a subtle contrast of flavours underlying it. It could be made with white or brown rice and my preference is for the brown for its greater flavour. That is why in many of the recipes I refer to using 'Japanese brown vinegar', but if you can't find it, a colourless one made of white rice will be more than fine.

In Japanese cooking the rice vinegar is typically blended with other ingredients for complexity and balance rather than used alone. You will see examples of this in the recipes for Japanese vinegar sauces in this book, where it is variously mixed with mirin, soy, dashi stock and so on.

It is used to bring balance to salad dressings, quick pickles (which I think of as the equivalent of *sunomono*), vegetables and fish dishes, and makes for a lovely light mayonnaise. And then there's sushi.

AKASU RICE VINEGAR

There is a nearly (only nearly) forgotten rice vinegar of Japan known as either *akasu* or *kasasu*, a type of vinegar made from aged sake lees sediment left behind from making sake. This is categorically not the same as the modern industrial rice vinegars that mix sake lees with distilled alcohol. *Akasu* uses those lees, yes, but ages them for two years or more so they deepen in colour and flavour. Traditionally, the lees would be aged in wooden boxes.

The resulting vinegar is a deep brown that when used in the traditional way with sushi gives it a fetching reddish tint. It came to prominence towards the end of the Edo period in Japan, from the early 1600s to the mid–late 1800s. Raw fish on vinegared rice became popular, with *akasu* being used in with the rice. Edo was the old name for Tokyo, so if you come across *edomae* sushi – or Tokyo sushi – *akasu* rice vinegar is what could/should/would be used.

It's a vinegar available to buy in Japan still, and if you are very lucky maybe even outside of Japan at a specialist store. Otherwise modern sushi is made with a sweet preparation of rice as described on page 190.

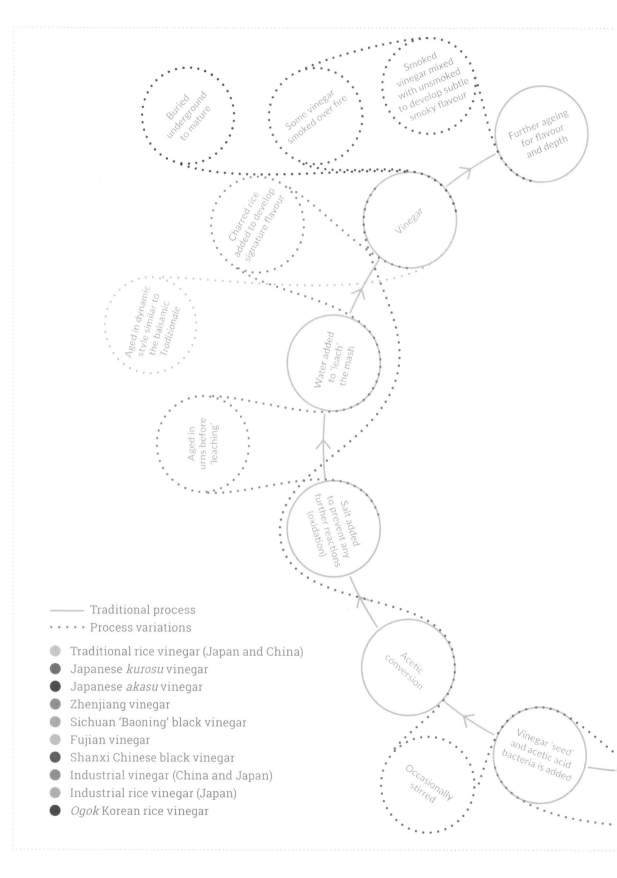

Buried underground to mature

Some vinegar smoked over fire

Smoked vinegar mixed with unsmoked to develop subtle smoky flavour

Further ageing for flavour and depth

Charred rice added to develop signature flavour

Vinegar

Aged in dynamic style similar to the balsamic Tradizionale

Water added to 'leach' the mash

Aged in urns before 'leaching'

Salt added to prevent any further reactions (oxidation)

Acetic conversion

Vinegar 'seed' and acetic acid bacteria is added

Occasionally stirred

———— Traditional process
• • • • Process variations

Traditional rice vinegar (Japan and China)
Japanese *kurosu* vinegar
Japanese *akasu* vinegar
Zhenjiang vinegar
Sichuan 'Baoning' black vinegar
Fujian vinegar
Shanxi Chinese black vinegar
Industrial vinegar (China and Japan)
Industrial rice vinegar (Japan)
Ogok Korean rice vinegar

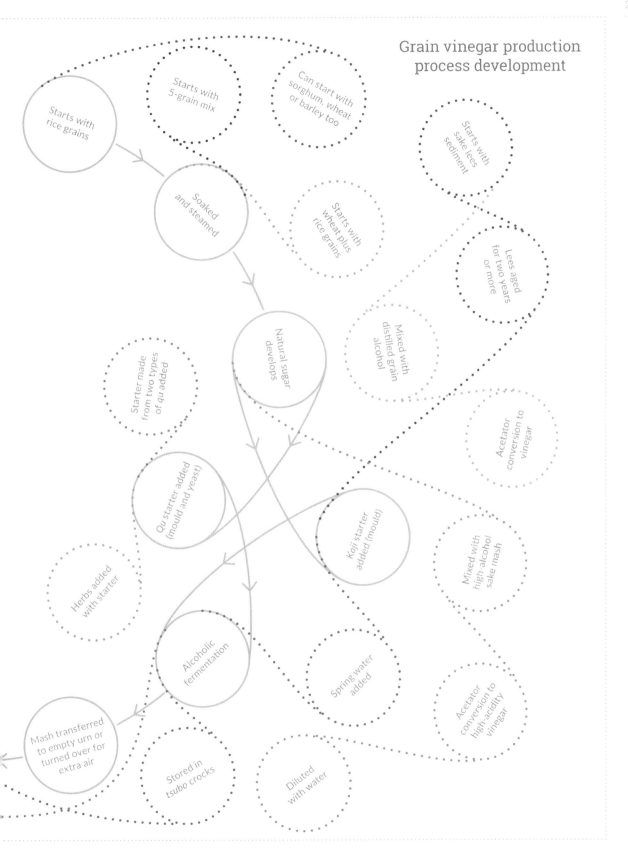

Grain vinegar production
process development

Starts with
rice grains

Starts with
5-grain mix

Can start with
sorghum, wheat
or barley too

Starts with
sake lees
sediment

Soaked
and steamed

Starts with
wheat plus
rice grains

Lees aged
for two years
or more

Natural sugar
develops

Mixed with
distilled grain
alcohol

Starter made
from two types
of qu added

Acetator
conversion to
vinegar

Qu starter added
(mould and yeast)

Koji starter
added (mould)

Mixed with
high-alcohol
sake mash

Herbs added
with starter

Alcoholic
fermentation

Spring water
added

Acetator
conversion to
high-acidity
vinegar

Mash transferred
to empty urn or
turned over for
extra air

Stored in
tsubo crocks

Diluted
with water

Chinese

The old Chinese proverb that includes vinegar as one of the seven essentials of daily life tells us not just that the Chinese have life's priorities pretty well sorted, but also that for centuries vinegar has played a vital and respected role in China. (The other essentials are firewood, rice, oil, salt, sauce and tea.)

Actually, it is not just centuries – it has been millennia. Texts and records from the Zhou Dynasty of 1027–221 BC and onwards mention rice wine being produced and fermented to vinegar. As time goes on, the early evidence for grain vinegar in China builds and builds and includes China's oldest agricultural writings, with Chinese characters for the elements used to make vinegar.

By the time of the Song Dynasty in the first century AD, vinegar was being widely used, in particular for preparing fish in a way we would think of now as being rather like sushi. Both Chinese 'sushi' and Chinese vinegar-making techniques travelled to Japan and were taken up there with gusto. While the first of those is now thought of as being more of a Japanese speciality, the Chinese kept strong their love of vinegar.

Modern mentions of Chinese vinegar tend to refer to Zhenjiang or Chinkiang Chinese black vinegar. That is a wonderful deep vinegar and certainly the easiest to get hold of outside of China. Yet it is just one of several Chinese regional speciality black vinegars that are prized for their flavour, heritage and methods of making. There are generally considered to be four main types that each owe their provenance to their particular region: Zhenjiang, Shanxi, Sichuan and Fujian (which is reddish-black). I am also including brief mentions of another two – Qishan and Chishui – just because I cannot resist, and they have interesting local significance.

Even these half-dozen vinegars barely scratch the surface of this great nation's vinegar portfolio. Go to a Chinese market and you will be faced with twenty or more different types of vinegar. Setting aside the fruit vinegars (and there is reason to think the Chinese fruit vinegars actually came first historically), your choice of grain vinegars may begin with rice but from there extend to sorghum, maize, barley, wheat or any combination of those. They will all be rooted in local distinctions, of course, as different areas across China have the propensity to grow particular types of grain (for example, rice in the south, sorghum in the north), and they would each want to cultivate vinegar of a particular style to go with other aspects of their local cooking. Then think that the natural micro-organisms in the air that make fermentation happen would be different from place to place, and you realise it stands to reason that there would be different grain vinegar styles across the country.

The Chinese government has, at varying points over the last forty years or so, tried to introduce standards and definitions across its grain vinegars. When classified as 'brewed', that means they bear some relation to the traditional style. And then there are artificial vinegars which really don't.

There have – obviously, inevitably – been huge strides made in how the brewed vinegars are produced. I cannot vouch for how much of what is produced now is really, genuinely produced according to authentic processes. The big commercial producers are making their vinegar in a largely industrial way, with as much or little respect to tradition as their commerciality allows. Some of them do have a premium line that has a greater focus on authenticity, and some smaller sellers are selling the big-brand vinegar just under another name.

Then there are the smaller producers, old craftsmen or new artisans, who are trying very hard to keep the traditional vinegar flame alive. Sweet-and-sour is a well-known and much-loved aspect of Chinese cooking – let one of these vinegars bring the sour to your cooking if you can.

Zhenjiang aromatic vinegar

On the east coast of China is Jiangsu province, which has some of the most fertile land in China. There you will find the city of Zhenjiang (about 170 miles inland from Shanghai, if you want to get some mental geographic bearings), which gives its name to China's most enduringly known grain vinegar. Zhenjiang is also known as Chinkiang, and so is its vinegar. It is sometimes called 'aromatic' because, well, it is. This is the almost inky black, mildly sweet, mellow and quite complex-flavoured vinegar that is the go-to choice for a Chinese dipping sauce. When Western recipes talk about Chinese black vinegar, this is what is meant. It has an acidity of around 4.5–5%, making it mild but still useful to cook with too, as maybe a meat marinade or tenderiser.

It is made by fermenting glutinous, sticky rice. Traditionally, its process would have been based upon the one described on page 202, where the fermentation is of a solid, not a liquid. The grain is mixed with a *qu* of yeasts and mould to turn its starch to sugar and then to alcohol.

Zhenjiang is distinctive as it uses two different types of *qu* starter, not just one. The alcohol mash would be seeded with vinegar from the last batch – known as the *pei* – and then stored in an urn for its acetic conversion. The urns would be covered with a rice straw lid (the Japanese go more for ceramic ones), and once the conversion to vinegar was complete they would be salted to stop any more reactions, and then allowed to age before leaching with water to produce the end result. The leaching stage of washing the 'vinegar' through with water is when charred rice would be added to give the Zhenjiang its distinctive dark colour and its flavour.

Modern Zhenjiang vinegar production is dominated by Hengshun, who have been making it since 1840, and they produce with what they describe as a 'traditional method but with innovated approach'. Their factory is also home to the region's Zhenjiang vinegar museum, and they are rightly proud of the heritage they are to some degree the international guardians of. Interestingly, they also produce aged versions of the Zhenjiang vinegars, and these more mature versions, which can be three years, six years or ten years old, come with more body and depth.

Zhenjiang Chinese black vinegar is really the only one of the regional Chinese vinegars that is widely available beyond China.

Shanxi aged vinegar

In the north of China is Shanxi province, home to another wonderful black vinegar. It is not nearly as well known outside of China as Zhenjiang is, but it is worth knowing about as you might get lucky and find it in some Chinese produce outlets. Or discover it in China itself, of course.

The main difference from Zhenjiang black vinegar is that the Shanxi version is made primarily of sorghum grain, with other grains such as wheat, rice or barley added as the maker wants; pea is also added for flavour differentiation. The basic way of making it follows the general rice and grain vinegar processes of the region, but it is what happens once it has become vinegar that is exciting.

After the acetic conversion is complete, some of the vinegar is smoked over fire. That is then mixed through with the unsmoked vinegar so that the smokiness is subtly underlying. The fascination for me doesn't end there. The vinegar is then aged outdoors for at least a year, which is typically much longer than most Zhenjiang black vinegar. Through the summer the heat of the sun will evaporate and intensify it, while in the winter the ice has to be removed. The result is a dark brown, richly flavoured, slightly smoky, pretty exciting-tasting, aged vinegar.

If you have any doubt as to how fundamental this vinegar is to the cuisine of the Shanxi province, bear in mind that in its capital of Taiyuan is the Ninghuafu black vinegar shop, where locals queue around the block to refill their multi-litre plastic bottles with their region's speciality vinegar.

Sichuan 'Baoning' black vinegar

We're heading now to the south-west of China, to Sichuan province, which is the home of so much iconic Szechuan food and where another famous and ancient Chinese black vinegar can be found. The city of Langzhong used to be known as 'Baoning', and that is the name by which this vinegar goes. It stands out from the others for being a herbal vinegar. Its main grain is wheat bran, but also in there are sixty or so Chinese traditional herbs. Too many for vinegar bottle labels to even think about listing, but you can expect to find elements of liquorice root, hawthorn and cinnamon. In the seventeenth century came tales of a Sichuan monk who lived to over 100 years of age, reputedly thanks to his daily dose of this vinegar.

It is typically mellower and sweeter than Zhenjiang vinegar, and ideal for use in Szechuan cooking – of course.

Fujian red vinegar

From the classic black vinegars to one with more of a reddish hue. It is a particular kind of yeast in the *qu* starter that gives this its red colour, and it hails from the Fujian province on China's south-east coast. There is another distinctive and exciting thing about this vinegar: in the traditional way of making it, it is aged in a dynamic way similar to that of sherry vinegar or *Tradizionale* balsamic, in that some of the vinegar is moved from urn to urn as it ages, to be at least three years old by the time it is 'ready'. Use as a dipping sauce for fish.

Qishan vinegar

Qishan City is in Shaanxi province (which slightly confusingly neighbours Shanxi province and its more famous black vinegar). In Shaanxi, this is the vinegar that their wonderful Qishan noodles would be impossible to imagine without. It is another sorghum grain vinegar.

Chishui 'sun' vinegar

This is a very old, very traditional-style black vinegar that is made in Guizhou province in the south of China. It is known as the 'sun' vinegar for its very long production process, which centres upon large numbers of urns of vinegar left out in the sun for years to allow the vinegar to mature and develop. Interestingly – and possibly worryingly for the future of this local speciality – a patent has been applied for that would enable Chishui sun vinegar to be made more quickly. This might mean that there is more of it produced and that it can be enjoyed further afield, but I only hope that at the same time the traditional processes can be protected.

IN THE KITCHEN
Chinese Black Vinegar

The Chinese black vinegars share similar uses:

- Try adding them to stir-fries, soups and noodle dishes.
- They make for an excellent dipping sauce, either on its own, mixed with grated ginger, or reduced by gently simmering it with mirin, soy sauce, sugar, water and spices of your choice to thicken, then left to cool. Try the latter with steamed buns or dumplings.

- I use them in meat recipes that can take the black vinegar's weight and benefit from its sweetness. Sometimes that is as a marinade, making use of the high acidity compared to other grain vinegars.
- Use as a finish or to deglaze a pan.
- They are also very good in sauces such as mayonnaise and roast meat gravy.

My final word here on Chinese grain vinegars is that while those mentioned are all versions of deeply coloured and flavoured vinegars, China does have a heritage of also producing the colourless or light-amber rice vinegar that would traditionally be made using polished rice, similar to Japanese *komesu*. Japan did, after all, learn how to do this from China. Such lightly coloured and flavoured vinegars are useful for some dishes, but I fear it will a be rare Chinese version that has been made in anything like traditional style. Most 'clear' Chinese rice vinegars – or at least the ones I have encountered – are made in an industrial way, and are in my view better swapped for a good Japanese one (or even a cider vinegar) for cooking with.

Korean

Korea also has a long heritage of producing vinegars, going back over 1,000 years. Like Japan, Korea was heavily influenced by China, and this shows in the production and use of its vinegars. On the one hand they are believed to have significant medicinal properties, while on the other hand, vinegars feature heavily in Korea's cuisine to balance out its bold flavours.

There were – and are – many Korean fruit vinegars such as peach, tangerine, persimmon and black raspberry, as well as flower vinegars and honey vinegars, but in particular there are grain vinegars. These are very similar in style to the Japanese grain vinegars. The lighter vinegars, which are clear or amber, would traditionally be made from polished rice, and the deeper coloured and flavoured versions from unpolished rice.

One South Korean grain vinegar deserves special mention: *ogok* ('5-grain') vinegar. Made from a mix of grains and to a traditional process that is very similar to that of the Chinese and Japanese grain vinegars mentioned earlier, the really interesting bit comes at the end of the acetic fermentation when the clay urn containing the vinegar is buried underground for over a year to mature, and for its flavours to both round out and develop.

Malt Vinegars

Every day, thousands of London commuters pass through the landscape of the city's vinegar heritage and past its remaining landmarks. I don't imagine many realise it as their train trundles through London Bridge, but this is the area that in the 1800s was home to the core of London's malt vinegar industry, to vinegar-makers who had been drawn there by the volume of breweries on that south side of the River Thames. For this is another well-worn story of vinegar production that is inextricably tied to the production of alcohol. Just as the French with their wine industry have wine vinegars and the Japanese have sake and rice vinegars, we Brits – and other nations with a tradition of beer drinking – have malt vinegars.

MALT VINEGAR PRODUCTION

Malt vinegar is barley that has been malted into beer or ale (without hops added), and then acetified into vinegar. Malting is not the most straightforward process, making it all the more remarkable just how ingenious the ancient Egyptians were for knowing – around 5,000 years ago – how to malt their native barley grain into beer that was known as *hequa*. Tomb-paintings of the time show their beer-making. Malt vinegar was its natural result, and one that happened quite quickly due to this being a beer that didn't keep for long.

It doesn't matter a jot to me that the ancient Egyptians did not have a full scientific comprehension of what was going on in that conversion; what matters is that they knew how to ferment barley into malted beer, and valued the vinegar that ensued as a preservative and a medicine. We now know that this is what was happening:

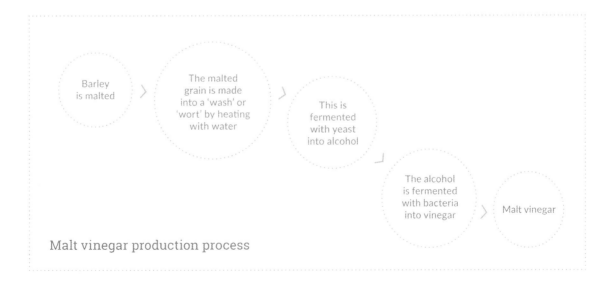

Barley is malted > The malted grain is made into a 'wash' or 'wort' by heating with water > This is fermented with yeast into alcohol > The alcohol is fermented with bacteria into vinegar > Malt vinegar

Malt vinegar production process

This apparent simplicity belies the choices that can be made at each stage that will affect the flavour profile of the vinegar. The very joy of having so few ingredients and stages gives the artful producer of malt vinegar (as with any vinegar) ample opportunity to craft something distinctive, flavourful and interesting.

The grain: barley is the grain of choice for brewing beer, but its starch isn't of itself ready and able to be fermented into alcohol. It has to be malted – hence the name – to release its starches and sugars that can then become alcohol. The process involves soaking the barley, allowing it to germinate so that the sugars are accessible, then applying heat to stop that germination. The management of that heat and the roasting that follows are what affects the character and colour of the malted beer, and therefore the malted vinegar.

As is always the way with vinegar, the characteristics and quality of the base ingredient are very important, and this is just as true with malted barley. Not all barleys or malts are the same by any means. There are many different varieties, few I think more exciting than Orkney's ancient 'bere' barley. (Pronounced 'bear' as in 'Paddington'.) It is not as high or fast yielding as more modern varieties, but has a distinctive flavour and heritage, and for obvious reasons is the malt barley of choice for Orkney Craft Vinegars (see page 268). It's easy for a malt vinegar-maker to choose a high-yielding modern varietal of barley, but the flavour will be flat in comparison. I remember tasting the wort of Orkney bere before it was fermented into alcohol – when it was just the malted grain heated with water. It was so delicious even at that stage that my friend and I were tempted to siphon some off to use as cooking liquor. There is no doubting how well that boded for the end result vinegar.

Roasted malt: I've already mentioned that it is the roasting stage of the malting process that affects the character and colour of beer and malt vinegar. So the clever vinegar-maker must decide what depth of both those things they want to end up with, and balance the roast accordingly.

The 'classic' British malt vinegar is rich brown – but it need not necessarily be so. It would be perfectly possible to make a pale, straw-coloured malt vinegar, yet that is not what the public expects. Even the Victorian British public demanded their malt vinegar to be brown. That can be achieved by using more intensely roasted barley, or by adding concentrated malt extract or (shudder) caramel.

I look forward to the day when we can enjoy greater variety of roasts of malt vinegars for different purposes.

Ageing: some interesting things happen when malt vinegar has the time to relax in a wooden barrel. As producers of sherry and balsamic vinegars know very well, the vinegar can mature in there and take on some elements of the wood that develop the vinegar's character. Echoing wine and balsamic vinegar ageing, however, commercially-minded producers are choosing to age the vinegar in huge tanks, which – even if they are wooden – will struggle to have an organoleptic impact on the vinegar's profile.

Look out for malt vinegars that have been aged for several months in wooden barrels (best of all former whisky or sherry barrels) because that is where the wood and ageing can play a role.

Pasteurising and filtering: I strongly believe that pasteurising and filtering also result in a loss of flavour – and a malt vinegar is all about flavour. Have a try of an unpasteurised, unfiltered one and enjoy.

Non-brewed condiment

Sometimes people tell me with a bit of embarrassment that they don't like vinegar. I try to take this in my stride and dig a little deeper into what they mean. And nine times out of ten, they mean they don't like chip-shop vinegar on their chip-shop chips. I can live with that. It is, after all, just one type of vinegar and used in a rather in-your-face way.

What I find much harder to live with is the nagging doubt that what they have been having and hating is not really malt vinegar at all. It could be the 'non-brewed condiment' that sadly too many chippies have on their counter: a manufactured mix of acetic acid, water, colourings and flavourings that is trying to emulate malt vinegar more cheaply. Of course they barely manage it. Of course nobody likes it. And of course that affects how people think of malt vinegar – because they believe that is what it is.

So please, do me, you, the malt vinegar industry and Britain's malt vinegar heritage a favour: if you find yourself in a chip-shop, ask what the vinegar is. Make sure it is actually vinegar. Know the difference.

BRITISH MALT VINEGAR

Britain's beer/ale vinegar replicates others across the world, in that it charts the peaks and troughs, twists and turns of the alcohol industry it stems from, and of society as a whole.

Barley has been brewed into beer in Britain since around the fifth century AD, when the Angles and the Saxons brought beer over with them. Through the medieval period, barley was a really important crop for food and for making ale. Rather than being made to be a fun drink, the ale was calorifically sustaining and a much better bet safety-wise than the filthy water of the time that too often carried diseases. Ale was being produced in significant quantities across the country, but was not being stored particularly securely, and – as the ancient Egyptians knew all too well – was apt to turn into vinegar that was known in the Middle English of the time as *alegar* (see page 17 for more on the etymology behind the words for vinegar).

Beer retained its popularity through Georgian times so that when industrialisation hit through the eighteenth and nineteenth centuries, beer-making was ripe for investment and development. Alongside greater understanding of how vinegar was made, and improved vinegar technologies, huge strides were made in building steam-powered breweries, developing yeasts and better movement of produce around the country.

The old method of movement of goods by horse and cart had meant that beer – and its vinegar – was seldom being traded far from where it was made. The advent of steam trains opened up a breadth of markets for breweries to grow into. There's a fascinating insight into this given by Hill, Evans & Co. in Worcester, founded in 1830 and one of the largest producers of vinegar in the world (if not the largest) in the nineteenth century, with a site that occupied seven acres and produced 9 million litres of malt vinegar each year in its heyday. From their position in the Midlands they were in a very good spot to get their wares out. To do it, they actually had a branch of railway line specifically built in 1872 to connect their malt vinegar distribution to the national rail network. A fact so very telling of the scale of the business and its importance.

Compare that level of production to modern-day Sarson's, the UK's go-to malt vinegar producer. They dominate the current market and as of recent reporting make 6 million litres of malt vinegar each year. So 6 million litres by modern-day Sarson's versus Hill, Evans & Co.'s 9 million litres in the mid-1800s. Staggering – especially when you realise that at the same time that Hill, Evans & Co. were making all this vinegar up in the Midlands (and supplying the vinegar that went into Lea & Perrins Worcestershire Sauce), on London's South Bank there were some other pretty big malt vinegar producers, too.

The famous names of Victorian London's malt vinegar production boom were centered upon the Bankside and Bermondsey area of London Bridge. There was Potts Vinegar Manufactory next door to the Barclay Perkins Brewery. Vickers & Slee who merged with Champions. Beaufoy Vinegar Factory, originally where Waterloo station is now, had to move to South Lambeth Road when the station was built. The white bell tower on top of the vat building remains a distinctive landmark.

British malt vinegar production in the twentieth century mirrored what happened to the nation's beer consumption, and it is not a happy tale from the producers' point of view. In 1913 there were 36 million barrels of beer drunk in Britain. The restrictions on alcohol during World War I led to that plummeting to 13 million barrels in 1919, and it has struggled ever since to get back to its prewar height. This was duly accompanied by a steady decline in the number of malt vinegar manufacturers as the century proceeded. It became a saga of malt vinegar mergers and closures: Crosse & Blackwell took over Sarson's in 1929, along with Champion & Slee. They then merged with Beaufoy (by then Beaufoy Grimble & Co.) in 1932 to become British Vinegars. Hill, Evans & Co. were out of business by 1965. Nestlé took over British Vinegars in 1979.

It is fascinating how in barely 200 years the British malt vinegar industry went from being rough and ready and localised, to an explosion of expansion, productivity and demand, to a decline that only the Sarson's brand weathered well.

Within the British Vinegars consolidation Sarson's managed to keep their brand name on the bottles. It is still there, even as ownership of the brand has continued to change hands between big food producers. They understand very well just how commercially strong the Sarson's name is. Production in London only ceased relatively recently in 1991 – lucky modern-day Londoners who have Maltings Place SE1 as their address are actually living in the renovated Sarson's vinegar works – and moved to a production base in Greater Manchester, currently as part of the Japanese company Mizkan.

And so Sarson's remains the iconic British vinegar, not just the iconic *malt* vinegar. They take pride in retaining aspects of the traditional malt vinegar production, and I doff my cap to them for the way they have been an indefatigable protector of not just their brand but the mainstream presence of British malt vinegar in recent years. Even if it is mainly – or only – thought of as an accompaniment to fish and chips. At its heart the process they still use follows the key basic principles shared with their Victorian vinegar-making forebears.

A MODERN REVIVAL IN MALT VINEGAR

I say with relief and joy that in recent years Britain is starting to rediscover its malt vinegar heritage, and there are some small producers coming through: craftsman vinegar-makers who are grabbing a moment of revived interest in our nation's food heritage and in quality produce, and making discerning choices in key areas of malt vinegar production.

That revival is being emulated in other malt-vinegar producing nations to whom I now need to make my apologies for having pretty much ignored them in my malt vinegar history precis. My only defence is in being so very proud of the vinegar heritage of my nation. That said, I am fully aware that there are some cracking malt vinegars to be had elsewhere too – including Austria, Germany and Canada.

Canada

Canada is in the top four or five countries producing barley, depending on the yield each year. There is a long history of beer brewing in the country, ever since European settlers first introduced Canada to beer.

Through the 1800s, more and more breweries opened up in Canada, with many around the Toronto area of Ontario in particular. Toronto changed significantly through the nineteenth century from being a largely agricultural area to embracing trade and manufacturing. Its population almost doubled over the period of a decade thanks to immigration. The beer breweries played a fundamental role in this evolution, helping to draw people to Toronto. The many nearby rivers and creeks gave the breweries ready access to water as an ingredient and to power the mills, and the growing population was thirsty.

Malt vinegar was a productive sideline for these breweries, and a useful one to have in their back pocket when the Canadian Prohibition of 1918 hit hard. Some, such as the Toronto Brewing and Malting Company, which reinvented itself as the Toronto Vinegar Company, were able to capitalise on that by switching the focus of the brewery from beer to malt vinegar.

Canadian Prohibition lasted only a couple of years, and in the period afterwards the revived Canadian beer industry came to be dominated by a very few big commercial producers. Only more recently has a craft beer revival come round, and on the back of that the nation is rediscovering its love and heritage for malt vinegars, too.

IN THE KITCHEN
Malt Vinegar

For fish and chips, of course, but then so much more besides. A mayonnaise made with malt vinegar takes on fabulous depth and the same applies for using it in many other finishing sauces. It's a great choice for a meaty gravy that can take its strength of flavour. I suggest using it at the beginning of cooking a casserole for extra depth, or it is great for pickling. Really it is fabulous anywhere that can make use of its rich flavour and mellow under-notes.

Sam Britten of Orkney Craft Vinegar cooked a version of this when I was visiting, and he has happily allowed me to include my way of doing it here. He – and I – make it with his 'bere' malt vinegar, which is produced using Orkney's ancient bere grain. It is one of the few examples of Britain's ancient vinegar being revived by an artisan.

The buttery sauce and fatty scallops are gorgeously tempered by the sharpness of the vinegar and its sweet, malty note. A few barely dressed rocket leaves are all else that is needed.

Scallops in Malted Butter Sauce

16 shelled scallops
2 tablespoons olive oil
140g butter
75ml malt vinegar
salt and freshly ground
   black pepper

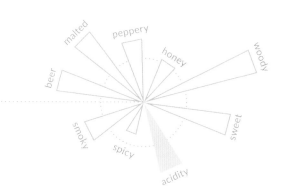

serves 4

Pat dry and season the scallops. Heat the oil in a large frying pan, then sit the scallops in the pan. Turn them after 2 minutes, when they should have taken on a gentle brown colour. Give them another minute, then add half the butter. Let it melt and, as it does, use it to baste the scallops; you will need to gently tilt the pan.

The butter will quickly turn a nutty brown, and at this point pour over 50ml of the vinegar. Cook for another 30 seconds, then lift the scallops out. Turn up the heat, add the remaining butter and vinegar and allow to bubble, stirring all the time, to reduce to a lovely sauce. Pour over the scallops and serve with a grinding of pepper over the top.

VINEGAR VARIATION
Try a sherry vinegar.

Parched peas are a tradition of my ancestral county of Lancashire – black peas cooked until almost mushy, then smothered in lots of salt and malt vinegar. They're still often enjoyed on Bonfire Night, and I remember my mum telling me about having them as a little girl in the late 1940s, when it was her town's turn for 'Wakes week'. That was the holiday the Lancashire cotton mill towns took in turn, originally so the mills could close for cleaning and repair. They may not have travelled far for the holidays but she could look forward to a cup of parched peas (sometimes served with crispy bacon).

All of which is to say that black peas and malt vinegar are a great combo, and one which I think does not just need to be filed under nostalgia. Hence this recipe, which layers up the classic recipe pairing with fresh notes of lemongrass and mint.

Parched Peas with Bacon, Rocket and Lemongrass

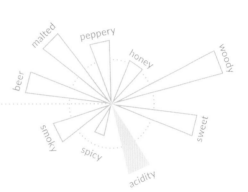

150g black peas (also known as black badgers or carlin peas)

25g unsalted butter

1 tablespoon olive oil

150g diced pancetta

1 trimmed lemongrass stalk

4 tablespoons malt vinegar

150g rocket (or watercress, baby spinach, or a combination of leaves)

6 sprigs of mint

60g Parmesan cheese

salt and freshly ground black pepper

Serves 4 as a lunch or starter

Soak the peas overnight in plenty of water. Drain and rinse them, then cover in plenty of fresh water and simmer with a lid partially on until fully tender. They will take about an hour, but start to check after 45 minutes – you want them soft but not collapsed. Keep back a cup of the cooking liquid, then drain the peas.

Heat the butter and oil in a large frying pan and add the diced pancetta to fry it off. Finely chop the bottom half of the lemongrass stalk and add to the pancetta pan. When the pancetta is nearly crisp, stir through the cooked black peas, malt vinegar, 2 tablespoons of the reserved cooking liquid and lots of salt and pepper. Once the pancetta is properly crisp, turn off the heat and put a lid on the pan, leaving it to sit in its own steam and cool down.

Arrange a bed of the leaves on a serving plate. Spoon over the pancetta and black pea mix. Finish with torn mint leaves and shavings or crumblings of the Parmesan. For a heartier lunch, serve with crusty bread that is toasted and rubbed with olive oil and garlic.

VINEGAR VARIATION

Not many choices here, but a maple vinegar could be a superb alternative.

A meal for a winter's night, with plenty of mash and mustard, and a glass of something red and hearty. The gravy is where the malt vinegar element comes in and is well worth knowing about for toad-in-the-hole or any other sausage-related meals.

Oven-baked Pork and Venison Meatballs

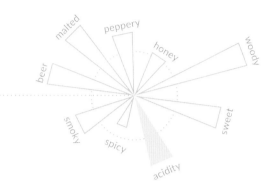

FOR THE MEATBALLS
400g pork mince
400g venison mince
3 tablespoons olive oil
2 medium red onions, diced
2 sprigs of thyme
½ teaspoon ground cloves
**2 tablespoons cherry vinegar
or red wine vinegar**
1 garlic clove, minced
80g dried breadcrumbs
(not panko)
salt and freshly ground
black pepper

FOR THE GRAVY
20g butter
3 onions, sliced
1½ tablespoons soft dark
brown sugar
4 tablespoons malt vinegar
2 tablespoons plain flour
750ml beef stock

serves 6

Mix together the pork and venison mince in a bowl, then set aside.

Heat 2 tablespoons of the oil in a large frying pan and gently cook the onions until soft and only just taking on some colour. As they cook, add some salt and the thyme sprigs. When the onions are done, add the ground cloves, cherry or red wine vinegar and the minced garlic. Cook for another few minutes to soften the garlic and reduce the liquid, then set aside to cool.

Once the onion mix is at room temperature, remove the thyme stalks and combine the onion mixture with the mince. Add the breadcrumbs, season well, and use your hands to mix it all together. Roll into 18 walnut-sized balls and put them in the fridge to firm up for at least 1 hour.

In the meantime, make the gravy. Melt the butter in a medium saucepan and cook the onions slowly until softened and starting to colour. Stir in the sugar and malt vinegar and let the vinegar evaporate, its flavour seeping into the onions. Take the pan off the heat and stir in the flour.

In a separate pan, warm the stock. Return the pan with the onions to a medium heat and, spoonful-by-spoonful, stir in the warm stock. Simmer gently for 20 minutes or so to reduce and thicken to a good gravy consistency. Season to taste.

The meatballs and gravy can both be prepared ahead of time and stored in the fridge for up to 3 days, as long as you return them to room temperature before baking. When you are ready to eat, preheat the oven to 220°C/200°C Fan/Gas Mark 7. Pour

VINEGAR VARIATION
I cannot in good conscience give an alternative to malt vinegar here. OK, maybe a balsamic or maple vinegar.

the remaining tablespoon of olive oil into a roasting tray and put it into the oven to get hot. Then sit the meatballs in the tray with gaps between them and bake for 20 minutes.

Warm the gravy on the stove, and at the end of the meatballs' 20 minutes cooking time, pour the gravy over the meatballs in the roasting tray. Reduce the oven temperature to 180°C/160°C Fan/Gas Mark 4 and return the tray to the oven for 10 minutes before serving.

The very essence of the good old British chip shop is its chips doused in salt and malt vinegar. Well, this recipe has all these basic elements in the form of a rather neat roasted new potato. Very nearly as tasty cold as they are hot.

Salt and Vinegar Roasted New Potatoes

16 new potatoes
3 tablespoons olive oil
2 tablespoons chopped
   flat-leaf parsley
malt vinegar, to taste
salt

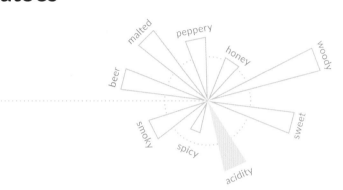

serves 4

Bring a pan of water to the boil and cook the potatoes for 10 minutes until only just becoming tender. Remove from the water and let them sit in the empty pan for a minute or so to dry them out. You can prepare to this point ahead of time.

Preheat the oven to 220°C/200°C Fan/Gas Mark 7.

Sit the potatoes on a baking tray and score a cross in each one, cutting quite deep but being sure not to go all the way through. Use a pastry brush to spread the oil over each potato.

Roast the potatoes for 25–30 minutes until nicely crisped and golden. When they come out, sprinkle liberally with salt and vinegar and scatter over the chopped parsley. Serve, with the vinegar bottle on the table – how much vinegar you choose to have on a potato is a very personal choice.

VINEGAR VARIATION
Malt vinegar is the chip-shop classic, but you could go for red wine vinegar instead, or vermouth vinegar.

You know that feeling of over-indulgence of meat and carbs at the Christmas feasting table? If so, then these are just what is needed, right at that moment, to pep up the palate no end. Bacon is wrapped around prunes as per a normal devil, but these devils are a little bit different, having been pickled for a week or so in cloves, cinnamon, coriander seeds and lemon. It turns them into just the best thing for Christmas.

Pickled Devils on Horseback

250g caster sugar
200ml malt vinegar
3 cloves
1 teaspoon coriander seeds
1 cinnamon stick
½ teaspoon allspice berries
2 broad strips of lemon zest
1 star anise
1 bay leaf
24 Agen prunes
12 rashers of streaky bacon

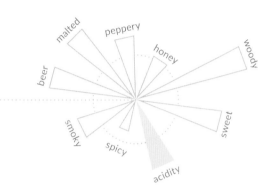

makes 24

Put all the ingredients, except the prunes and bacon, into a medium saucepan. Add 200ml of water, bring to the boil, then reduce the heat and let it gently simmer for 15 minutes. Set aside to cool.

Put the prunes into a sterilised pickling jar. Pour over the cooled pickling liquid and make sure the prunes are totally covered. Seal and set aside for at least a week, or up to 2 weeks.

To make the devils on horseback: preheat the oven to 190°C/170°C Fan/Gas Mark 5.

Lift the prunes out of their pickling liquid and remove the stones. Cut each bacon rasher in half and wrap each prune in a strip of streaky bacon. Secure with a cocktail stick, place in a roasting tin and cook for 15 minutes.

VINEGAR VARIATION
Try using a white wine vinegar or a red wine vinegar.

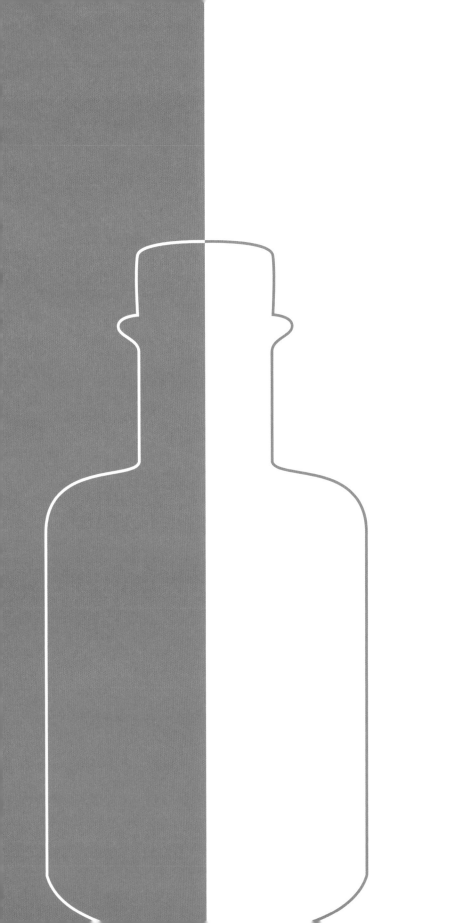

EXTRACTED AND INFUSED VINEGARS

Extracted Vinegars

HONEY VINEGAR

In the section on fruit vinegars, I made a claim that those were (probably) the very first, the very oldest types of vinegar. Honey vinegar could be a contender for that title, though. It is known that the production and drinking of honey wine goes back to the ancient Greeks, and possibly earlier. There is evidence of honey vinegar in northern China around the same period, too. And right there already I have touched upon one of the most glorious things about honey vinegar: it is a vinegar that has long been truly international.

Look at the history of the Romans, the Chinese, the Spanish, the Celts and many more, and you will find honey. And where there is honey there are people fermenting it into alcoholic honey wine, with vinegar the inevitable next step. I am saying 'honey wine' when the word I really want to use is 'mead', because to me as a Brit that is what our heritage honey wine is. But I know it might not be yours. Honey wine in different times and places could be ambrosia (Greece), hydromel (France), ogol (Ethiopia) or many others, reflecting again its worldwide spread.

All of which makes your chances of encountering interesting honey vinegars in interesting places very high. For all of them, the honey will have first been diluted before the alcoholic fermentation can take place. Think how sweet honey is, and you can imagine that if left in its natural state and not diluted it would take a very long time for the sugars to be converted to alcohol. Often honey vinegar-makers will mention the attributes of the particular water they have used in making the honey wine, and this is why. When there are so few ingredients, the quality of every one of them matters.

From honey wine, the conversion to vinegar is typically done in quite a traditional way. This is in part due to the smaller volume of honey vinegar that is produced. It is not like making large commercial quantities of wine vinegar, cider vinegar or rice vinegar. Honey vinegar isn't a product on that scale so will often be made in small batches.

I often think the surprising thing about honey vinegar is how little like honey it can taste. Which I don't necessarily mean as a bad thing. The honey has gone on quite a journey before it becomes vinegar, and on its way necessarily loses much of its overriding sweetness. The resulting flavours are subtle – of honey, with notes of the varietal of the particular nectar. A vinegar from robustly-flavoured buckwheat honey will, for instance, be wonderfully different from a vinegar made with something light like orange blossom as its honey base. All of which is to say, don't be drawn to honey vinegar for a presumption of sweetness. Be drawn to honey vinegar for its underlying essence of honey, for a vinegar with a rounded flavour that is very versatile.

That is the case for twice-fermented honey vinegar, anyway. But given the increasing appetite in the vinegar market for bitter-sweet vinegars, it is perhaps inevitable that there are other styles coming through where honey plays a different role.

Some producers are introducing honey into vinegar either at the acetic fermentation stage of making, say, a wine vinegar, or even at the end once the vinegar conversion is complete. The result is a vinegar with its honey much more flavour-forward and, of course, sweeter. Do note, though, that the overall acidity of the vinegar is likely to be lowered when the honey is added. Sometimes these are labelled as 'condiment' vinegars. They are supremely delicious for all kinds of sauces, salads and drizzling, but it is a factor to bear in mind if you intend to do something like pickle or escabeche with it.

IN THE KITCHEN
Honey Vinegar

This is such a wonderfully useful vinegar. It can be used wherever a cider vinegar or white wine vinegar might have been, and is a decent alternative to rice vinegar and to the lighter fruit vinegars. So I am talking about sauces, salad dressings, marinades, pickles, meringues, drinking vinegar shrubs and more besides.

This is (currently, at least) my favourite vinegar to add to a gin and tonic – just a few dashes will do.

MAPLE VINEGAR

There is a wonderful world of vinegars produced from the sweet sap of trees, and the bridge to that from honey vinegar is maple vinegar – meaning vinegar made from maple syrup that is double-fermented into vinegar. I find maple vinegar does rather better than honey vinegar in terms of retaining its original characteristics. Maple vinegars have a distinct, pleasing sweetness and caramel tones, with lovely woody flavours and smells.

It is a vinegar I have so far only encountered in Canada, which obviously makes sense given the country's associations with maple syrup. Around 70 per cent of the world's maple syrup production is in Quebec. (Vermont State in the north-east of the USA is also a significant producer, so I have hopes of finding maple vinegar there, too.) The syrup is made from the sap of various kinds of maple tree. I don't mind admitting that prior to discovering maple vinegar I hadn't given too much thought as to how this store-cupboard staple is produced, but now that I have it is fascinating: the trees store starch in their trunks and roots during the winter, and as the weather warms that starch becomes sugar and rises up the tree in the sap. Early European settlers to Canada and the north-east of America learned from the indigenous peoples there just when and how to drill small holes into the trees to allow the sap to run out and be collected. After that it is just a matter of heating the sap to evaporate the water and reduce it to a concentrated sweet syrup.

That is the traditional process of maple-syrup-making, anyway. It will probably come as little surprise to you that the driving forces of business have resulted in producers finding ways to extract more of the sap at a faster rate and turning it into sellable syrup as quickly as possible. Flavour will never be the winner under such pressures, understandable as they are.

To turn maple syrup into vinegar it has to first be diluted, just as for fermenting honey. The concentration of sugar is otherwise too high and it would take too long for the sugars to convert to alcohol. The pathway to vinegar is the familiar one: sugar is fermented to alcohol; alcohol is fermented to vinegar.

When tasting a maple vinegar, the key things to look out for will be the quality of the maple syrup that was the starting ingredient, and clues to the traditional methods of its production. I think barrel-ageing can play a key role too in developing the flavour of a maple vinegar.

IN THE KITCHEN
Maple Vinegar

It is great as a dish-finisher, for ceviche, over desserts, into cocktails or for making shrubs.

If you are lucky enough to get hold of a really good maple vinegar with a great balance of sweetness and acidity, multi-layered flavour and slightly viscous texture, think about using it as an alternative to balsamic vinegar.

COCONUT AND PALM VINEGAR

How I would love to be able to write that my first encounter with coconut vinegar came via the romance of a walk along a beach in Goa, with coconut trees all around and a meeting with a local toddy-tapper. The truth is actually closer to having a vindaloo in England – but the images those two tales conjure up are not necessarily as far apart as they might seem.

Vindaloo as a traditional dish of Goa has its origins in the cooking influences of Portugal, which for many years had the governance of this beautiful state on the western coast of India. To many Brits, the mention of vindaloo sends a shiver down the spine, with memories of overly spiced curry-house versions. As British-Indian cooking has matured in recent years, so I urge you to put any such thoughts out of your head. True vindaloo is made by marinating meat in spices and vinegar, then cooking it in the marinade along with other elements of your choosing, such as tamarind, onions and ginger. The vinegar is a very important part of the dish, acting as a tenderiser of the meat via the marinade and contributing to the sweet-and-sour flavours.

Locally, traditionally, the vinegar used for vindaloo and many other Goan dishes would be coconut vinegar. In the Philippines, too, where there is also an abundance of coconut palm trees, there is a culinary culture of using coconut vinegar

Coconut-water vinegar

A sort of side note concerning rarely-found coconut-water vinegar: this is not the same thing as coconut vinegar. Coconut vinegar is – as mentioned – double-fermented sap from the tree. Coconut-water vinegar is double-fermented coconut water, a way of using what is often considered locally as a waste material from the coconut. It is most likely to be found in Africa as a way of maximising the value of the coconut trees' produce.

(known as *sukang tuba* – *suka* meaning vinegar). It is every vinegar story across every nation: vinegar magicked up from whatever the local crops are.

It is made from the sap – also known as the 'toddy' – of the coconut palm tree. Traditionally, the sap would be collected by a toddy-tapper, who'd climb the tree to open the vein that carries the sap up the tree and attach an earthenware pot to collect the sap that drains out. This is not as dramatic or damaging as it may sound. The vein is closed off for the extremes of the afternoon so that the tree has time to recover its lost fluids.

The sugar in the sap is fermented into alcohol – in Goa this is the *feni* spirit that is served up neat over ice with a slice of lime or in cocktails. What follows is the acetic fermentation into vinegar, and the traditional Goan way of doing that would be to leave the coconut palm alcohol in an earthenware pot sealed with muslin and thick clay. It is left completely untouched for several months to allow bacterial nature to take its course and produce vinegar. Much modern coconut vinegar-making is, of course, rather more technological than that.

The resulting vinegar is clear, maybe slightly cloudy, but basically of no colour. It has a slightly sweet smell, but not in a coconut-y way. Nor is the flavour particularly resonant of coconuts. Not at all, actually, on the first tasting, but I do find the coconut builds slightly as a pleasing after-taste. Mainly this is a sharp-tasting vinegar with little roundness to it.

'Other' palm vinegars

The coconut palm is by no means the only type of palm tree that is used to make vinegar. I started this section with coconut vinegar as I think that is the one with the highest profile. But it is not the oldest, the one with the highest production or indeed with the most culinary uses in some of the regions where it is produced.

The ancient Babylonians were making vinegar from the sap of the date palm tree many thousands of years ago. Along with the juices of the pressed date fruits, date palm sap was fermented into a wine and then into a vinegar for cooking and preserving. Date palm vinegar is still produced in modern Middle East countries where date trees are prolific.

I think there are two other palm vinegars particularly worth being aware of. Firstly, vinegar from the nipa palm that in the Philippines is known as *sukang Paombong*. *Suka* for 'vinegar', and *Paombong* for the town in the Bulacan region where it is a speciality and of huge importance to the local economy, given that this is one of the most popular Filipino vinegars for cooking with. It is a little cloudy to look at, with subtle citrus notes through it. Secondly, there is the vinegar from the palmyra palm, which is also known as the toddy palm. Somewhat confusingly so, as toddy is the generic term for saps from other palms too.

(If you are wondering whether this kind of toddy is anything to do with the 'hot toddy' drink so often reached for in the face of the British cold, then I hope you will indulge a non-vinegar side-note: when Sri Lanka was Ceylon, and Ceylon was under British governance, the British colonials got rather a taste for the alcoholic drink made from fermenting toddy sap, which was locally called *tārī*. Versions of the word and the spirit-based recipe were in time appropriated by the Brits back home.)

For all the palm vinegars the basic principles of the collection of the sap, its fermentation and the resulting vinegar are very similar to those outlined earlier for coconut vinegar. And just to be clear: palm-oil trees, about which there is rightly so much worry in terms of environmental and social impact, are a different type of palm tree altogether.

IN THE KITCHEN
Coconut and Palm Vinegars

Coconut vinegar is an important ingredient in Goa for soups, salads and speciality meat dishes, such as the xacuti and sorpotel curries – and, yes, vindaloo too. To make any of these without coconut vinegar, the best alternatives would be cider vinegar, malt vinegar or rice vinegar.

In the Philippines, coconut vinegar is mixed with chilli, lime or kumquat juice and soy to make a sauce that can be used in myriad ways – and is especially good over pork.

Use these vinegars for all manner of Filipino and Goan cooking. Then beyond that for meat marinades and pickling where you want acidity for tenderising or preserving, but without especial call for flavour.

SUGAR CANE VINEGAR

One of the many things that intrigues me about vinegar is the sheer resourcefulness and will with which it is, and has been, made around the world. Vinegar appears wherever there is a crop that contains sugar – making it more of a surprise than it should be to realise that sugar cane itself is made into vinegar.

Sugar cane vinegar can be found across the top sugar-cane-producing nations, and few more so than the Philippines, which is in the top ten of countries producing sugar cane. Sugar cane is a hugely important crop for the Philippines, behind only bananas and pineapples in cash terms. It matters to its export economy and it matters to the significant numbers of people who work in the industry. Little wonder, then, that given the Filipino cooking culture makes significant use of vinegar, it also embraces sugar cane vinegars of different types.

Sukang Iloko (or '*Iloco*')

This is a darkly coloured cane vinegar, ranging from dark yellow to golden brown. It is a speciality of the Ilocos region (hence the name) in the north-west of the Philippines, but its popularity and use spreads across the country. It is made from molasses as the by-product of sugar refining – another example of the inspiring waste-not-want-not approach to produce that vinegar traditionally plays a role in.

The thick molasses are first fermented to *basi* wine. Traditionally, that would be done in clay jars sealed with banana leaves. Botanicals and fruits would be added, and if left to ferment beyond turning to alcohol the *basi* would in due course become aromatic *sukang Iloko* vinegar. Its profile sits somewhere between a cider vinegar and sherry vinegar.

It is used in so much of Filipino cooking, from the national dish of *adobo* (meat, seafood or vegetables marinated in a mix of *sukang Iloko*, soy sauce and peppercorns, then cooked in the marinade), to *empanadas* and salad dressings.

When buying a dark cane vinegar it pays to read the label on the bottle. Sometimes caramel is added to give colour and sweetness. I imagine there could be an argument that caramel is made from sugar too, so what's the difference? The difference is huge. Adding any ingredient at the end to modify a vinegar is only done because the maker is not happy with how the vinegar turned out. Inevitably it is a lower-quality vinegar – though it could still be tasty and useful to you.

Sukang Maasim

This vinegar is colourless, clear and maybe slightly cloudy (in lesser-quality versions, 'cloudifiers' are added at the end to achieve this).

It is a sharper, flatter sugar cane vinegar than *sukang Iloko*. As I have just said, that one is made from the dark molasses that result from turning sugar cane into sugar. When you think what molasses are, the depth that comes with its vinegar is easily imagined. By contrast, *sukang Maasim* is made as a result of the sugar cane being pressed for its juice and sap, which becomes syrup and is double-fermented into vinegar. The sweetness is fermented away to give a not especially interesting vinegar. That is easy for me to say with a wealth of vinegar options at my disposal, of course. Without those, I daresay the appeal of *sukang Maasim* for preserving or basic cooking would grow significantly.

IN THE KITCHEN
Sugar Cane Vinegars

Sukang Maasim can be made into a Filipino-style dipping sauce for deep-fried prawns or grilled meats, with chopped chillis and spices stirred into it. Or use it as a marinade for meats, or as an alternative for lighter rice vinegars.

The deeper *sukang Iloko* is also good as a dipping sauce – maybe mixed with sugar, soy sauce, garlic and chilli for a typically Filipino condiment. Think also of *sukang Iloko* for Filipino *adobo*, *empanadas*, meat stews and salad dressings. And it can be reduced over heat in a pan to a syrup and used as a sweet glaze, similar to a balsamic. Reduced or not, try it as you might a balsamic or fruit vinegar.

There are lots of choices with this shrub. Drink it soft, by using it as a cordial and topping up with sparkling water or ginger ale. Drink it hard, by mixing a splash into a whisky or gin cocktail. Or use it to oomph-up a less-than-brilliant sparkling wine by pouring a teaspoon or so of shrub into a glass and topping up with the wine.

The shrub's mix of sweetness, fruit and acidity also makes this a good choice for using as a dessert sauce. Try it drizzled over a steamed chocolate or ginger pudding, over a slice of Madeira cake or over ice cream.

Pear and Thyme Shrub

800g ripe pears
150g caster sugar
250ml honey vinegar
6 bushy sprigs of thyme

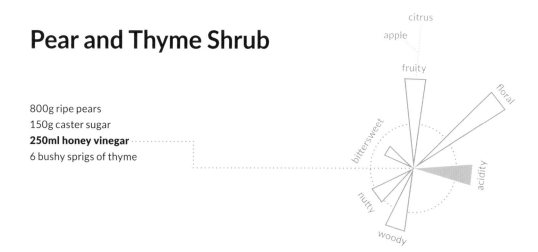

makes approx. 300ml

Peel, core and chop the pears. Put the fruit flesh into a bowl and press at it with a masher to start to break it down. Stir through the sugar, cover and set aside for 2 days in the fridge.

After the first day of maceration, pour the vinegar into a non-corrosive jug or bowl, pull the leaves off the thyme sprigs and stir those into the vinegar. Cover and set aside in the fridge.

Once the fruit has had 2 days of releasing its juices, strain the pears through a sieve into a bowl. Push at the fruit to get as much juice out as you can (the fruit left behind in the sieve makes a great puree for desserts or to have with yoghurt). The strained liquid will be thicker than you want for a shrub, so strain again, ideally through a finer sieve or one lined with muslin. As it strains, pour over the vinegar and thyme mix and leave for 30 minutes or so for it all to strain through together.

VINEGAR VARIATION
Try using cider vinegar or white wine vinegar.

Transfer the fruit syrup and infused vinegar shrub to a sterilised glass bottle and store for at least 3 days in the fridge before using.

Cucumbers in season have a surprisingly intense flavour given that they are 95 per cent water. Out of season they can taste like little other than water. So buy the best you can as seasonally as you can, keeping an eye out for the shorter 'ridge' cucumbers, which have a knobbly skin and are particularly good. The vinegar's job here is to bring out as much flavour as possible to produce a deliciously summery accompaniment to warm-weather chicken salads or salmon – especially the pickled salmon on page 162.

Minted Cucumber Ribbons

1 ridge cucumber or
  ½ regular cucumber
1½ teaspoons
  nasturtium vinegar
¾ teaspoon salt
1 tablespoon chopped
  mint leaves

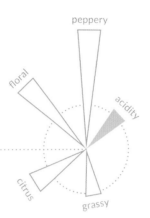

serves 4

Use a vegetable peeler to remove a strip of skin from one edge of the cucumber. Discard (or eat it, or use it to garnish a gin and tonic), then keep peeling ribbons of flesh from the same area, which should now be edged by a thin strip of green skin. Go as far as the seeds, then repeat on the opposite side of the cucumber. Do the same on the remaining two sides of the cucumber, then pile all the ribbons into a bowl. Sprinkle over the vinegar and salt, and toss everything together with your fingers.

Set aside at room temperature for 10 minutes or so for the flavours to meld together. Then sprinkle over the chopped mint, toss again and serve.

VINEGAR VARIATION
Any herb-infused vinegar or slightly sweet white wine vinegar (such as Moscatel) will work very well, as would a champagne vinegar. A light rice vinegar is an interesting option, too.

Honey vinegar is mixed with actual honey here, for a dressing that gives a really sweet bite and is excellent with this slaw of red and white cabbage, fennel, horseradish and herbs. Serve with sausages, chicken, cold roast beef sandwiches or fish.

Honeyed Slaw of Red and White Cabbage

300g red cabbage (approx.
    ½ cabbage), finely sliced
150g white cabbage (approx.
    ⅓ cabbage), finely sliced
1 fennel bulb, trimmed and
    finely sliced
3 tablespoons freshly
    grated horseradish
125ml honey vinegar
100ml extra virgin olive oil
1½ tablespoons honey
a handful of fresh leafy
    herbs, such as basil,
    tarragon, dill, chervil,
    parsley or a combination
salt

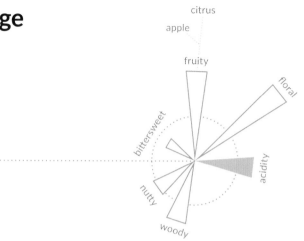

serves 4–6

Place the cabbage and fennel in a large mixing bowl.

In a separate bowl, whisk together the grated horseradish, vinegar, oil, honey, and a couple of good pinches of salt. Pour over the cabbage and fennel and toss well. Set aside for anything between 30 minutes and overnight (if you have the time – and in the fridge if overnight), then tear in the herbs and toss before serving.

VINEGAR VARIATION

Use cider vinegar, white wine vinegar, rice vinegar, or any fruit vinegar you think would pair well with the veg.

Sweetly spiced, or spicily sweet – either way, choose young, perky summer carrots for this dish rather than the slightly more weathered winter ones. They carry their own sweetness, which is emphasised by the raisins and sharply balanced with the vinegar and spices of the vinaigrette. Be sure to keep back a handful of the leafy green carrot tops if there are any, to add before serving.

This is less of a meal-type salad, and more of a 'to go with things' kind of salad, maybe as part of a tapas-style lunch or with a piece of fish.

Sweetly Spiced Carrot Salad

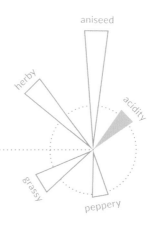

3½ tablespoons
   tarragon vinegar
½ teaspoon ground cinnamon
¼ teaspoon ground cumin
50g raisins or sultanas
450g carrots
75ml rapeseed oil, or olive oil
1½ teaspoons honey
a large handful of leafy carrot
   tops, or flat-leaf parsley,
   roughly chopped
salt

serves 4–6

Mix together the vinegar with the cinnamon and cumin in a bowl. Stir in the raisins or sultanas and set aside for 10 minutes.

Meanwhile, use a mandoline or vegetable peeler to slice the carrots into thin ribbons in a large bowl.

Drain the spiced vinegar into a separate bowl. Toss the soaked raisins into the carrots.

Make a vinaigrette by whisking the oil into the spiced vinegar along with the honey and more salt than you otherwise might. Add to the carrots and toss round.

Add the carrot tops or parsley to the salad bowl, check the seasoning, then set aside for at least 10 minutes at room temperature before serving.

VINEGAR VARIATION
Another herb-infused vinegar such as bay or thyme would be lovely, or go for honey vinegar, rice vinegar, coconut vinegar or cider vinegar.

Here, the mackerel is briefly marinated in an infused vinegar, then griddled and piled up on dressed watercress with some toasted flaked almonds over the top. I'd have this with a dollop of mayonnaise (see page 45) and maybe some buttery new potatoes.

Griddled Fresh Mackerel

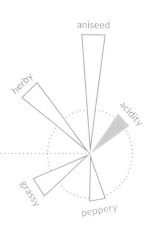

3 tablespoons
   tarragon vinegar
5 tablespoons extra virgin
   olive oil
4 fresh mackerel fillets
   (so 2 whole fish, filleted)
15g flaked almonds
a large handful of watercress or
   other leaves
1 tablespoon chopped
   flat-leaf parsley
salt and freshly ground
   black pepper

serves 2

Combine the vinegar and oil in a bowl with some salt and a good grinding of pepper.

Slash the skin of the mackerel fillets three times, then lay them in a shallow bowl and pour the marinade over. Set aside for a few hours in the fridge (or at least as long as it takes you to get ready for griddling).

Lightly toast the flaked almonds in a hot, dry frying pan for a minute or two until golden. Set aside.

Get a griddle pan good and hot, then lift the fillets out of the marinade and lay them skin-side down in the griddle. Turn after 3 minutes and give them another 3 minutes. Alternatively, you can cook them under a grill or on a barbecue.

As the fish is cooking, dress the watercress with a couple of tablespoons of the fish marinade; taste the marinade first in case you want to add more seasoning, oil or vinegar.

VINEGAR VARIATION
Use any other herb-
infused vinegar such
as bay or dill. Garlic or
chilli vinegar would work
well, as would a white
wine vinegar (especially
Moscatel), a red wine
vinegar, vermouth
vinegar, rice vinegar or
apple cider vinegar.

Arrange the dressed watercress on serving plates. Sit the cooked fillets on top of the leaves, drizzling over any juices left behind in the griddle pan. Finish by sprinkling over the chopped parsley and flaked almonds.

Mignonette sauce is a classic accompaniment to raw oysters. Traditionally, it is made with red wine vinegar mixed with shallots and cracked black pepper. But I am not that keen on pieces of shallot with my oyster as it slips down my throat, so prefer to infuse the vinegar with the shallots first to take on their sweetness and flavour, then strain the shallots out for serving.

Oysters with Mignonette Sauce

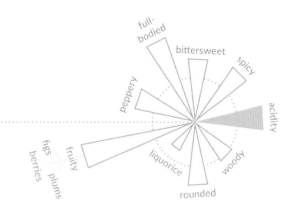

12 oysters

MIGNONETTE SAUCE
100ml red wine vinegar, such as Cabernet Sauvignon
2 banana shallots, finely chopped
freshly ground black pepper

makes 12

Infuse the vinegar a good hour or so before you want to serve: pour the vinegar into a bowl and add the shallots. Grind over some pepper and set aside for an hour at room temperature. Strain, then transfer the infused vinegar to a serving bowl or jug.

Shuck the oysters (see page 83) and sit them on a bed of ice in a serving dish. Spoon a little sauce over each oyster before eating.

VINEGAR VARIATION
Vermouth vinegar is fabulous here, or try a rice vinegar or herb-infused vinegar such as tarragon.

Any smoked fish can be used here – as long as it doesn't need to be cooked. Smoked halibut would be my choice, but smoked salmon is great too. Whatever you go for, the smoked fish, smooth potato and crisp apple is bound together with a vinaigrette and lots of herbs for a tasty lunch or light supper dish. Serve with a few salad leaves on the side to serve as a lunch or starter; this is, in many ways, just a more elegant version of a potato salad.

Smoked Fish, Potato and Apple Stack

400g waxy potatoes, skins on
4 teaspoons Dijon mustard
4 teaspoons honey vinegar
4 tablespoons olive oil
½ teaspoon caster sugar
1 crisp, medium-sized
    eating apple
1 tablespoon chopped chives
3 tablespoons
    chopped tarragon
180g smoked halibut or
    salmon, shredded
1 tablespoon capers, drained
    and chopped
salt

You will need: a 9cm pastry
    cutter or chef's ring

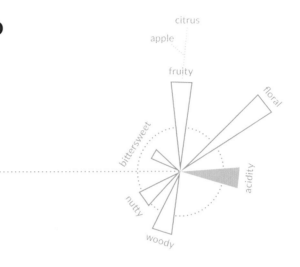

serves 4

Bring a large pan of water to the boil and cook the potatoes for 15–20 minutes until just tender. Drain, then leave the potatoes to sit in the pan off the heat, with a lid half-on, for around 15 minutes so they finish cooking in their own steam.

Meanwhile, prepare the dressing by whisking together the mustard, vinegar, olive oil, sugar and a good pinch of salt.

As soon as the potatoes are cool enough to handle, rub off the skins and cut the potatoes into 1cm dice. Gently toss them in the dressing.

Quarter, core and dice the apple, then gently toss that into the potato mix along with the chives, tarragon, smoked fish and capers.

Put the chef's ring or pastry cutter onto a plate and pack with a quarter of the smoked fish mixture. After a few minutes, carefully remove the ring and repeat for the other three servings.

VINEGAR VARIATION

A sweet white wine vinegar such as Moscatel can be substituted for the honey vinegar. Or try apple cider vinegar, mango vinegar, pear vinegar, coconut vinegar, a herb- or flower-infused vinegar or light rice vinegar.

This is such a lovely dish of intense flavour. The saffron and lightly spiced, lightly zesty vinegar bring out the best in the potatoes. It makes an excellent side dish. Don't worry if it looks as though the potatoes are going to be lurid orange at the beginning – the colour will mellow as the flavours pervade the potatoes.

Saffron-roasted Potatoes

1 teaspoon saffron threads
**4 teaspoons spiced
   orange vinegar**
700g waxy potatoes, scrubbed
4 tablespoons olive oil
salt and freshly ground
   black pepper

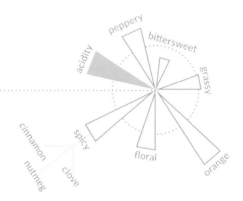

serves 3–4

Grind the saffron threads in a pestle and mortar, then transfer to a bowl. Gently heat the vinegar for 30 seconds over a low heat and pour over the saffron. Leave to infuse for 20 minutes, or at least for the time it takes you to prepare the potatoes.

Preheat the oven to 200°C/180°C Fan/Gas Mark 6.

Cut the potatoes into slices 4–5mm thick – there is no need to peel them first. Tip into a baking dish. Add the oil to the saffron-infused vinegar and pour the whole lot over the potatoes. Mix to combine, and season.

Transfer to the oven for 30 minutes, stirring halfway through. The potatoes are ready when tender and lightly crisped.

VINEGAR VARIATION

Instead of spiced orange vinegar, use a good white wine vinegar, and while the saffron is infusing in it, add the grated zest of ½ orange and a few gratings of nutmeg.

The punch of flavour and acidity of vinegar – good vinegar – is absolutely crucial to steak tartare. Which makes it all the more curious that in most recipes it only really features by way of cornichons as a carrier for the vinegar. I think it's far better to use it as an ingredient, allowing a choice of vinegar and how to balance it.

The idea of eating raw beef doesn't bother me. Not when I know it is fresh and well sourced. But I regret to say that the usual serving of a raw egg yolk on top of the beef tartare holds absolutely no appeal. I don't think it is because it is raw – I just think it looks ugly. So I get my raw egg element via a dollop of rather luscious mayonnaise.

Steak Tartare

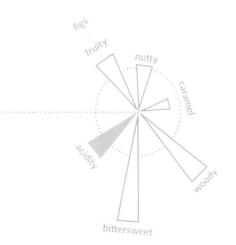

200g trimmed beef steak fillet
1 small shallot, finely diced
2 teaspoons finely chopped
    flat-leaf parsley
2 teaspoons finely
    chopped mint
2 teaspoons finely
    chopped tarragon
25ml maple vinegar
2 tablespoons mayonnaise
    (see page 45), or 2 egg
    yolks if you prefer
salt and freshly ground
    black pepper

serves 2

Dice the beef as small as you can; you are aiming for 2–3mm cubes. Put them into a bowl with the shallots, chopped herbs and the vinegar, and mix to combine. Taste, and add a little more vinegar if you think it needs it and doing so won't make it too loose to hold its shape when piled up. Season well.

Pile the tartare onto two plates. To create a neat shape, pack into a greased 7cm biscuit cutter as a mould. Put a spoonful of mayonnaise on top to serve (or for a more classic finish, skip the mayonnaise, make a shallow indent in the top of each steak tartare and sit an egg yolk in it before serving).

VINEGAR VARIATION
A fruity red wine vinegar
would be good; or a fruit
vinegar that you know
will go well with beef –
think berries or apples.

Baking with buttermilk makes cakes extra light and moist. For this recipe, 'real' buttermilk is replicated with a mix of milk and lavender-infused vinegar. The lavender notes are given a helping hand with some lavender flowers ground into the mix, too. Layer up with sweet mascarpone and raspberries, and this cake manages to be both light and decadent.

Lavender and Lemon-thyme Victoria Sponge

FOR THE SPONGE
200ml full-fat milk
1 tablespoon lavender-infused vinegar
220g granulated sugar
1 teaspoon dried or fresh edible lavender flowers
250g plain flour
1½ teaspoons baking powder
½ teaspoon bicarbonate of soda
¼ teaspoon fine salt
125g soft unsalted butter
3 large eggs
½ teaspoon vanilla extract

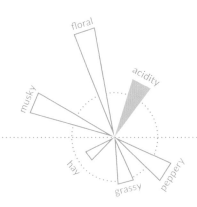

FOR THE FILLING
300g mascarpone cheese
50g caster sugar
a few drops of vanilla extract
3 tablespoons raspberry jam
100g raspberries

TO FINISH
1 teaspoon lemon thyme, finely chopped
2 tablespoons caster sugar
sprigs of edible lavender, lemon thyme flowers or lemon thyme leaves

serves 8–10

Preheat the oven to 180°C/160°C Fan/Gas Mark 4. Grease and line two 20cm round cake tins with baking parchment.

Make the 'buttermilk' first by stirring together the milk and vinegar in a bowl, then set aside for 10 minutes. It will become a little lumpy as the acidity of the vinegar reacts with the milk (this is meant to happen!).

Use a spice grinder or pestle and mortar to grind together the granulated sugar and lavender flowers and set aside.

Sift the flour, baking powder, bicarbonate of soda and salt into a large bowl. In a separate bowl, cream together the butter and ground lavender-suffused sugar until light and fluffy. Beat in the eggs, one at a time, followed by the vanilla extract. Now fold in a little of the dry ingredients, then a little of the buttermilk mixture, and carry on with this process until it is all mixed in. Make sure to mix well after each addition.

Divide the sponge mixture evenly between the two tins and bake for 30 minutes. They are ready when coming away from the sides of the tin slightly and a cake skewer comes out clean. Let them cool in the tins for 10 minutes before turning out onto a wire rack to cool completely.

For the filling, beat together the mascarpone, sugar and a few drops of vanilla extract until smooth. Spread the jam on one of the sponge layers, sit the raspberries on top, then spoon over the mascarpone mix. Don't try to spread the mascarpone, just dot it over. Sit the other sponge on top and gently press so that the mascarpone falls around the berries.

Combine the chopped lemon thyme and caster sugar in a bowl and dust it over the top of the cake. Finish with edible lavender, thyme sprigs or leaves to decorate.

VINEGAR VARIATION

You could swap the lavender-infused vinegar for another suitably floral infusion, such as rose, and use rose petals in the sugar. Or use white wine vinegar or a light fruit vinegar, with either lavender or rose petals in the mix and on the top.

My favourite pancakes to make and eat every Shrove Tuesday are the stacks of slightly risen *crempog*, which are a Welsh tradition. If you aren't familiar, think of American pancakes and you are on the right lines – but these are distinctly smaller and lighter. Mighty tempting for an indulgent breakfast, afternoon tea or dessert with some cream or yoghurt on the side.

Buttermilk is the traditional ingredient for its acidity, which reacts with the bicarbonate of soda to give a characteristic bubble and rise. Here, that is replicated with a mix of milk and infused vinegar. Add a handful of raspberries to the batter, and the quick cooking in the hot griddle or frying pan gets the raspberries going just enough to release their flavour without them losing their shape. Their sweetness marries gorgeously with the gentle acidity of the pseudo-buttermilk.

Raspberry Drop Pancakes

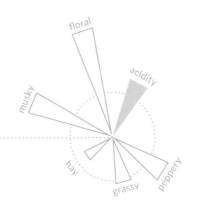

200ml whole milk

**1 tablespoon herb- or flower-
   infused vinegar**

25g butter, plus extra for
   cooking and serving

180g plain flour

1 egg, beaten

¾ teaspoon bicarbonate of soda

90g raspberries

honey, golden syrup or maple
   syrup for drizzling

makes 16

Stir together the milk and vinegar in a bowl or jug and set aside. Melt the butter and set aside to cool.

Sift the flour into a large mixing bowl, then use a hand whisk to mix in the melted butter and the milk and vinegar mixture until you have a smooth batter. Then whisk in the egg. The batter can be made to this point a couple of hours before using.

Just before you're ready to start cooking, whisk in the bicarbonate of soda then gently fold through 70g of the raspberries, keeping the rest for serving.

Grease a frying pan or griddle with a small knob of butter and heat it until good and hot. Make a pancake by dropping 1 tablespoon of the batter into the pan and then repeat, doing four or five pancakes at a time. Allow to cook for a couple of minutes until bubbly and puffed up and the underside is golden brown. Flip them over and repeat on the other side.

VINEGAR VARIATION

Try honey vinegar,
cider vinegar or white
wine vinegar.

Keep the pancakes warm while you finish the rest (adding more butter to the pan as necessary), building up stacks of pancakes as you go with a little butter, a few raspberries and a drizzle of honey or syrup between each layer.

Infused Vinegars

This book is not intended as a guide to making vinegar, as you may have guessed by now. I have considerable respect for passionate home vinegar-makers for all their will, creativity, endeavour and commitment. My reason for not making it much myself – and for not using this book as a platform to persuade you to make it yourself either – is simply that there are so many skilled, creative craftspeople-come-alchemists out there making wonderful vinegars from exciting base produce, and those are the vinegars that I want to bring into my cooking.

All of which makes much of this section of *The Vinegar Cupboard* something of a departure. For I am about to recommend ways of making your own vinegar infusions. A wonderful way to create your own blends of flavour, which suit how you want to cook and eat, and I can vouch for the marvellous feeling of pride you will have at your own creativity, too.

Infusing vinegar is an age-old idea and simplicity itself. At the most basic level, it is just about immersing the chosen flower, herb, spice or fruit in the vinegar to release its flavour. From there come all kinds of ways to craft a blend of flavours.

Wine vinegars, cider vinegars, rice vinegars and palm vinegars are all especially suited to being infused. I would say this is the place to use a vinegar with a flatter flavour. There is little point in choosing one that is packed with its own flavour, which you then have to worry about balancing and matching. Go for a plain vinegar and allow the flavours you are infusing to shine through.

On the following pages are some ideas to get you thinking, but first, here are my general tips

The basic method is to immerse the infusing ingredient(s) in the vinegar for the periods indicated in the recipes that follow, then strain the infusing ingredient(s) out

Store your infusions in the dark at around 18°C

The quantities and infusion times on the following pages are a guide. The result will depend on the vinegar, the infusing ingredient(s) and how intense (or not) you want it to be. Test after the times given, and if not quite strong enough then strain out the infusing element, refresh with new, and leave for a while again to deepen in flavour

Flower infusions

Borage

Use eight flowers to infuse in white wine vinegar for about a fortnight to give a vinegar of mild cucumber freshness that is wonderful in so many summer dishes. I'd use a few dashes in a summer gin and tonic, and more than a few dashes in a jug of Pimms. It is best to try to remove the stamen inside the flower head before using to infuse (it is a bit bitter).

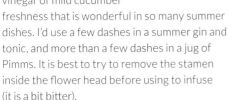

Chive blossoms

I much prefer using these to infuse a vinegar than chive leaves. And I much prefer using the resulting chive-infused vinegar to any sprinkling of chopped chive leaves. The flavour is so much more subtly onion-y, and the blossoms give the vinegar a very pleasing blush. Infuse two blossom heads for two weeks.

Elderflower

Use two bouncy heads of elderflower, with the blossoms picked off the central stems that hold the head together. Don't be tempted to wash the elderflower as you will be washing away flavour, too. Infuse for about a fortnight. Think of the classic elderflower pairings of gooseberries and mackerel when using this; transfer to a spray bottle to use as a finishing spritz for all kinds of summer dishes.

Lavender

Go slightly steady with this as it is easy for the lavender to overwhelm. Use three or four sprigs and infuse for about a fortnight.

Nasturtium

Infuse half a dozen flowers for about a fortnight.

Orchid

One of the most beautiful of vinegar infusions as these long, elegant leaves sit in the bottle and catch the light. Pick the leaves from two large orchids and infuse them for a fortnight. A vinegar with notes of cucumber, again, but a little crisper and fresher.

Rose

Immerse the petals of two or three rose blossoms for about a fortnight.

Violets

Infuse half a dozen flower heads for about a week in – this is important – white wine vinegar, to give the most fabulously coloured bluey-purple vinegar.

Fruit infusions

In the section on fruit vinegars I mentioned that there can be a bit of a confusion as to whether a fruit vinegar is the fruit itself that has been double-fermented to vinegar, or vinegar with an addition of the fruit. In the case of the latter I'd say that this is closer to being an infused vinegar than a fruit vinegar. It may seem as though I am dancing on the head of a pin by making that distinction, but I feel there is a huge difference in what the two things are and how they taste.

Certainly for the home vinegar-lover, it is easier to make an infused fruit vinegar than to double-ferment. Bear in mind that the juice of the fruit will dilute the vinegar a little and therefore lower its acidity, so choose a vinegar of slightly higher acidity (say, 6% or 7%), or be aware that when you are using it the acidity may be lower than if un-infused.

Use 350ml of vinegar, and try the following infusions:

Apricots

Chop two apricots and immerse them in the vinegar for a month. (Don't use the stones as the flavour will be too strong.)

Cherries

Mash 50g of very ripe pitted cherries to break them down before immersing in the vinegar for about a month. This is possibly my favourite of the fruit vinegars: great as a marinade for game and fish, as a drinking vinegar shrub, for deglazing and over chocolate.

Figs

Two fresh or dried figs, cut into quarters and left in the vinegar for about a fortnight.

Oranges

One to avoid, I think. Not because orange vinegars aren't lovely and versatile – they are – but because infusing them at a domestic level doesn't really work that well, and the orange vinegars available to buy are infusions too (often with spices in as well), just infused more successfully.

Quince

Hard fruits such as quince will not give freely of their juice or flavour, so you need to heat them first. Roughly chop a quince and sit over a low heat in a saucepan until fully soft. Cool, then add to the vinegar and leave for about a month.

Herb infusions

There are no end of creative possibilities for both the making and using of herb vinegar infusions. Do note that their colour and sprightliness wilt as the infusing time goes on.

Using 350ml of vinegar, add a couple of sprigs of your chosen herb and leave it in the vinegar for about three weeks. Think about thyme, sage, rosemary, basil (which will turn the vinegar rather red – that is fine), dill, oregano, parsley…

Possibly the most celebrated of herb-infused vinegars is France's 'four thieves' vinegar. It did, after all, save lives in the late eighteenth century as plague was spreading through France, but somehow thieves seemed immune from catching it. Four young boys, who were thieves,

were caught and questioned about why that was. They put it down to using as a disinfectant a vinegar prepared by their mother – it was an infusion of lavender, rosemary, mint, other herbs and garlic. Thereafter the herb-infused vinegar was soaked into scarves that villagers would hold against their nose and mouth to fend off the plague.

It is not dissimilar to old recipes for medicinal vinegar tonics in New England, with herbs and spices infused into their cider vinegars.

'Four thieves' vinegar is still being made and sold in France, but here's a simple way to make your own.

'Four thieves'

750ml white wine vinegar
6 garlic cloves, chopped
1 teaspoon black peppercorns
3 sprigs thyme
3 sprigs rosemary
3 sprigs sage
3 sprigs lavender
3 sprigs mint

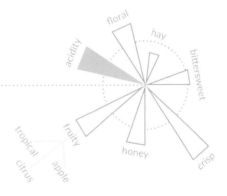

makes 750ml

Simply infuse the white wine vinegar with the garlic, peppercorns and herbs. Seal and store for six weeks to infuse, then strain out the solids and reseal the vinegar.

Spice infusions

There's a Filipino vinegar called *suka pinakurat*, which is an infusion of spices such as chilli or ginger into coconut vinegar. It is pretty hot by all accounts and pretty popular. Coconut vinegar lends itself well to being infused with spices as it doesn't have much flavour of its own to rival them. For similar reasons, any other palm vinegars or a cane vinegar are good for spice infusions. Otherwise, do be sure to go for a mild-flavoured wine, cider or rice vinegar.

Use 350ml of vinegar, and try the following infusions.

Chilli

For your own version of *suka pinakurat*, sit one or two dried chillis in the vinegar for a fortnight.

Lemongrass

Infuse one stalk of lemongrass for one week. Note that this can be a surprisingly intensely flavoured infusion.

Clove

1 teaspoon of cloves infused for one week.

Vanilla

There's a temptation to be so attuned to using vanilla in sweet dishes that it is easy to forget that vanilla is actually a spice. Slice down the length of a vanilla pod and sit it in the vinegar for 2 weeks. The resulting infusion is terrific in salad dressings or for tomato dishes, and is also a good choice for meringues and fruit salads.

Horseradish

Another of my favourite infusions; I choose a red wine vinegar for this one. Infuse 1 tablespoon of grated horseradish for a fortnight.

Peppercorns

I like to use a mix of peppercorn colours for a rounded flavour. Immerse 1 tablespoon of peppercorns for 1 week.

INFUSED BLENDS

These are just a handful of ideas based on the tip-of-the-iceberg infusions above. A rule of thumb when making a blend is to use less of each element than you would if it was the sole infusion, with the balance in favour of the lead infusion.

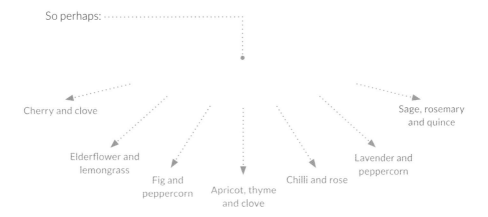

So perhaps:

Cherry and clove

Elderflower and lemongrass

Fig and peppercorn

Apricot, thyme and clove

Chilli and rose

Lavender and peppercorn

Sage, rosemary and quince

I could play this game all day … and have been known to.

MORE VINEGARS

Wherever there is starch there is sugar. Where there is sugar there can be alcohol. And where there is alcohol there is vinegar just another fermentation away. So it is no surprise at all that there are crops being turned into vinegar that defy my neat categorisations throughout this book. Not so many as to throw a spanner in the works, but a few that are well-worth mentioning.

ASPARAGUS VINEGAR

Think for a moment how fabulously sweet asparagus is when it is slap-bang in its season. Now imagine the very essence of that sweetness and flavour being captured in a vinegar. I don't mean essence of asparagus infused into vinegar – I mean asparagus that is pressed, fermented to asparagus wine, then fermented to an intense and delicious vinegar. Look out for it in Austria, where both Gölles and Gegenbauer produce it. Quite possibly others, too.

BENIMOSU (SWEET POTATO VINEGAR)

This deep red vinegar made from purple sweet potatoes is a Japanese speciality. The starchiness of the sweet potatoes has to first be converted to sugar by steaming them. From there the process follows the method of other Japanese vinegar production by using *koji* yeast mould to ferment the sweet potato to alcohol, before bacteria is added to convert it to vinegar. It is typically aged for about a year before selling.

Benimosu is acclaimed for its health benefits thanks to the high levels of polyphenols that are naturally found in purple sweet potatoes, and which (as with apple vinegar) are intensified in the vinegar-making process.

There are two types of *benimosu*: a 'plain' one that is great for cooking with, or using in salad dressings, pickles or sushi rice; and a honey-sweetened version that makes a fine ice cream sauce or addition to cocktails.

BLACK BEAN VINEGAR

This is another vinegar that is high in polyphenols, again thanks to the natural properties of black beans. It is a Chinese vinegar that can take nine years to develop – not something that you will find easily, but worth taking note of if you do.

WHEY VINEGAR

What to do with all the whey left behind as a by-product of cheese-making? Turn it into vinegar, of course. OK, maybe not 'of course'. But whey vinegar is a thing, and a clever thing too, as it is a way of utilising the cheese 'waste' that results from cheese production. It is not an especially new idea, having first been done at a commercial level around 100 years ago for markets in France and Austria, where it was sold as 'lactavinegar'. That name gives the clue as to how the vinegar is made. Its lactose is a form of sugar, which – as has been this book's repeated refrain – is what is needed to be turned to alcohol, and from there to vinegar.

It's one to keep an eye out for in Austria, Switzerland, Japan and New Zealand, where it is often sold as a health tonic vinegar to aid digestion.

VINEGAR
PRODUCERS

This list can only possibly scratch the surface of all the varied and versatile vinegars being produced around the world.

Fruit Vinegars and Fruit Balsamic Vinegars

Gegenbauer, Austria
Gegenbauer sources fruits for its vinegar from Austria or wherever they are exceptional, leading to an extensive range of flavour-packed fruit vinegars, including Sicilian melon vinegar; Turkish *baglama* vinegar; Italian pomegranate vinegar; and Austrian tomato, raspberry and cherry vinegars. Their blackcurrant vinegar and cucumber vinegar are hard to beat.

Gölles, Austria
I especially like the fact that many of their vinegars come in a spray bottle, which is ideal for vinegar-spritz finishes to a dish or drink. They have truly cracked how to make a good raspberry vinegar, and their superb range includes fruit balsamic.

Isle of Wight Tomatoes, UK
Arreton Valley on the Isle of Wight gets more sunshine than pretty much anywhere else in the UK, which has more than a little to do with how tasty its tomatoes are. When turned into a fruit balsamic blend of oak-smoked tomatoes steeped in balsamic vinegar for several weeks, the marriage of flavours works very well. Just the right balance of rich, sweet and acidic to be useful for sauces, dressings and desserts.

National Fruit Collection, UK
Brogdale Farm is home to the National Fruit Collection, which oversees the protection/development of thousands of varieties of fruits. They work with a local cider-maker on fruit cider vinegars, where soft fruits such as strawberries and cherries are part-fermented and added to the cider vinegar. They burst with fruit flavour, but do note that these are low acidity so not suitable for preserving. Great for drinking vinegars, salad dressings and all kinds of drizzling.

Nordhavn Vinegar Brewery, Denmark
Set up by ground-breaking chef and restaurateur Claus Meyer of Noma fame, with all the attention to detail, quality and innovation that are the hallmarks of the rest of Claus's work. The cherry, blackcurrant and rosehip varieties are particularly exciting, as is the balsamic plum. Just delicious.

Uchibori, Japan

A Japanese vinegar-maker at the forefront of the nation's vinegar-drinking craze. This fourth-generation family business used to be mainly known for its culinary vinegars; now it focuses on fruit vinegars for drinking or drizzling, though not really for cooking with. If you go to a Japanese department store and see the Oaks Heart range being sold in a vinegar bar, that is Uchibori.

Balsamic Vinegars

Many of the balsamic vinegar producers do private label work, meaning that their balsamics are sold under various different brand labels, potentially all around the world. This creates an impression of there being rather more different balsamic producers than there actually are. It also makes it all the more important to know how to read the bottles to better gauge what you might be buying (see page 76). That said, the following are worth keeping an eye out for.

Acetaia San Giacomo, Reggio Emilia

Run by Andrea Bezzecchi, who re-opened his family *acetaia* on the death of his father. Given his time as President of Reggio Emilia's *Tradizionale* Consortium it is all the more interesting that while there is obvious and justifiable pride here in the *Tradizionale* they produce, they have a forward-looking stance on producing a range of balsamic blends.

Nero Modena, Modena

A collaboration between businessman Alessandro Calveri and Marina Spaggiari, who pretty much has *Tradizionale* balsamic running through her veins. Her love for its heritage has an impact on the quality and flavour of the vinegars through the range. I rather love their handy carry-with-you sachets of 10ml of balsamic. Now you need never be caught short without good balsamic again.

They operate three of their own labels and do private label work, too. In the UK I buy Belazu balsamic because I know it is Nero Modena.

Sherry Vinegars

Páez Morilla, Spain

The family *bodega* of Antonio Páez Lobato – aka Jerez's 'Vinegar King' – to whom the expansion of interest in sherry vinegar outside of Andalucía is credited. Páez Morilla still produces delicious vinegars across the spectrum of grape varieties and ages, including some very special twenty-five-year-old ones. (The drive out of Jerez airport into the city might well take you past the roundabout on Avenida Reina Sofia that is dedicated to Antonio.)

Valdespino, Spain

One of the oldest sherry *bodegas*, producing a very lovely sherry vinegar that at time of writing is quite easily available to buy in the UK from good actual or online delis.

Ximénez Paula Coll, Spain

A collaboration between Bodegas Ximénez-Spínola and the prestige olive oil company Oleum Flumen. This small, family-run *bodega* is unusual for only working with Pedro Ximénez grapes. They produce limited batches of wonderful wines, and allow Oleum Flumen to develop some of their sherry into this rich vinegar. Sometimes available in even smaller batches is a version of the vinegar produced and sold directly by Bodegas Ximénez-Spínola.

Wine Vinegars

Badia, Spain

I met my vinegar soul-sister at Badia in Catalunya: Judit Badia (a chemical engineer by training), who with her sister (an artist) and father together run the family's wine vinegar business. The sisters bring a modern, feminine, strong and open-spirited edge to how vinegar happens here. The really good stuff comes under the label of Gardeny. Their Moscatel is my go-to salad dressing vinegar; the Vermouth vinegar is exceptional; as is the Merlot vinegar, which at a tasting I went to was described by locals as being like the Catalan region's 'old-style' wine vinegars.

Borocet, Hungary

This small producer makes wine vinegars from the Tokaj region's sweet Aszu wine. They have a version aged for five years in barrels, and others with herb or floral infusions.

Cult Vinegars, UK

Small-batch wine vinegars, sophisticated in their flavour and design, but simple in every other way. Owner Jonathan Brown buys wine (very good wine, often at auction), makes it into vinegar in an almost literal kitchen-table-business, then bottles it for selling in small vials with pipette tops that are perfect for finishing a dish.

He also wants to encourage more of us to make our own wine vinegar, and I think his is the right way of going about it: he sells bottles of mother-of-vinegar to get you started, and beautifully designed, minimalist vinegar crocks; the idea is to pour into that your unfinished glasses or bottles of wine. An elegant way of making the most of any wine waste.

Doktorenhof, Germany

Based in Germany's Palatinate wine-growing region, the second largest wine region in the country. The extensive range includes vinegars from Riesling, White Burgundy and bitter-sweet wines with grape must added.

Fleuriet, France

Wine vinegars made in Rouillac from the Pineau des Charentes AOC wines. Françoise and Philippe Fleuriet began their vinegar-making in the proud wine vinegar style – that is to say, by accident. This has resulted in small-batch vinegars used in some of the best restaurants in France. The Fleuriets age the wine in barrels (with names scribbled on them), then allow them to slowly and naturally acetify into vinegar over several months.

Hilbilby, Australia

This vinegar-maker is better known for its cider vinegar tonics, but I rather love that they also do a raw and unfiltered red wine vinegar made from the red wine of Sutton Grange in Victoria.

Katz, USA

Strictly speaking, Albert Katz is an olive man, not a vinegar man. An award-winning olive man at that, with thirty acres of olive groves in California. But Albert recognised a little while ago that California – while abundant in wine – was somewhat lacking in wine vinegar. Olive oil and vinegar being such natural bedfellows, he began making vinegar in the slow Orléans style using Californian wines. The state's prize grape variety of Zinfandel is represented in the range, as is Sauvignon Blanc, and there's a super red wine vinegar blend of Merlot, Zinfandel and Cabernet Sauvignon.

   Available in delis around the USA. Nobody in my acquaintance is allowed to make a visit to New York or any major city without promising to scout out and bring me back a Katz vinegar.

Michel Pouret, France

From the hundreds of vinegars of Orléans' vinegar-making heyday, there is just one left: Michel Pouret.

Minus8, Canada

This company now does several other fine vinegars but started as an ice-wine vinegar producer – 'Minus 8' refers to the temperature at which the grapes are harvested and pressed. The vinegar is barrel-aged in the *solera* method (see page 115) of Andalucían sherry and wine vinegars, resulting in a vinegar that is deep amber, dense, nutty and woody. The wine vinegar range has been expanded to encompass those produced from particular grapes – there's now a Riesling and a Concord version.

Philippe Gonet, France

Vinegars made from the breadth of wines in the Arbois AOCs. Best of all (maybe) is the vinegar made from the region's speciality, *vin jaune* – a very exciting vinegar that manages to be fresh, fruity and nutty all at once. A close rival for my affections is a vinegar made from another local speciality wine, Macvin, which is *vin jaune* fortified with local *marc* brandy.

Vinegar Shed, UK

Andy Harries launched Vinegar Shed to bring to the UK the kinds of small-batch artisanal vinegars that were – until he was doing it, anyway – virtually impossible to find. He has a great eye and palate for delicious vinegars with interesting back-stories.

Cider Vinegars

Aspall, UK

OK, not so much one to look out for as Aspall vinegar is a UK market-leader sold all over the place, but it can be so easy to dismiss the commercial big-guns and I think that would a shame in Aspall's case. There is real pride here in what they produce. The one to look for is the organic cider (or 'cyder' as they put it) vinegar which isn't produced by Frings acetator as is the main cider vinegar range but by a slower production process that was pioneered in the 1970s by John Chevalier Guild, one of a long line of Chevaliers at the heart of Aspall. The result is a more rounded, flavoursome cider vinegar.

Carrs Ciderhouse, USA

In the heartland of America's New England cider apple vinegar heritage is this young orchard on the north-west slope of Mount Warner, with a view over the Connecticut River Valley. Husband and wife, Jonathan Carr and Nicole Blum, began the orchard in 2007 and its youth means they were able to choose the exact apples they wanted. The soil here grows intensely flavoured apples, which translate into really good cider and cider vinegar.

Famille Dupont, France

The Dupont family have been working to reinvigorate their Normandy farm estate for nigh on forty years, with considerable success. They make excellent Calvados, cider and, more recently, cider vinegar of exceptional flavour, with all the qualities of their cider. They also do a very interesting *aigre doux* cider, which is a sweet and sour blend.

Le Grande Epicerie, France

The Paris food hall in which you will find many different cider vinegars from farms across Normandy and Brittany.

Little Stour Orchard, UK

Sarah and Michael Bowers luxuriate in taking two years to make their '10 Acre' cider vinegar with the apples from their ten-acre (hence the name) orchard a little inland from the famous Kent coastal towns of Ramsgate and Margate. The apples are juiced on a 180-year-old oak press, then naturally fermented for up to a year to become cider. After a second fermentation into vinegar they are matured in oak barrels.

National Fruit Collection, UK

Brogdale Farm in Kent is home to the National Fruit Collection and oversees the protection/development of thousands of varieties of fruits. They work with a local cider maker to make small-batch raw cider vinegar using apples from the National Collection, including many heritage varieties.

Pierre Huet, France

Another family-owned Normandy estate. There is quite an extensive range of products here, including a small number of vinegars produced at the estate. There is an apple cider vinegar; a vinegar that is fermented with raspberries; and a pear 'cider' vinegar. You get the real flavour of the fruits with these.

Sunnycrest Orchards, Sharon Springs, USA

Mention New York and it is hard for the mind not to jump straight to thoughts of the City. But venture beyond the bright lights and the state of New York borders the well-known apple-growing New England states, and has swathes of land that are similarly rural. Upstate New York has a strong agriculture community and heritage, which includes cider apples. Some of those farms also produce cider vinegars, such as the Farm Girls Vinegars ACV produced here.

Japanese Rice Vinegars

Iio Jozo, Japan

A fifth-generation vinegar-maker in the Kyoto region, which stands out for growing (organically) its own rice. This gives them total control over every stage of how the vinegars are made. And they are made with love, care and time. The extensive range is made to traditional methods. They do an *akasu* and modern brown rice vinegars made with pleasingly high proportions of rice, so they will actually have some flavour to them.

Murayama Zosu, Japan

A Kyoto-based vinegar-maker with an increasingly far-reaching appeal. They produce a lot of vinegar, and while some is made fast with an acetator, some is made more traditionally. Look out for the Chidorisu, which is a good-flavoured, very versatile, light rice vinegar.

Sakamoto Kurozu, Japan

Established in the mid-1970s, but producing *kurozu* following centuries-old traditions. They are based in Kagoshima in Kyushu, where visitors can see the *tsubo* jars in the sun, go to the visitor centre, watch a video on how it is made – and best of all, buy the vinegar. Not that you have to go to Kyushu to get Sakamoto Kurozu; it is available across Japan and internationally at specialist Japanese stores. There is the youngest, mildest amber *kurozu* that has aged for at least a year, and then gradings of *kurozu* with more age and a deeper colour/flavour.

The Wasabi Company, UK

The heartland of England's watercress beds is an unlikely place to find some very interesting Japanese rice vinegars … and yet there they are. From wasabi to rice vinegar is obviously not too much of a mental leap for The Wasabi Company, and they are importing a range from Marushosu Jozomoto in Wakayama. Very exciting for anyone who fancies trying some excellent Japanese vinegars and vinegar sauces made with interesting flavours.

Uchibori, Japan

I mentioned on page 262 that Uchibori are doing all kinds of exciting things with fruit vinegars and drinking vinegars. Their brown rice vinegar is top-notch, too.

Chinese Black Vinegars

This is difficult. Zhenjiang black vinegar is not very hard to find outside of China, but much of the mass-market product is mass-made. Try to buy the best quality you can in specialist Chinese produce outlets. If you're lucky, you might find other regional black vinegars there too. Within China, try to find the local vinegar.

Hengshun, China

There is good reason Hengshun have stayed in business for nearly 200 years and are one of the most popular Zhenjiang brands within China as well as outside. Go for their aged black vinegars if you can.

Ninghuafu, China

Remember how the locals of Taiyuan in Shanxi queue down the street for their refills of this (see page 212)? If they can bother to do that, then I recommend you grab a bottle whenever – if ever – possible.

Sichuan Baoning Vinegar Co., China

Until relatively recently this company had exclusive rights to Sichuan's famous herbal vinegar. It is still the one you are most likely to find.

Malt Vinegars

Artisan Malt Vinegar, UK

This vinegar-maker was really the first modern UK malt vinegar producer to reinvent malt vinegar for the modern market, following the idea that it could be made in a craft – nay, artisanal – way. Produced in Cornwall and matured in barrels for several months.

Minus8, Canada

Small-batch malt vinegar in the style of an IPA (India Pale Ale). A gorgeous deep amber colour with more complexity and freshness than any other malt vinegar I have tried. Very versatile.

Orkney Craft Vinegar, UK

Malt vinegar from Orkney's ancient bere barley grain. The creativity that seems to run throughout the Orkney Islands is nowhere more evident than here, with Sam Britten and his father-in-law, Keith. Sam used to be a chef and a miller, and how well those two attributes come together in malt-vinegar-making, with Keith providing ingenuity of production. A delicious, deeply flavoured malt vinegar that matures for several months in oak barrels after careful acetifying. Particularly exciting is their malt vinegar aged in Bruichladdich barrels, a whisky made from bere.

Spinnakers, Canada

This is a great example of a modern craft beer-maker accidentally 'discovering' that one of their beers had been left sitting around had turned to vinegar in its bottle, and was really rather good. Now they do it on purpose.

Honey Vinegar

Acetum Mellis, Italy

This Italian producer makes lots of different honeys, but it is their *miele millefiori* (mixed-flower honey) that is fermented into honey wine and then to honey vinegar. They also do some aged versions.

Castell de Gardeny, Spain

This is the premium range of Catalunya vinegar producer, Badia. Of the many wine vinegars they produce, one is an 'orange blossom condiment'. Orange Muscat wine is made into vinegar, then blended with orange blossom honey that is also from Catalunya. They call it a condiment to reflect the lower acidity, but this is a lovely vinegar.

Katz, USA

To California, where Katz Vinegars, who do such fabulous wine vinegar varieties, also do a blend of sweet late harvest Viognier wine with their own Californian honey. Note, this is one of those honey vinegars where the honey isn't fermented into alcohol – it is added to the wine at the stage of acetic fermentation. So it is giving sweetness as well as flavour.

Orkney Craft Vinegar, UK

The producers of Orkney's bere malt vinegar also make a glorious honey vinegar. It is actually honey and meadowsweet – a reference to a very old flavour combination in a drink, and to the meadowsweet that grows wild all over the Orkney Islands.

Uchibori, Japan

Honey vinegar from deeply coloured and robustly-flavoured buckwheat honey. The resulting vinegar retains the crop's intensity.

Maple Vinegar

Minus8, Canada

Another fantastic vinegar from this vinegar-maker is 'Maple8'. From a starting base of Quebec maple syrup, it becomes a vinegar that is then aged for four years in oak barrels, resulting in a gorgeously bright amber colour, with a medium-thick consistency. Its identity as maple syrup is very much there, beautifully tempered with 5% acidity. A vinegar that when I first tasted it made me say 'wow' out loud to absolutely no one.

Coconut and Other Palm Vinegars

My friend Kate Hawkings – restaurateur and drinks supremo – did the Goan legwork for me in finding a good local source of coconut vinegar to bring back to London for me to try. It came in a refilled water bottle so I have no idea what it was, but would say that if you find yourself in Goa or the Philippines, your best bet is to seek out whatever the locals are using.

Green Gold Gourmet, Philippines

They do a range of *suka* vinegars, including spiced and sweetened. Available internationally, too.

Infused Vinegars

Doktorenhof, Germany

What a range is to be found here! Using the base of their own very lovely wine vinegars, Doktorenhof produce so many fruit, herb and spice infusions. All the ones I have tried have had a great balance of infusion with the base vinegar. There's fig, cinnamon, rose, saffron, ginger, elderflower, lemon, to name a few...

Erste Kamptaler, Austria

This Austrian vinegar-maker produces wine vinegars and fruit vinegars, and also has quite the range of herb- and spice-infused vinegars, too. There's basil, dill, paprika, chilli, garlic, wild garlic and more.

Hilbilby, Australia

A 'Fire Tonic' infusion of raw, unfiltered cider vinegar with – get ready for this – 'raw local honey, chillies, turmeric, garlic, horseradish, ginger, carrot, celery, red onion, brown onion, apple, orange, lemon, mustard seed, parsley, rosemary, oregano, thyme, juniper berries, peppercorns, bay leaves, Szechuan pepper & Himalayan pink mineral salt'. It packs the punch you would imagine but with more balance than you might think. For drinking and dressing.

Uchibori, Japan

Japan's *sakura* cherry blossom is revered across the country in its fleeting season. The blossoms are often preserved by pickling in plum vinegar, drying, then salting them for use as a sweet or savoury ingredient. Uchibori produce the vinegar infusion of the *sakura* and it is wonderful.

Womersley, UK

These vinegars are fruit, herb and spice infusions in white distilled vinegar, giving Womersley a blank flavour canvas with which to develop their blends. They are delicious, and there are some interesting combinations as well as more familiar ones. The orange and mace is one of my favourites.

I often see infused vinegars at food markets and craft fairs. It always pays to take a moment to ask what the base vinegar used was. Hopefully it will be a well-made wine, cider or rice vinegar, as you might use if infusing it yourself.

RECIPES
BY VINEGAR
TYPE

F

fig vinegar
pumpkin soup with enoki
mushrooms 189

flower-infused vinegar
beetroot pickled with dill and
orange 150

lavender and lemon-thyme
Victoria sponge 248

raspberry drop pancakes 251

ricotta 151

smoked fish, potato and apple
stack 244

see also lavender-infused
vinegar; nasturtium vinegar

fruit vinegar
balsamic-ripple ice cream 96

beetroot and garlic soup 79

beurre noir 42

braised pig's cheeks with
liquorice 90

chicory and caraway salad 181

cranberry sauce 46

green beans and spring onions
with sesame 184

lavender and lemon-thyme
Victoria sponge 248

oysters with tarragon butter 83

pan deglaze 49

partridge with red cabbage
and quick-pickled balsamic
onions 84

roasted grapes 93

slaw of red and white
cabbage 238

steak tartare 247

stuffed red cabbage leaves 104

see also apple vinegar; cherry
vinegar; dark fruit vinegar;
fig vinegar; mango vinegar;
orange vinegar; pear vinegar;
quince vinegar; red fruit
vinegar

G

garlic vinegar
grilled fresh mackerel 241

H

herb-infused vinegar
béarnaise sauce 44

beetroot pickled with dill and
orange 150

elderberry pontac sauce 50

garlic and herb pork chops 92

grilled fresh mackerel 241

mayonnaise 45

minted cucumber ribbons 237

pan deglazes 49

pot-roasted loin of pork with fig
and walnut stuffing 168

raspberry drop pancakes 251

ricotta 151

smoked fish, potato and apple
stack 244

soused sardines with *agrodolce*
onions 166

sweetly spiced carrot
salad 240

see also tarragon vinegar

honey vinegar
beetroot and garlic soup 79

chicory and caraway salad 181

cinder toffee 171

cucumber pickled with spices,
garlic and bay 144

elderberry pontac sauce 50

fried eggs 142

garlic and herb pork chops 92

pan deglaze 49

pear and thyme shrub 236

pot-roasted brisket with
honey 86

pot-roasted loin of pork with fig
and walnut stuffing 168

raspberry drop pancakes 251

slaw of red and white
cabbage 238

smoked fish, potato and apple
stack 244

soda bread 155

soused sardines with *agrodolce*
onions 166

sweetly spiced carrot
salad 240

J

Japanese black vinegar
pumpkin soup with enoki
mushrooms 189

Japanese brown rice vinegar
chicory and caraway salad 181

green beans and spring onions
with sesame 184

mayonnaise 45

nanbanzuke fish 194

pickled radish, samphire and
parsley *amasu* salad 183

pickled whole garlic 186

plum and bay Japanese
shrub 180

sauces 192–3

Japanese *kurosu* vinegar
honey baked figs 201

steamed sea bass rolls 197

L

lavender-infused vinegar
lavender and lemon-thyme
Victoria sponge 248

M

malt vinegar
apple and chestnut soup 100

beetroot pickled with dill and
orange 150

braised pig's cheeks with
liquorice 90

oven-baked pork and venison
meatballs 224

oysters with tarragon butter 83

pan deglaze 49

parched peas with bacon,
rocket and lemongrass 223

pickled devils on
horseback 227

pot-roasted loin of pork with fig
and walnut stuffing 168

poulet au vinaigre 170

T

V

W

INDEX

Acknowledgements

My heartfelt thanks to:

Firstly, team Absolute: Meg Boas for seeing the possibilities behind the idea; Jon Croft for making it happen; Emily North who has been just the most wonderful editor and this rookie author will always thank you for it; Rachel 'M' for editing endeavours; and Marie O'Shepherd for the beautiful design work with Anika Schulze. (Also Adam O'Shepherd and Polly Webster for their gorgeous food styling and photography.)

Kate Howell, Claire Ford and the Borough Market team who have been so very supportive, believed in the subject and continue to be just wonderful to work with. Not least with the Borough Market Cookbook Club, and so special thanks to those members who were part of my gang of recipe testers: Bron, Marian, Elain, Marc, Tracy-Ann, Steph, Caroline, Charlotte and Mark.

Gen Taylor – my Guild of Food Writers co-Chair, without whom I simply wouldn't have been able to write this while doing that, too. Kate Hawkings – for introducing me to Scrivener, making me giggle at some necessary times and for being my occasional international vinegar-hunter. Rachel Roddy – whose support and enthusiasm at the early stages helped give me faith, and who took me on a very fun balsamic tasting in Rome. And also to so many food-writing peers and friends who listened to me on the journey to getting my debut book off the ground and have offered heaps of advice and support along the way too: especially Jayne Cross, Hattie Ellis, Charlotte Pike, Claudia Roden and Ken Hom.

Elly James – because while we didn't do a book together, you made me think I could, and taught me how to do a half-decent book proposal. Gudrun Dewhurst at Advantage Austria for insight into the vinegars of that region. Wayne Lee and Julian Bird for giving me the space and time to do this. Rosemary Moon for being the most welcoming of hosts as I went vinegar-hunting in Orkney.

Henry Chevalier Guild, for belief in the importance of spreading the vinegar love and being at the end of the phone for vinegar insights when needed. Belazu and George Bennell for your support, too, and introducing me to my vinegar soul-sister, Judit Badia. She is rivalled only by Marina Spaggiari – thank you, Marina, for so patiently listening to and answering all my questions. Indeed, thanks go to all the wonderful vinegar producers whom I have encountered along the way, especially those who shared with me 'the secret of the vinegar makers'.

One of the very largest thanks of all goes to the Jane Grigson Trust. I can't possibly ever really say just how much winning the Award has meant to me and the development of this book. Particular thanks to Geraldene Holt and Sally Holloway.

Lastly. It took a while to get this book off the ground and at various points along the way I occasionally indulged myself in thinking how, in my first book, I might thank my wonderful husband. Well here I am and somewhat lost for words now. Save to say that without his unstinting support I simply would never have become a food-writer. He enabled and supported me in taking a career-leap into the unknown; and was there with a dry martini and a hug whenever the struggle to turn a dream into a reality seemed too hard. So thank you, my James.

CREDITS

Publisher Jon Croft
Commissioning Editor Meg Boas
Senior Editor Emily North
Art Director and Designer Marie O'Shepherd
Junior Designer Anika Schulze

Food Styling Adam O'Shepherd
Photography Polly Webster *pollywebsterphotography.com*
Copyeditor Rachel Malig
Proofreader Margaret Haynes
Indexing Zoe Ross

About the Author

Angela Clutton is a food writer and food historian. She has written on food and drink for publications including the *Daily Telegraph*, the *Independent* and *Country Life*; and she regularly writes for Borough Market for whom she is also a recipe developer, demonstration cook and hosts the hugely popular Borough Market Cookbook Club. Television work includes being the featured food historian on BBC TV's *Rip Off Britain, Food*.

Until recently, Angela has been the co-Chair of The Guild of Food Writers. *The Vinegar Cupboard* won the Jane Grigson Trust Award 2018.

© Orlando Gili

BLOOMSBURY ABSOLUTE
Bloomsbury Publishing Plc
50 Bedford Square, London, WC1B 3DP, UK

BLOOMSBURY, BLOOMSBURY ABSOLUTE, the Diana logo and the Absolute
Press logo are trademarks of Bloomsbury Publishing Plc

First published in Great Britain in 2019

A catalogue record for this book is available from the British Library.

Library of Congress Cataloguing-in-Publication data has been applied for.

ISBN
HB: 9781472958112
ePUB: 9781472958105
ePDF: 9781472958099

2 4 6 8 10 9 7 5 3 1

Printed and bound in China by C&C Offset Printing Co.

Bloomsbury Publishing Plc makes every effort to ensure that the papers used in
the manufacture of our books are natural, recyclable products made from wood
grown in well-managed forests. Our manufacturing processes conform to the
environmental regulations of the country of origin.

To find out more about our authors and books visit www.bloomsbury.com and sign
up for our newsletters.